What people are saying about

Poltergeist!

The Poltergeist is perhaps the most discussed, argued over and misunderstood phenomena that could infest one's home or workplace. This book is set to become a definitive work on the subject. The author takes you on his personal quest to try and discover the truth behind this complex and often contentious subject. A quest that takes the reader on a journey from the phantom drummers of the seventeenth century to The Cage in present day Essex, with stops along the way at Borley Rectory, Amityville, Columbus, Ohio and Enfield – with a spot of mongoose-hunting on the Isle of Man. But this is no travelogue, this is a fascinating study and update of an often-contentious area of paranormal experience.

Do we need another book about Poltergeists you may ask? The answer is a resounding YES, we certainly do need this book about Poltergeists!

Steve Parsons, author of *Ghostology: The Art of the Ghost Hunter* (White Crow Books, 2016), presenter on several ghost hunting shows including *Most Haunted*

T0302785

Poltergeist!

A New Investigation Into
Destructive Hauntings,
Including "The Cage – Witches Prison",
St Osyth

Poltergeist!

A New Investigation Into
Destructive Hauntings,
Including "The Cage – Witches Prison",
St Osyth

John Fraser

6TH
BOOKS

Winchester, UK
Washington, USA

JOHN HUNT PUBLISHING

First published by Sixth Books, 2020
Sixth Books is an imprint of John Hunt Publishing Ltd., No. 3 East St., Alresford,
Hampshire SO24 9EE, UK
office@jhpbooks.com
www.johnhuntpublishing.com
www.6th-books.com

For distributor details and how to order please visit the 'Ordering' section on our website.

ISBN: 978 1 78904 397 6
978 1 78904 398 3 (ebook)
Library of Congress Control Number: 2019941564

Design: Stuart Davies

UK: Printed and bound by CPI Group (UK) Ltd, Croydon, CR0 4YY
US: Printed and bound by Thomson-Shore, 7300 West Joy Road, Dexter, MI 48130

We operate a distinctive and ethical publishing philosophy in
all areas of our business, from our global network of authors to
production and worldwide distribution.

Contents

*The scientific man does not aim at an immediate result. ...
His work is like that of the planter – for the future. His duty
is to lay the foundation for those who are to come, and point
the way.*
Nikola Tesla, 1934

Preface

In medicine a group of symptoms which consistently occur together is called a syndrome and is given a name even if the underlying cause is not known. If a poltergeist was a medical diagnosis it would undoubtedly be a syndrome as well. A syndrome of strange and often frightening symptoms which includes:

- Objects disappearing or being thrown.
- Inexplicable rapping noises sometimes of a type that seem to indicate intelligence behind them.
- Occasional pools of water forming for no apparent reason.
- Victims sometimes appearing to be scratched by some unseen hand or force.

This is a syndrome which if we are being honest no specialist in the field of research yet truly understands. Perhaps I would go even further and say there are few if any that could honestly call themselves specialists at all!

Yet despite this very distinctive type of phenomena capturing the imagination in fiction and film, when it comes to the factual written word, analysis and case studies of this 'Noisy ghost' (a direct translation from the word's meaning in German) seem to be relatively rare. To prove my point as I wrote this introduction I did a google of "Poltergeist Books" and excluding fiction the front end of the list included:

Poltergeist! A Study in Destructive Haunting (Colin Wilson, 1981)
On the Track of the Poltergeist (D. Scott Rogo, 1986)
And even:

Ghosts and Poltergeists (Herbert Thurston – published as far back as 1954)

To put this in perspective, it is fair to say that none of these authors could have even thought about doing a similar Internet search at the time of writing.

Is it possible that the 'real life' poltergeist is fairly mundane when compared with its best-selling fiction counterpart? Do books based on case facts and theories fail to capture the imagination in the same way as for example this quote below?

One [poltergeist] bit a woman, leaving puncture wounds all over her body. Another attacked the contents of a warehouse full of glasses and mugs. Yet another lifted furniture into the air, then sent objects flying in another house.

The strange thing is that this quote is actually from the summary given on another old book on poltergeists, *The Poltergeist*, written in 1972, primarily meant as a serious academic study by the psychologist William G. Roll. Who needs to make up stories when the apparent truth in dry academic terms can be quite as intense as that?

Guy Playfair, my colleague in the Society for Psychical Research (SPR), was one of the main investigators of the famous case of 'The Enfield Poltergeist' in the late 1970s and was consulted on a drama based on the events (*The Enfield Haunting* – Sky TV, 2015). During a question and answer session about the case and the television show, he stated his objections to a dramatized event that was added to the production which did not actually happen – an incident when an unseen force flung the actor who was playing him off his feet and against the wall. His argument wasn't simply that the production company had used too much 'artistic licence' – his complaint was about the pointlessness of making things up, when the real life events were even more dramatic. He was confused that they would add this bit of fiction, but not even mention dramatic real incidents such as a gas fire being literally ripped out of the wall into which it had been built! Perhaps it was just as well for all concerned that Playfair did not have a formal consulting role in *The Conjuring 2*, the very successful US movie 'loosely' which based on the Enfield incidents, to the extent that his entire character was written out!

I must admit to being equally confused as to why a power that can cause such force does not get more 'real life' coverage?

Perhaps this is partially explained by the fact that unlike some 'traditional' well-known hauntings those involving the 'syndrome' of Poltergeist phenomena are often centred on particular people rather than places – and if ethically investigated may not ever fully be reported due to the needs of anonymity. Poltergeist activity taking place in a family home – which is already causing great stress – is far more complex to put 'on the record' than strange events in an old haunted house already in the public domain. There is also the problem that whilst many traditional hauntings seem to be long term, many poltergeist cases only last a few weeks, and some as we will see may be one-off events that are put down as being simply 'just one of those things'. Whilst this may explain the relative shortage of fully usable case studies, it does not really explain the shortage of books about what the phenomena is.

Reverting back to my random googled list of books on the subject, the 1981 book by Colin Wilson *Poltergeist! A Study in Destructive Haunting* is one in which I was already very familiar, and approaches the subject from a particularly interesting angle.

Wilson was an author who made his initial breakthrough with his best-selling book *The Outsider* published in 1956 when he was only 24. He considered himself to be primarily an 'Existential Philosopher', whose earlier writings have been compared by some to those of the American 'Beat Culture' of the 1950s–60s such as Jack Kerouac and Allen Ginsberg. This comparison being valid in their rejection of standard values, their portrayal of the human condition and their shared need to make some kind of mind-altering spiritual quest beyond mundane existence. Wilson only later found a fascination in what can be termed the paranormal through his interest in the way the mind works when a paranormal experience is either created or experienced.

For those whose appetites for Wilson's 'Existential Philosophy' need a little more filling, Gary Lachman's biography of Wilson *Beyond the Robot* (TarcherPerigee, 2016) is a very good place to start. With the added 'Existential' bonus that the historian Lachman in 'another life' was a bass guitarist in the mid-1970s for Blondie, the New York punk rock/new wave band who ultimately found worldwide fame.

What is particularly interesting about Wilson's *Poltergeist!* book is that he starts with what would be his expected philosophical angle and looks for evidence of powers within us that might create poltergeist type phenomena. Gradually, however, he comes to the conclusion that any intelligent behaviour shown is far more likely to come from an outside entity rather than from within. One of the defining moments for Wilson's shift of belief was his witness testimony gathering for a late 1960s poltergeist outbreak in Pontefract in Yorkshire. Though the outbreak was based in a normal council (local government) owned house, the activity became rightly or wrongly associated with a ghost of a monk, and it became known as the case of the Black Monk of Pontefract. More will be said later about this case, but what perhaps swayed Wilson the most was when a resident of the house was literally pulled up the stairs by her own cardigan, which he thought unlikely to be the actions of her own (sensible) conscious or unconscious mind. In the end he more favoured a theory in which an independent entity is somehow trapped in the ground and can come to life when focusing through the mediumistic powers of the right people and become latent again when those people move on:

> *Perhaps waiting for another provider of energy to offer it the chance
> to erupt into the space and time world of humanity.*[1]

Wilson's is one of the last major books to be published around the poltergeist theme, written in a style that is very readable, and that truly makes some speculations about their cause. I therefore decided on the slight association of titles between my book and his as a tribute to Wilson, whose work I respect as one of the seminal works on the subject. Also, though, to show that my book to some extent reassesses his work, and shows that there has been some new and important research since the time of his publication. A book that when even making mistakes is written with an intense 'hairs bristling on the back of your head' kind of style.

If poltergeist phenomena, is indeed a 'syndrome' – it is equally valid to call the lack of written progress on the subject an 'enigma' as well. Since the previous publications mentioned, there has certainly been progress within our understanding of the subject which I hope the coming chapters will clearly show. Whilst it is still true no book at this stage can fully define what a poltergeist is, I hope the following pages will at least put the 'enigma' of silence about this 'noisy ghost' aside once and for all. I think the importance to do this will become more self-evident with the oncoming realisation that – unlike other types of apparent paranormal phenomena – those within the 'Poltergeist Syndrome' could well be far more easily open to future objective proof.

And whilst it may sound clichéd to say it – when it comes to the poltergeist – truth can indeed be stranger than the best-selling fiction!

Chapter 1

Poltergeists – The only provable spontaneous form of the 'paranormal'?

(Is proof of more traditional ghosts always to be 'spirited away'?)

In the early 1970s Alan Gauld and Tony Cornell, members of the Society for Psychical Research, put on a grand demonstration of a ghost detecting unit they had invented known as S.P.I.D.E.R. This was certainly originally an abbreviation for something, but few if any in the SPR can remember what!

Andrew Green, a well-known UK ghost hunter of his time, stated in his book *Ghost Hunting: A Practical Guide* (Mayflower Books, St Albans, 1976) that:

> *It consisted of a camera linked to a tape recorder, linked to photo-electric cells, linked to a noise and vibration detector, a small electric bulb, a sensitive wire circuit and a buzzer. The idea was that if anything made a noise in a room that had been wired and sealed then the camera would automatically take a photograph... the tape recorder would also be switched on and the light and buzzer... But the problem was to decide on how sensitive the pieces of equipment should be. If it was too sensitive, someone sneezing in the next room for example would cause all the equipment to operate: the lights would come on, the buzzer sound, the camera would flash...*

Despite the grand demonstration during twenty years of use it picked up little of interest. It was lately the subject of debate at an SPR council as to whether it was an eyesore as it 'gathered cobwebs' in a storage area of our new Kensington headquarters.

Just a few years later in 1977 first-time investigator Maurice Grosse began an investigation of what became known as the

Despite a new headquarters housing an excellent library, and detailed archives dating back to 1882, even the Society of Psychical Research, along with its counterparts in the USA and Europe, has not yet fully succeeded in explaining the 'Poltergeist Syndrome'.

Enfield poltergeist (he was soon to be helped by SPR colleague Guy Playfair). Whilst cameras and tapes were used there was no need for sophisticated equipment; the phenomena spoke for itself!

Grosse was to find amongst many other events:

- Marbles that flew through the air and landed on the floor without rolling
- Doors and drawers that opened of their own accord
- Door chimes that swung
- Objects (teaspoon, cardboard box, fish tank lid) that jumped.[2]

7

Amongst the other dozens of witnesses was a police constable WPC Heeps who saw: "A chair slide across the floor" about three or four feet, and although she immediately examined the chair she could not explain how it had moved.[3]

They also included George Fallows, an experienced reporter from the *Daily Mirror*, who stated that

> *I am satisfied the overall impression of our investigation is reasonably accurate. To the best of our ability, we have eliminated the possibility of total trickery, although we have been able to simulate most of the phenomena. In my opinion this faking could only be done by an expert.*[4]

It is this quote from the reporter George Fallows that perhaps sums up the strength of many types of poltergeist phenomena – they are **either** paranormal or faked. There is no current normal theory of physics that lets marbles fly or lids of fish tanks jump – if they did indeed happen without human help either science has been totally turned on its head or the paranormal exists – or just quite conceivably both! (Let's not after all forget that many things that would have been considered as paranormal – the inconceivability for example within the medieval world that the earth could be round without us falling off – have now been long incorporated into mainstream science.)

Reverting back to more traditional ghosts and fast-forwarding on through three decades of inconclusive paranormal research, we would find that despite the brave failure of S.P.I.D.E.R., 'ghost detecting' equipment far from being put on the back burner was by the turn of the millennium becoming a whole new industry in itself. By 2003 the American 'Ghost Hunter' Joshua P. Warren in his book *How to Hunt Ghosts* was recommending as well as the basics such as camera, tape recorder, torch (flashlight), the following equipment as standard:

- Electromagnetic field meters, for detecting changes in electromagnetic energies.
- Infrared meter, for detecting changes in heat sources.
- Audio enhancer, to enhance barely audible sounds. (Warren though at least acknowledges that in an occupied location it might be difficult to separate any paranormal noises from natural ones.)
- Electrostatic generator, any device that breaks up natural electric bonds, thereby spraying ions into the air. (If the materialization of ghosts depends on electrostatic charges, this should enhance ghostly activity, Warren argues.)
- Strobe light, to illuminate objects that move too fast to be perceived.
- Tone generator, to investigate the possibility that a paranormal experience becomes more likely when tones are generated at a particular range.

He also in specific circumstances recommended the use of a Geiger counter to measure background radio activity. Though even as a 'fearless' investigator my reaction to this would be ghost or no ghost – if a Geiger counter goes off – I'm not staying anywhere near that 'haunted' house!

The more serious point here, however, is, what are ghost hunters trying to measure? Where is the evidence that ghostly materialisation depends on electrostatic charge? Surely at least there must be a theory to connect ghostly appearances with electromagnetic energies, as on both sides of the Atlantic this piece of equipment seems indispensable in paranormal investigation?

Paradoxically the only theory there is in fact reverses their use as 'Ghost Detectors' – and finds through their readings a plausible natural explanation.

Measurements made at supposedly haunted sites by parapsychologists William G. Roll (the author of one of the

Poltergeist books mentioned in the preface) and Andrew Nichols found that natural underlying levels of electromagnetic fields were higher than expected in a majority of cases, and speculated that the effect it had on the brain may lead to naturally occurring unusual experiences that may be seen as paranormal.[5]

Similar research has also been done by the engineer Vic Tandy with regards to the effect that low frequency sound tones known as Infrasound may possibly have on the effect of peripheral vision and the possible strange experience that could create. So much of Warren's ghost detecting equipment actually becomes potential 'Ghost Busting' equipment instead, and others are simply random devices no more useful than taking a microwave oven into a haunted house. At least with the latter you could warm up some soup to keep you awake!

The problem with investigating traditional ghosts is that:

- We do not truly know for sure if they actually exist!
- If they do exist in a paranormal sense we are not yet sure what they actually are!

So how can we detect something when we don't know the form that it takes?

However, why does this make them any less provable than poltergeist phenomena, which I pointed out previously is also in truth just an unexplained 'syndrome' of strange events? As we shall see, the way that academic study of the paranormal has developed is quite a large factor in this.

In 1984 the University of Edinburgh quite bravely took a grant from the estate of author Arthur Koestler and set up the 'Koestler Parapsychology Unit'. This brought to the UK for the first time a significant if limited academic effort to look for theories behind apparent paranormal events. (Efforts in this realm had actually begun in the USA as far back as 1935, when Joseph B. Rhine set up the Duke Parapsychology Laboratory at Duke University.)

Since Edinburgh University's involvement there are now about a dozen UK-based universities that take an interest in anomalous phenomena. This is quite impressive but also in some ways an unbalanced involvement – as all are based around psychology departments. Psychology is of course a social science with little formal involvement from such 'hard' sciences as physics whose laws would need to be refined or reinvented if such phenomena were proven.

This has led perhaps inevitably to a large amount of resources going into efforts to look for explanations with regards to things seen and heard that are internal to the mind – to seek predominately for natural mind-based explanations when somebody experiences something they regard as a ghost.

Taken to extremes some recent universities studying the subject have even given its study a whole new title – that of 'Anomalistic Psychology'. The traditional title 'Parapsychology' was long seen as being a neutral term – literally the study of beyond conventional psychology – making no assumptions as to what we will ultimately find. The new study of 'Anomalistic Psychology' by its very definition is biased already, making the assumption that ghost-like experiences are likely to have psychological explanations. This is even admitted by those who practise it. Goldsmiths College, part of the University of London, uses the following definition in an introduction to its department:

> *Anomalistic Psychologists tend to start from the position that paranormal forces probably don't exist and that therefore we should be looking for other kinds of explanations, in particular the psychological explanations for those experiences that people typically label as paranormal.*

Explanations put forward by those in this discipline for a ghost-type experience include:

Confirmation Bias – This is the psychological tendency to interpret evidence as confirmation of one's existing beliefs or theories.

Top-down Processing – The acceptance that thought comes before perceptions of the senses, and can use contextual information in pattern recognition. This can lead to false perceptions in the brain's search for meaning – a favoured example given by Chris French of Goldsmiths College being the perception of satanic phrases amongst certain Christian Fundamentalists when a heavy rock album from the group Black Sabbath was played in reverse. In reality of course no such phrases were present. Anomalistic psychologists argue quite simply that such factors would lead to a general inaccuracy of eyewitness testimony.

Concentrating just on these factors, however, means that anomalistic psychologists indulge in a certain amount of prejudgement of natural cause when people see or hear ghosts. As Barrie Colvin, a council member of the SPR and a very experienced front-line investigator, puts it:

> It is important to recognise that anomalistic psychologists tend to offer a generalised view of what normal forces and normal psychological conditions might or could account for ostensibly paranormal phenomena. However, and this is important, **they do not actually consider the evidence at all**... [and] in order to move forward, it is true that psychical researchers need to be increasingly aware of the arguments put forward by anomalous psychologists. Similarly the latter need... also to consider the available and considered evidence put before them.[6]

Now personally I would also criticize the lack of objectivity and open-mindedness in the anomalistic psychology approach. In doing so though I would also admit that certainly, with regards to visual phenomena, much of the research that has been done by them has a definite persuasive quality – especially with regards to 'corner of eye' sightings and fleeting glimpses.

What is often overlooked by ghost hunters, but never forgotten by anomalistic psychologists, is that what we remember is a construct of the mind, and not necessarily an accurate reflection of what actually happened. A famous video experiment by Daniel Simons of the University of Illinois, Department of Psychology, is an amusing example of this. Here a man blatantly walking around in a gorilla suit was not noticed by only about 50% of observers when asked to observe how often a basketball was passed amongst others in the video film. Whilst this is an experiment in non-observation, it does show the likelihood when the process is reversed that something which isn't there could also be 'observed' if within the observer's expectations.

In summary if we can't recognise a 'gorilla type' sighting, how are we supposed to show that our 'paranormal type' sighting is in fact that? Risking just one further animal analogy – this is the 'elephant in the room' that has long stopped sightings of apparitions from becoming 'solid' paranormal evidence.

Further insights into the theories of 'anomalistic psychology' were given by the psychologist Richard Bentall in his paper "The Illusion of Reality" (1990), arguing in the paper's abstract that:

> The available evidence suggests that hallucinations result from a failure of the metacognitive skills involved in discriminating between self-generated and external sources of information. It is likely that different aspects of these skills are implicated in different types of hallucinatory experiences.

A theory though must also have some evidence, but this to be fair to some extent has been provided by psychologists R. Lange and J. Houran, who tested this idea by taking two groups around an old house (with no reputation of ghosts). One group was told to look out for paranormal activity, the other was not. It was perhaps not surprisingly the group with the expectation of the paranormal who experienced the greater number of unusual experiences.

One of the reasons I am sympathetic to some extent about these theories is that similar may possibly have happened at an investigation which I carried out in a previous incarnation of Vice Chair of the historic (London-based) Ghost Club at the end of the last millennium. This took place in the remains of Clerkenwell's old House of Detention – a long-disused remand prison now a museum. Obviously any investigation has by its nature some expectation of happenings, but when in what was a claustrophobic underground prison museum this surely takes any sense of expectation to very significant new heights.

The House of Detention already had a reputation for being haunted and was also a fascinating slice of history – being rebuilt from an older prison in 1845 to become London's biggest remand centre detaining as many as 10,000 prisoners a year. Though demolished in 1890 the entire underground level was left intact. This section was reopened in 1983 as a tourist and visitors' attraction – a combination of serious prison museum and chamber of horrors. Previous to our visit footsteps had been heard and the manager of the 'Museum' had also lost count of the number of people who heard a little girl's 'heart-rending' sobs reverberate from the inner depths of the jail. (Surprising as it may seem children were imprisoned there too.) Previous investigators had apparently seen a sighting of a woman with "light parted hair who gradually faded away". (This in itself is a near perfect example of a fleeting glimpse apparition which the anomalistic psychologists would try to rationalise.) A BBC crew had filmed an aborted interview there when the investigator could no longer take the sense of an inhospitable presence and had to flee the building. Well-publicised incidents such as that could only add to the sense of expectation and tension.

It was perhaps not surprising then that my team of Ghost

Club investigators had some very strange experiences. This included the more (psychically) sensitive investigators picking up the presence of entities such as a prison overseer who was graphically described as being:

Skinny and emaciated with a strong and unhygienic body odour!

But while presences were sensed in abundance, little objectively speaking actually happened that night.

One particular former colleague of mine called Lionel Gibson had experiences which he took detailed notes on that perhaps show how plausible the arguments of our more sceptical psychologist 'friends' can be.

In his questionnaire, which we at the time asked all investigators to complete, Lionel described himself as an

Ex journalist ex international Civil Servant... with some ability when it comes to separating fact from fiction.

With regards to any psychical abilities Lionel stated that:

Very rarely do I happen to have strange feeling about a particular building... [and that] I do range this on a low scale when it comes to psychical abilities.

On paper at least about as objective a person as you could possibly want an observer to be!

So what did Lionel 'experience' at the House of Detention?

He started his report by stating clearly that he did not 'see' or 'hear' anything out of the ordinary that involved any of his five senses. He then added, however, that he gradually sensed a:

Chorus of discordant voices. Shouting, screaming, pleading, crying, begging!

15

Later when he passed an unlit cell he was overcome with sadness and felt his name had been called out, and how someone was trying to tell him something without words that:

He was being unjustly imprisoned for a crime of murder he did not commit. He wanted me to help him to tell the authorities in charge of his case.

Just at the point when another investigator interrupted his strange trance-like state, a curtain seemed to descend on these very deep impressions leaving Lionel with just a strange feeling of guilt.

At the end of his report, however, Lionel level-headedly stated that he would:

Prefer not to express any opinions or possible explanations regarding my experiences, which is ironic considering my own propensity to consider events in an intellectual framework.

Atmospheric and claustrophobic enough to trigger paranormal type experiences through an investigator's own heightened expectations?

Lionel had experienced something profound at the House of Detention but whether that thing was internal or external even he was not in a position to say. Now if an experienced observer can't be sure of the objective truth of what he has experienced, does the impact of expectation not push us into a 'cul-de-sac' when it comes to proving the more traditional apparitional type of ghost? Even if we are convinced enough ourselves, how can we really convince others that our mind and perceptions are not simply being distracted by an unusual situation, in the same way as it was for many who missed the gorilla when keeping their eye on the basketball?

For any open-minded instigator making this jump from impressions and fleeting glimpse observations to proof is presently nearly impossible to do. Lionel by implication understood this in his report and deliberately made this point very clear.

Before concentrating more on the type of phenomena provided in poltergeist cases in the coming chapters – it is worth pointing out that more recently there has been an attempt to 'open up' the apparent cul-de-sac that applies to brief visual and audio evidence of the 'conventional' apparitional-style ghost.

In the same way that an **extensive collection** of individually imperfect witness testimonies gradually proves a criminal case in court – why can it not also provide proof of the paranormal?

Who would be best to construct such an argument – in an ideal world a paranormal investigator who happens to also be a qualified barrister?

Could any such person actually exist with an expertise in two such different fields? In the strange world of paranormal investigation the answer in this case is yes – one of my colleagues in the Ghost Club and latterly in the SPR just happens to manage to fit these criteria exactly.

Alan Murdie (LLB) is a fascinating character, a mix of a razor-sharp mind and old-fashioned and charming English eccentric, and the only person I have known to wear a Victorian-style monocle rather than glasses for reading (or just for effect?). I came to know him first when he was Chair of the Ghost Club – at about the same time I was organising the House of Detention investigations as the Vice Chair. Alan's tenure as Chair continues the tradition of a Club that has been a famous meeting point for those intrigued by the paranormal (who have often themselves turned out to be either intriguing or famous or both). Founded in 1862 the club's members in the past have included Charles Dickens, the war poet Siegfried Sassoon, Harry Price (famous for his investigations on Borley Rectory), Peter Cushing (who acted in so many horror films as well as the original *Star Wars* movie), Peter Underwood (who wrote over 40 books on the paranormal), and more recently Maurice Grosse who investigated the famous Enfield Poltergeist.

As well as being Ghost Club Chair and a member of the Council of the Society for Psychical Research, Alan still has time to publish specialist studies in law as well as the paranormal. I suspect no other author has such a contrast in publishing titles. These vary from *Haunted Edinburgh* to *Environmental Law and Citizen Action*. From *Ghost Hunting: A Practical Guide* to *Q & A on Intellectual Property Law*.

At the 37th SPR Conference in Greenwich, London in 2015 Alan presented what may become a truly ground-breaking paper:

'EXTRAORDINARY EVIDENCE' VERSUS 'SIMILAR FACT EVIDENCE': PROVING THE OCCURRENCE OF PSI OUTSIDE THE LABORATORY

Here he argued effectively against dismissing witness evidence in the way that most sceptics seem to. He stating that doing so:

is not a scientific exercise but a philosophical and social process, and it appears that this expression is used primarily as a sceptical sound bite in the context of psychical research and parapsychology, rather than any working principle for the analysis of data.

And that:

Rather than shunning of so-called anecdotal testimony, the courts accept that collections of what may appear to be isolated facts or reports, emerging from the testimony of different witnesses, or from forensic traces, can constitute cogent proof to a standard beyond reasonable doubt.

Also pointing out that:

Since 1894 across much of the English-speaking world, a principle known as similar fact evidence has been applied when proving the commission of serious crimes and offences. Similar fact evidence enables separated collections of isolated testimony to be taken together to act as cogent proof of guilt.

It is this concept of similar fact evidence that is potentially so relevant when it comes to sightings of ghosts – the well-established legal concept that if enough people say they have experienced or seen something, there comes a point when the evidence is overwhelming and, in the case of the legal process, this is deemed to show guilt beyond reasonable doubt. If such evidence can be used in courts where the consequences are so important to the victim and accused, why is it dismissed when it comes to paranormal proof?

Or as Alan concludes in more legal terminology:

Existing collections of data accumulated by psychical researchers and parapsychologists over many decades may therefore constitute cogent evidence for the existence of PSI effects if analysed from a similar fact approach.

What made this so interesting to me was the fact that at around the same time I had noticed that when it came to investigating apparently haunted houses, whilst so much equipment was used very little witness testimony was taken; and any testimony that was actually taken would normally extend to just the immediate owner(s) of the property. This by itself would be subject to all the psychological theories that anomalistic psychologists put forward.

Perhaps the first (of very few) modern collation of witness testimony was the tenancy of Harry Price at Borley Rectory in the 1930s, thought to be the most haunted house in England at the time. Here, however, the observers he chose were given instructions in advance, sometimes of a leading nature, through what became known as Price's 'Blue Book' of instructions. These included an instruction to go to the summer house just before dusk and see if you can observe the phantom nun walking on the path specifically now referred to as the nun's walk – hardly a prompt to encourage neutral observation! Such a scenario is also of course very different to going back to a case and picking up information later.

There have been numerous haunted sites that have been thoroughly investigated since, by many different witnesses, be it Chingle Hall in the 1990s or Woodchester Mansion more recently. Both of these cases were as a result of the trend for owners to rent out premises to paranormal investigators. In neither of these cases, however, was any attempt made to bring the collection of witness testimonies together.

The fascination that I had with background research of this type actually extended back to a case I had previously investigated around the turn of the millennium, when a single lady with a young child had felt unable to stay in her fairly modern council apartment in south London. She had just been upgraded from one to two bedrooms and with wallpaper bought but not yet put up there seemed little motive for fraud. The lady had reported an entity which she described as a tall dark male that had the appearance of being in his mid-thirties who had a tendency to stand in the bedroom corner – sometimes interacting with her, with sensations such as being pushed. She would also feel as if the empty side of her bed was "indented" at times – as if with a presence, which under any circumstances, but particularly when there is only one adult in the house, must be regarded as being particularly frightening.

Over and above the phenomena itself – what made this case particularly interesting was when talking to her neighbours, and to the lady herself, they also reported that the previous two families had told them of similar experiences in the apartment – providing potential 'similar fact' evidence of just the type that subsequently Alan Murdie had argued for.

In this case, however, the vulnerabilities of the occupier were far more important and with the help of some rather official-looking 'Ghost Club (founded 1864)' note paper we wrote to the relevant council authorities. Here we explained level-headedly, whatever the truth of the facts, the perceptions of the occupier of what was making her tenancy there impossible. The case quite surprisingly also drew the interest of her local Member of Parliament and between all our efforts the housing authority took a surprisingly enlightened approach. They offered her a similar apartment a few streets away which she gladly accepted.

It would of course have been unprofessional to contact the next set of occupiers and ask if by chance they had seen the ghost of a tall dark man, so from a witness research point of view this case reached a dead end. It did, however, whet my appetite for such an approach and some years later just (by coincidence?) as Alan was writing his paper a similar case emerged.

This was the well-publicised case of the former holding cells known as 'The Cage' in St Osyth, Essex. Now converted into a small residence but famous locally for the fact that the accused witch Ursula Kemp had been kept there prior to her execution in Chelmsford. The fact that it was well publicised meant that the owner had no need for the confidentiality that any good investigator should normally offer as a matter of course.

Now this location was especially interesting in its range of witnesses. Firstly, the owner Vanessa Mitchell who ultimately had to leave the premises because of the phenomena; second her initial lodgers and friends who had also experienced things. Thirdly, following Ms Mitchell's departure there had been numerous paranormal research teams visiting the building. With the help of a small grant from the SPR I managed to interview through various means about two dozen witnesses to the phenomenon and did indeed find that some 'trend events' seemed to stick out – corroborated from several sources often with no connection with each other. This would have significantly reduced the chances of psychological explanations fitting the facts.

Now the case of 'The Cage' will be discussed in much more detail later both for its long-term ability to prove the visual and 'normal' audio paranormal effects through witnesses but also because of the fact that it had significant poltergeist elements as well. (It would be so much easier if paranormal phenomena fitted into neat poltergeist/non-poltergeist patterns, but whilst there are trends that is certainly not always the case.)

It will take far more than just one investigation though before Alan Murdie's very interesting theories can become an established way of research, and until then we will still see the caseloads of electronic gadgets – the 'whistles and bells' going off in the night, which may seem impressive but are often nothing but meaningless noise!

Whatever the merits of Alan's paper and my parallel research on 'The Cage', any progress that will be made is still something for the future. To the best of my knowledge there has been very little similar research done since. Perhaps the reader, if also an active investigator, would care to indulge in a similar follow-up exercise? If he or she does please let me know of the results.

Any such exercise of course takes a great amount of time and patience, and yet when it comes to poltergeist phenomena it seems, unlike the 'apparitional' ghosts, to be much more practical to identify – perhaps slightly rarer but as we will see later perhaps not as rare as it seems. If an object is on one side of the room and then is suddenly thrown to the other – this is no corner of the eye phenomena; it can plainly be seen to have moved. If that movement can be caught on camera once fraud is excluded there is de facto proof of the paranormal. No psychological explanations for any sceptic to hide behind as an excuse for his or her non-investigation! The same is the case with poltergeist type sounds that go beyond the distant sound of footsteps and seem often to comprise of rapping sounds which appear to communicate in an intelligent way.

An interesting investigation going back to my Ghost Club days was that at a historic Jacobean House – Charlton House in the South of London, with poltergeist activity which had been reported by others in the past. As in most investigations in large places our team broke up into groups. It was Group B (as they were imaginatively called) that experienced a particularly fascinating event. Whilst they did not get any record on film their written record seems clear and without any hint of ambiguity to be picked over by those who follow anomalistic psychology.

The report as written by the group leader reads as follows:

Group B has started its second Vigil of the evening in The Grand Salon... nothing of note happened in the first 20 minutes... [When Fred] was approximately 10 feet away from the table [where a wooden ornament in the shape of a mushroom was placed] ... I heard a loud crash, the first thing I remember was Gideon looking to the back of the room... that's where he said he thought the noise had come from. I ran to the front of the room where Gideon and Fred were standing looking down at the mushroom. Gideon picked [it] up and we both checked to see if it was hot which it was not. Kathleen said she thought the object had come from her left-hand side which was very strange as moments before the object had been on the table to her right. She also said that she saw the object land on the floor in front of her and that it did not appear to continue to roll or move... The group from the next door came in... feeling that they were being watched [immediately previously] and had asked [for] some sort of sign to which seconds later they had heard the loud crash coming from the Grand Salon.

It is worth also noting that all who reported this incident stated that the crash was far louder than they thought could be possibly made by a small wooden ornament.

If you study these abridged notes it is clear that, assuming there was not mass collusion or sleight of hand trickery (the latter unlikely if the nearest person was ten feet away from the object), what happened to that object cannot be explained by nature. Assuming the incident happened – it was in essence the paranormal 'in motion'. The evidence of the poltergeist is simply as stark and persuasive as that! Of all the witnesses it was Gideon I knew the best. He had perhaps something of a hard-headed scepticism prior to that evening, but I think it would be fair to say his outlook on the 'paranormal' changed in just one night with just one event.

The conclusion of this is that it seems we need dozens of witnesses and numerous incidents of 'traditional' ghosts to get to the same stage of evidence as a one-off poltergeist incident can provide. Lionel Gibson in his report on the House of Detention was almost surely correct when he stated that he would prefer not to express any opinions or possible explanations regarding his experiences because they were likely subjective and potentially psychological in their nature. It was also possible that Lionel had a further and much stranger contribution in providing evidence of the paranormal.

A few years after the House of Detention incidents Lionel sadly passed on. With any relatives based in Argentina and many of his closer friends part of the Ghost Club, its Chair Alan Murdie took it upon himself to be executor of Lionel's estate. A simple legal process for a qualified barrister of course!

Whilst any legal issues might have been simple the logistical issues were far more complex. Lionel had a burial plot previously purchased in Paris so it actually proved necessary to repatriate the body there. By luck my wife then worked in this very specialist field and this issue was at least overcome. The other major logistic issue consisted of a fascinatingly cluttered and eclectically furnished small apartment in London which was owned by Lionel and which certainly needed some clearing prior to sale. This was something that for a while Alan often worked late into the night doing.

On several occasions when in Lionel's apartment strange poltergeist style events were to occur, which had such an effect on Alan that he decided to keep a full record. The most significant event happened when two other witnesses were present – when they all returned to the flat, to quote Alan's own words:

On entering the flat I went into the kitchen and was disturbed to see two objects lying on the kitchen floor. These were a small plastic watering can lying on its side and a Perspex box containing a silver ornament of a flowering plant. The box is a plastic and rectangular one measuring 34 centimetres by 10cms by 13cms; it weighs approximately 1 kilogramme. The box had been standing up against the wall next to the veranda door which was locked and blocked with a chair. Nothing else appeared to have been moved.

I was quite shaken by this as I had left the kitchen floor clear of any objects, since I had expected the relatives the following week and I did not want the flat to seem untidy.

Other events included an object falling off a mantelpiece in front of witnesses and unexplained banging on a wall. Now there are plenty of psychological factors that might give the impression late at night, in an eccentrically decorated and cluttered flat, of something flashing past your eyes – but few if any that might explain how objects can move when they are previously placed elsewhere.

With regards to the watering can incident Alan notes that Mary Rose Barrington, an extremely experienced SPR investigator, speculated that:

> The displacement of the objects had been purposive and might represent an attempt to draw attention to the need to water the remains of what had been a large pot plant situated in the kitchen.

However, knowing Lionel quite well I personally feel there might be another explanation.

It may be fair to say that anyone with a *"propensity to consider events in an intellectual framework"* would know that this incident was providing strong evidence. Now of course I speculate slightly here but this quote is a quote I used earlier, and one that in fact comes from Lionel's own notes regarding his approach to investigating phenomena It takes a good investigator to know what makes up strong evidence, and I couldn't help wondering if Lionel, after experiencing so much of the inconclusive subjective type evidence, had decided himself to provide something a little more 'solid' – an ad hoc poltergeist event to assist our hunt to discover the paranormal?

Whatever the motivation or cause behind this event – it sums up nicely the theme of this chapter, the strength of evidence that even a simple poltergeist act seems to bring when compared with the 'traditional' ghost. Game, set and match to the poltergeist as objective proof that the paranormal exists?

If things were only as simple as that, this book would simply extend to one chapter – the paranormal would be proved – science would be reinvented and a parapsychologist would again become a 'Nobel Prize' winner.[7]

Nothing, however, in the paranormal is simple – so the only thing we can conclusively prove for now is the need for a chapter two!

Chapter 2

A Brief and (Slightly) Alternative History to Our Subject

(Has this noisy ghost always been with us – perhaps just living round the corner?)

A Poltergeist is an alleged ghost, elemental, entity, agency, secondary personality, 'intelligence', power, spirit, imp, or familiar with certain unpleasant characteristics... mischievous, destructive, noisy, cruel, erratic, thievish, demonstrative, purposeless, cunning, unhelpful, malicious, audacious, teasing, ill disposed, spiteful, ruthless, resourceful and vampiric...![8]

Harry Price, the most famous Ghost Hunter of the first half of the 20th century, when writing one of the first mainstream books purely dedicated to the poltergeist, seemed just a touch intent on 'hedging his bets' as to what a poltergeist is and how it behaves.

I was particularly interested, however, that he included 'vampiric' in this very long list, as we will discover in a later chapter the connection that poltergeist and the vampire might well be close first cousins.

Apart from this long list of words showing Price's skill with using a thesaurus, it also showed that he only felt able to create a 'symptom' like list as opposed to a definition. This indicates that he may well have reluctantly agreed with the argument I made in this book's preface – that currently at least a poltergeist is simply a word for an undefined syndrome of possibly related strange occurrences. The best you can get from grouping Price's definitions together would be to classify a poltergeist as a paranormal entity 'with a sore head'!

Whilst Price's definition of what a poltergeist is lacks

precision, the same could not be said by that given by my former SPR colleagues Gauld and Cornell who, perhaps after tiring of experimenting with the "S.P.I.D.E.R." ghost detecting machine, turned their skills instead to a most unique and in-depth project. This being the analysis of 500 of the better recorded poltergeist cases, of which they published their findings in their 1979 book *Poltergeists*. These findings included that Price's "mischievous, destructive, noisy, cruel... entity" had a 64% propensity to move small objects, and even to move larger objects such as tables and chairs in 36% of cases. It could make rapping sounds in nearly half of all case (48%). This vast survey also showed that poltergeist cases had more traditional ghost-like tendencies – appearing as a human-like phantom in 29% of cases, and making vocal or groaning sounds nearly as often as visually seen (26%).

Whilst Price's *Poltergeist Over England* is arguably the much better known book out of the two, Gauld and Cornell's *Poltergeists* is undoubtedly the most encyclopaedic and seminal work on the subject to date. Whilst Price might have used a keen eye and reasonable amount of equipment when investigating phenomena at sites such as Borley Rectory, he could never claim to have gone to the same lengths as Cornell, who in 1961, prior to working with Gauld, decided to embark on some 'house shaking' experiments to discover whether poltergeist type phenomena could be replicated by geophysical effects.

So whilst Price spent time in old dark houses of some reputation, Cornell instead approached the Cambridge Borough surveyor and successfully asked if he could 'borrow' some houses scheduled for demolition. To which he would attach a robust vibrating device on the outer wall, and place test objects inside to see if they would move – along with some (brave) volunteers. Despite ultimately vibrating the houses so that its whole structure was clearly shaking as if in an earthquake and plaster falling from the ceiling (to the extent that it was agreed to be far more terrifying than investigating a 'real' poltergeist entity), only four insignificant object movements were found to have occurred. Cornell concluded that it was likely that those houses would collapse before any objects moved with the significance reported in classic poltergeist cases. What he also showed is the extent a good researcher should go to test out a natural theory – though if and only if your borough surveyor is sympathetic to your needs. This under-publicised unique experiment is also important in showing that progress is in fact possible in the understanding of poltergeists. There have been other examples of good experiments since, as we will see later. The problem of course is, whilst science keeps the subject at arm's length, there is no real central body or point in which to compare results – other than the far too rare published book on the subject.

What both the books of Price and Gauld & Cornell had in common was a good knowledge of the fact that poltergeist phenomena had existed long before the syndrome had been defined. Price for instance refers to a German case going back as far as 355 CE which involved the throwing of stones, people being pulled out of bed, raps and terrible blows being heard. He also refers to a slightly later case in 858 CE, in which Rudolf of Fulda, a German Benedictine monk, communicated with a spirit who appeared to make intelligent raps. Taken at face value these incidents are so very close in their nature to modern events, and have no cultural or religious reference to make it likely that they would be imagined, made up or exaggerated. Surely if just a mythological entity – a poltergeist would do something more interesting than stone throwing and rapping most of the time.

Gauld and Cornell find an alternative source to make the same point. Referring to relatively more modern cases discussed in *Disquisitionum Magicarum* written by the Jesuit Martin del Rio in 1599. Del Rio defines a particular type of "well known" demon renowned for causing "disturbances and annoyances" within the home. He then discusses an incident experienced by a "William of Paris" whose sleep was interrupted by the clattering of pots, *the throwing of stones* and ultimately being pulled out of bed. These examples clearly show that this phenomenon seems not to be related to a specific time and place or set of beliefs.

There are limits to how much we can learn from quoting sources which in turn quote earlier sources, which goes way beyond firm witness testimony and into the realms of hearsay. With regards to getting a historical perspective though, a few such cases are certainly required.

A historic case of particular interest is that of the Drummer of Tedworth, partly because the case was notable for having been investigated by Joseph Glanvill, a member of the newly-created 'Royal Society' (the world's oldest independent scientific academy). This made it one of the first haunting episodes to receive serious scrutiny, and to be written up in great detail in Glanvill's 1681 book *Saducismus Triumphatus*. Despite the fact that the case was investigated in detail, the conclusions were as based in controversy as most cases are today, and so give a good flavour as to the problems of serious research.

The fact that the Royal Society was newly created in itself says a lot, as this period of time was a transition phase between the days of superstition and days of enlightenment to come. It was only a few decades since the middle 17th century peak of witchcraft trials in the UK, when self-styled 'Witch-Finder General' Matthew Hopkins was responsible for the deaths of 300 women between the years 1644 and 1646. While in the USA the equally famous Salem witchcraft trials were still a decade away in the future.

The case itself took place in 1661 at the home of a local magistrate named Mompesson in Tedworth in Wilshire and involved the outbreak of violent sounding knockings and rapping noises all over his house – continuing nightly over a period of two months. Now the concept and causes of poltergeist rapping was of course unfamiliar to Mompesson, who connected this incident with that of his recent jailing of a 'nuisance' drummer named William Drury who had also been carrying forged papers. As well as Drury being temporarily imprisoned, Mompesson had ensured that Drury's drum had been confiscated.

Can poltergeist rapping be confused with drumming? If cross-referencing cases, the answer seems to be a definite yes. In the case of the Black Monk of Pontefract (briefly mentioned in our preface), Colin Wilson describes a period when the poltergeist was becoming more powerful and its drumming noises became deafening.

Whilst it was Mompesson's impression that this drumming was in some way caused by the witchcraft of Drury, the phenomena grew far beyond simply drumming and started to centre on Mompesson's children – again something we would notice as a far more standard poltergeist trait. It would make chairs, tables, trunks inexplicably move. (If you remember in Gauld and Cornell's survey, a common trait in 36% of poltergeist cases – whilst rapping scores even higher at 48%.) Objects were also thrown about. Scratching noises began to be heard in the children's bedroom – sounding to Mompesson as though they were made by "iron talons" – and followed the children around the house. Glanvill visited the premises and talked to witnesses. He also had experiences of his own including strange scratching coming from the children's bedroom and a strange heavy panting sound resembling a dog out of breath.

Over and above its strong poltergeist credentials, the Drummer of Tedworth case also had all the modern controversy of 'Confirmation Bias' evidence presented to fit into the writer's agenda.

Glanvill's *Saducismus Triumphatus* was never intended to be a book of science, and despite being a member of the Royal Society, the book is in effect an affirmation of the existence of witchcraft and an attack on non-believing sceptics. This sceptic believer 'conversation' is now over four centuries old and shows little or no desire to run out of steam or passion. The Tedworth

Drummer was an excellent example for Glanvill to put in a book whose conclusions were already pre-set in stone.

Glanville, however, was not the only well-known person to investigate this case. The architect Christopher Wren (famous for designing St Paul's Cathedral in London) also attended. A quote from his contemporary John Aubrey commenting about Wren's visit notes that:

He [Wren] could see no strange things, but sometimes he should hear a drumming, as one may drum with one's hand upon the wainscot; but he observed that this drumming was only when a certain maid-servant was in the next room; the partitions of the rooms are by borden-brass, as we call it. But all these remarked that the Devil kept no very unseasonable hours: it seldom knocked after 12 at night, or before 6 in the morning.

In other words, Wren clearly believed that the phenomenon was faked, showing our fact or fraud debate is also one many hundreds of years old, and that unlike other types of apparent paranormal phenomena, there is often little room for innocent interpretation.

Following the publication of Glanvill's book in 1681, twenty years after the initial outbreak, there is no recorded evidence of further phenomena taking place at the home of Mompesson. It is highly likely in fact that the phenomena died down long before Glanvill's book was published.

To show that Poltergeist phenomena is by no means something that only happens in Britain or even Northern Europe, there is a similar and equally famous case that occurred in the USA to the Bell family of Robertson County, Tennessee in 1817. As the concept of a poltergeist was not yet fully established, this became known as the 'Bell Witch' phenomena. Like the Tedworth Drummer it was initially blamed on an outside malevolent influence. In this case a deceased neighbour, Kate Batts, who may or may not have been cheated on a land purchase and who reputedly swore to haunt the family on her deathbed.

Whatever the catalysis was for the phenomena, like most cases it started with simple acts such as knocking and scratches. The phenomena then started to get more intense and just like the Tedworth case the family started to experience having their bedclothes pulled away, and also the throwing of stones and turning chairs upside down. In some ways the phenomena went beyond that of the Tedworth Drummer. A disembodied voice started to be heard which:

> spoke at a nerve-racking pitch when displeased, while at other times it sang and spoke in low musical tones.[9]

Betsy Bell, the 12-year-old daughter of John Bell, seemed to often be the centre of the phenomena, and would have her hair pulled and her face go red when apparently slapped by the poltergeist. (Bruising, scratching and other markings whilst not so common as other symptoms have been shown to occur in numerous other cases.)

Like the Tedworth case the publicity may have brought the interest of a famous person. In this case it was no less than General Andrew Jackson, who was subsequently to become the President of the USA between 1829 and 1837. (Such involvement in investigating cases by senior statesmen is not unique – Arthur Balfour the UK's Prime Minister between 1902 and 1905 had also served as President of the Society for Psychical Research in 1893.)

As Jackson never wrote about the case himself, the extent of his visit is based on a book by MV Ingram in 1894, *An Authenticated History of the Famous Bell Witch*, where he states that Jackson experienced the phenomena including the bed sheets being pulled away.

The main phenomena lasted four years although the occasional 'encore' still took place much later than this. More recently there have been reports of phenomena in the 'Bell Witch Cave', a cave very close to where the Bell's farm once stood. This switch has a similarity to the famous British Borley Rectory case, where following the demolition of the Rectory in the 1940s, the phenomenon seemed to transfer itself to the nearby Borley Church.

Our further case of particular interest, also like the Tedworth case, involved a member of the British 'Royal Society' which had since become far more established as a hard-headed scientific body. This case has become known as 'Bealings Bells', and concerned the inexplicable and constant ringing of the inner house servants' bells that took place at the home of Major Edward Moor who in 1834 lived at Great Bealings in Suffolk.

The refreshing difference here was that whilst Major Moor was a scholar he was not one with a theory to push, and far less likely to have fallen into the trap of 'confirmation bias'. It is clear from the book that he self-published in 1841[10] that he was simply genuinely baffled and wanted to get to the truth stating that:

The bells rang scores of times when no one was in the passage or back house or grounds unseen. I have waited in the kitchen for a repetition of the ringing, with all the servants present... Neither I nor the servants singularly nor together... could... work the wonderment that I and more than half a score of others saw.

On looking for further rational explanation over and above that of fraud the Major noted:

I am baffled to a sufficient cause of what I have thus seen and heard... The weather was calm. The known laws of electric theory seem inadequate in their normal explanation as are those of expansion of metals by change of temperature.

By his testing of the bell mechanisms and trying to pinpoint fraud, Major Moor, in many ways, became the first objective paranormal investigator as we know it today. As a poltergeist case it was somewhat atypical in that the poltergeist (assuming there was one) was basically a 'one-trick pony'. This becomes clearer when we look at Colin Wilson's attempts to make sense of poltergeist phenomena when he points out in his book *Poltergeist!* (p. 359) a list of no less than 19 symptoms that Guy Playfair believes the 'Poltergeist Syndrome' can have:

> *that in some cases only half a dozen of these appear – let us say raps, overturning furniture, apports 'possession' and outbreaks of fire. You always get them in the same order. You don't get puddles of water before stone throwing. You don't get fires before raps. So that there is a predictable behaviour pattern.*

Whilst Playfair's list may well have omitted bell ringing as a premier symptom, this would have simply been because of the fact that most of us no longer have servants to ring and those who do don't use mechanical bells. Bell ringing has been a common symptom in the past happening in amongst other places Borley Rectory until the wires were deliberately disconnected to stop further noise. However, what was different about 'Bealings Bells' is that the phenomena did not develop in any way. The bells rang and rang but nothing else occurred. This shows the difficulty any investigator will have in finding a theory that truly seems to apply in all cases. It could though be speculated that a poltergeist might aim for the point of least resistance (with regards to whatever energy is used), and maximum impact on the people who have to endure the phenomena. That being the case the constant ringing of pull bells could fit the first criteria and most definitely fits the second.

A virtually identical case took place in Douai, France in 1907 in the house of a mailman, his wife and five children, and a serving maid whom one assumes the pull bell was meant to call. One of their neighbours was an initial witness to the ringing phenomena and, noticing that the ringing sometimes took place at the very time she was discussing the phenomena, according to William Roll she stated that:

One might have thought that it was defying me.[11]

Despite 300 witnesses from the local area gathering to witness the ringing and the police ultimately being called in, no explanation was found.

Where the case of 'Bealings Bells' and for that matter the Douai case were far more typical, however, was the fact that the bells kept ringing and ringing and ringing... for exactly 56 days (or just two weeks in the Douai case) and then according to Major Moor the phenomena totally ceased – much like the Tedworth 'drumming'.

This time limitation of phenomena that seemed to be the case both at Tedworth and Great Bealings is often given as a reason for poltergeist phenomena not being as thoroughly investigated as that involving more 'traditional' ghosts. Barrie Colvin, when writing for the SPR's PSI Encyclopaedia, states that:

Poltergeist activity is very rare, and often lasts only a few days or weeks. By the time a case comes to the attention of parapsychologists it may have ceased, or have become too weak to provide unambiguous evidence.

But does the history of the subject actually back up this simple assumption?

I mentioned earlier that Gauld and Cornell actually surveyed 500 cases. Now, however impressive this seems, taken over several centuries, this does not in itself show them to be a common occurrence. This chapter was called an "Alternative History" of the poltergeist for a reason, because one of its purposes was to give a first hint that poltergeists are perhaps more common than we realise – and perhaps they are also active in the most unexpected places.

A traditional history of our subject would have also taken in other well-known pre-20th century cases as:

The Epworth Rectory Poltergeist whose phenomena started in 1716 and was investigated by the eminent scientist Joseph Priestley. (Famous for discovering that rather important substance called oxygen.)

The London 'Cock Lane' ghost whose noisy poltergeist type rapping in 1762 seemed to emanate from a daughter of a gentleman Richard Parsons, named Elizabeth. The famous English essayist Samuel Johnson was one of the witnesses and commented that:

> ... *The opinion of the whole assembly, that the child has some art of making or counterfeiting a particular noise, and that there is no agency of any higher cause.*

A case not often categorised in the history of the poltergeist would be the phenomena surrounding the Fox sisters of **Hydesville, New York** which started in 1848. We will look at this later in the next chapter and when we do please refer to Johnson's quote above to get a sense of the similarity between the facts of these cases – and to see if this quote would also apply to the Fox sisters.

However, as one of this chapter's main purposes is to show the potential common nature of this phenomena, our next stop will not be Cock Lane or Epworth or (as yet) Hydesville but on to my home town of Croydon!

I currently live in a Borough of London called Croydon, and within Croydon itself a smaller district known as Thornton

Heath. It is in effect an outer suburb of London. Now whilst London is a grand ancient city, Croydon has become a sprawling commuter-belt, a mix of modern and 19th century housing with very few older buildings still intact from when it was several villages.

Sadly Croydon's main claim to fame is the fact it rates quite highly in surveys of the most boring or unhappy places to live. Coming second to top (or second to bottom) based on a 2013 survey reported online in the *Croydon Advertiser* the long-running local paper.

The extent of this tag is unjustified. I rather like the place, and the *Croydon Advertiser* goes on to defend it explaining Croydon's plus points, such as the facts that:

- *Westfield and Hammerson have just committed £1bn to transforming our shopping centres.*
- *The Brit School, in Selhurst, has spawned talent including Adele, Leona Lewis and Amy Winehouse.*
- *The architecture – sure, it's not everyone's cup of tea, but Croydon is as close as this green and pleasant land gets to New York.*
- *The* Croydon Advertiser, *of course, serving the community since 1869 [which they admit is a shameless plug].*

In fact Croydon hit the national press when in a bid to re-establish its reputation the English National Trust started offering walking tours around our town. Sadly the headline in the *Daily Telegraph* was:

National Trust offers walking tours around 'Crap Town' Croydon

The point I am generally making is that whilst I find it a perfectly good place to live, it is not the traditional spot steeped in history in which we would expect to find paranormal activity. So if there have been significant active poltergeist cases near to where I live, is it not arguable that they can quite frankly be found anywhere?

On the plus side the *Croydon Advertiser* article also points out that Croydon is home to Croydon Minster, London's only 'Minster' approved church (an honorary title given to a large and significant church – though not quite a Cathedral).

Croydon Minster itself has a strong reputation for being haunted. A grey man is occasionally witnessed, who is believed to be the ghost of Archbishop Sheldon, checking his fire damaged tomb had been repaired. This, however, has no poltergeist features and is based on word of mouth (hearsay). I would need much better evidence than this to try to prove my point, and was strangely to uncover such a case barely 300 metres from where I live.

I had heard occasional reference to a Thornton Heath poltergeist over time and thankfully through the help of the Society for Psychical Research's (SPR) library I was even able to get hold of the original sourcebook on the subject *On the Trail of the Poltergeist* by Dr Nandor Fodor who, in the 1930s, was Director of Research for the "International Institute for Psychical Research" (now defunct). This pre-Second World War period was a special time for psychical research when there were actually some well-funded virtually full-time professional researchers in the field. The International Institute... was but one such organisation. Others included the SPR itself and the 'National Laboratory for Psychical Research' set up by Harry Price (who we became familiar with earlier) which used the generosity of his hosts The College for Psychic Studies and a whole floor of their impressive building in Queensbury Place in London, which still exists to this day. It was also the time in the USA when JB Rhine was setting up the first Parapsychology Lab at Duke University, North Carolina. Here he was also to identify the concept of ESP (Extrasensory Perception – receiving information paranormally from an external source), and more importantly to our subject matter clarifying that of PK (Psychokinesis – the power to mentally influence external objects without the use of physical energy). As I was to find out later this small house 300 metres away from me had received attention not just by Nandor Fodor but from Harry Price as well.

Whilst the other organisations I mentioned are still well known within paranormal investigation circles, the "International Institute for Psychical Research" has largely been forgotten, and on receiving Fodor's 1958 publication from the SPR Library I was fascinated to see that my return date stamp was the only one in the library sheet. It is unfortunate that this is the case, as whilst the connections and funding of many of these organisations started at least partially from those with a spiritualist leaning, Fodor's background came with an interest in the then fairly new 'science' of psychology – possibly making him the first (and long forgotten) parapsychologist. In fact he states quite categorically in the introduction (p. 8) that:

Poltergeist disturbance may represent an episodic mental aberration of a schizophrenic character arising from the severe traumatisation and consequent dissociation. Poltergeist psychosis would be its appropriate psychiatric description.

He proudly also announces (p. 10) that his manuscript of the Thornton Heath incident was sent to (arguably) the inventor of psychology Sigmund Freud, who stated after reading it that:

The way you deflect your interest from the question of whether the phenomena observed are real or have been falsified and turn it into the psychological study of the medium, including the investigation of her previous history, seem to me to be the right step to take in the planning of research which will lead to some explanation of the occurrences in question.

Freud indeed also had a keen interest in psychical research and the poltergeist, and was actually invited to join the "American Psychical Institute" by the pioneering American paranormal investigator Hereward Carrington – which Freud declined but with the interesting footnote that:

If I had my life to live over again, I should devote it myself to psychical research rather than psychoanalysis.

So in some ways it was just an accident of timing that the antics of the poltergeist was not brought much closer into social and behavioural sciences.

The incidents themselves came to prominence when in 1938 the Forbes family of Beverstone Road, Thornton Heath (husband, wife and a 16-year-old son) reported some strange incidents in their house to the local and national press. There was nothing suspicious about this in itself. In these long pre-Internet days, and when large telephone books only covered the local area, this was the obvious way of reaching out to paranormal investigators – and has been the way both the Enfield Poltergeist case and the incidents at Borley Rectory had also come to prominence.

This caused a series of reporters to attend the premises, from the *Sunday Pictorial*, the *Daily Mirror* and also Croydon's own representatives from the long running *Croydon Advertiser*. Fortunately Fodor had dated these newspaper reports and it proved possible, in the case of the *Croydon Advertiser*, to track down the original with the help of the research department from Croydon Central Library.

From Fodor's account, the team of two from the *Sunday Pictorial* was faced with a selection of flying objects which included eggs and shattering china and glass. Perhaps the most impressive phenomena of all were when Mrs Forbes was telling her story and a heavy crash was heard. On rushing out to the hall the reporters stated that they *saw a bronze fender (a low frame that borders a traditional fireplace) from an upstairs bedroom lying at the foot of the stairs. No one was upstairs at the time.*

The *Daily Mirror* reporters (the newspaper most closely involved with both the Borley and Enfield Cases) were a little more sceptical. Pointing out that:

the incidents [they experienced] only took place when we were off our guard.

And that:

nothing happened when Mrs Forbes was held.

The *Croydon Advertiser* attended the property at the very same time as Harry Price did, stating that:

A psychic investigator of International repute, Harry Price... was also a visitor at the house... During the evening he spent two hours there, said that what he was told was "remarkable", and declined an invitation to stay longer. He excused himself on the grounds that he had a long journey to make.

Harry Price did live in Pulborough, Sussex, which is 45 miles away, which may well have been a genuine reason for his evening visit being brief. Interestingly though when his *Poltergeist Over England* was published seven years later he did not think the case remarkable enough to include it. Had he stayed he may have thought differently though as the headline in the *Advertiser* stated:

Night in Haunted House – Reporter's Narrow Escape – Wardrobe Crashes on Bed!!!

Going on to explain that:

> *An Advertiser reporter... had a narrow escape from death or serious injury, when in this house of strange happenings a heavy wardrobe crashed down on a bed he was about to enter.*

In many ways the beginning of this case was more satisfactory than the conclusion. Fodor made that common mistake of confirmation bias spending as much time investigating Mrs Forbes' psychological background as gathering evidence for the poltergeist activities and coming to the conclusion that she was a neurotic with a disorganised psyche. Now I am not myself a psychologist but I suspect those terms have little true meaning in the more sophisticated approaches that are taken by qualified practitioners today.

Despite the fact that the phenomena continued and included scratch marks and burn-like marks appearing, Fodor started to think that much of it was subconsciously faked, and suggested she be tested under controlled conditions at his Institute. A poltergeist case then suddenly became much more of a 'medium' testing experiment, though, as we will see later, the two might well be related.

Initially Mrs Forbes passed Fodor's tests set with flying colours, even getting through some rather dubious ethical procedures when this 'victim' of a poltergeist (Forbes was of course not a professional medium) was stripped in daylight in a search for the small objects that seemed to magically appear. Of equal ethical dubiousness was the discussion within the Institute of a proposed experiment to see if the hapless Mrs Forbes could "apport" the Crown Jewels from the Tower of London. The reporting of this led to a libel case by Fodor against the London-based *Psychic News*, which Fodor won on the grounds that the experiment, though discussed, had not actually gone ahead.

Nothing was found on the occasion of the strip search, but

when X-rayed two small "apport" objects were apparently being kept hidden under Mrs Forbes' left breast. As to whether, as Fodor finally thought, this was evidence that the whole episode was consciously or subconsciously faked is very much open for debate. I suspect the reporter from the *Croydon Advertiser* who was nearly crushed by a wardrobe would disagree.

In pointing out a further difficulty in investigating the poltergeist, my SPR colleague Barrie Colvin states that:

Poltergeist activity typically arises in domestic family situations, which may sometimes be tense, and at unsocial hours – all of which complicates investigators' attempts to gain access.[12]

This intrusive historic case shows, if nothing else, that if investigators are to get access to domestic family situations they need to first learn that the needs of the family come first. Even today this is not always apparently the case.

This is not the only poltergeist case which is fairly well known and occurred within Thornton Heath. Confusingly the second case is known as the 'Thornton Heath Poltergeist' as well, and, though the tale is commonly told, it is far less easy to source which would potentially lay it open to accusations of hearsay. However, the story is quite appealing in its own right, and also puts my home area Thornton Heath even more on to the paranormal map, as a Birmingham-based film company (which is nowhere near Thornton Heath) felt compelled to make a well-produced albeit low-budget feature film based on the haunting, *The Thornton Heath Poltergeist* (2017).

This poltergeist tale happened in an older 18th century property, old by Thornton Heath standards, and began in the early 1970s when on one August night the family in question were woken by a blaring bedside radio.

The phenomena began to escalate despite the intervention of a local clergyman (and possibly because of the intervention of a local medium). It included a lampshade falling over, an ornament being hurled across the room, a Christmas tree starting to shake violently, and the common poltergeist phenomena of footsteps being heard. Louder noises included the sounds of furniture crashing when nothing had in fact been moved, and the sighting of a man in old-fashioned clothes by the couple's son. When we look later at the paranormal activity at The Cage (St Osyth) in more detail, we will see that this combination of object movement, footsteps and banging is far from being uncommon.

The medium told the family that the house was haunted by a farmer by the name of Chatterton, who had apparently lived in the house in the mid-18th century. Once the poltergeist had been given an identity there were also sightings of a grey-haired lady assumed to be Chatterton's wife.

The phenomena lasted four years but ceased after the family moved out. Though whether phenomena ceases or simply ceases to be reported in such instances is a point of contention.

One final Croydon tale worthy of mention took very little research due to its fame within the paranormal community, and my familiarity with the building itself. This case was all of a mile outside Thornton Heath in Central Croydon – a bar in Park Street, the functional and rather nondescript 1970s part of the town. It was one of the more famous cases in the UK at the time, featuring in pages 326–332 of Colin Wilson's *Poltergeist!* book. Wilson thought it important enough to give the case a six-page discussion. This was about the second longest entry in his book, apart from the Black Monk of Pontefract case. The bar at the time was known as The Kings Cellars, though has had other names since. Wilson describes it in *Poltergeist!* (p. 328) as being in 1980:

less of a public house than a kind of continental bar... The downstairs bar has been decorated to look ancient with imitation masonry.

This was a description that provoked my recollections of the odd occasion I had ventured in to this bar when in my early twenties. When I genuinely believed that, despite the 1970s' concrete outside, the bar was genuinely old. I can only assume that my powers of perception were dimmed by the fact that it was never the first bar I would visit during an evening.

The case was investigated by Guy Playfair and Maurice Grosse (who also investigated the even more famous Enfield Poltergeist case). Some of the phenomena which occurred included bottles and glasses falling off shelves, cold spots and malfunctioning electrical equipment. The telephones would malfunction without fault being found as would the electronic tills which acted randomly registering in one instance £999 for no reason (or the number 666 if you look at it upside down which of course just happens to be the biblical 'number of the beast').

It is interesting to note that one incident reported by the bar manager at the time involved all of the glasses on the top shelf vibrating as if a large lorry was going past, but there was no lorry, all was silent outside. This reminds me a little of the effect found by Cornell when trying to vibrate the condemned house in Cambridge – a possibility in this case of some kind of geophysical explanation?

However, there can be no geophysics to explain one of the strangest incidents which happened one morning when all of the ashtrays on top of the bar had been neatly emptied on to the floor creating a long line of ash. This seems to fit the profile of a poltergeist as being an intelligent prankster.

The bar manager seemed to think the cause might have been a girl who had apparently thrown herself off the nearby St George's House (sometimes known by locals as the Nestlé Tower as it was the long-time UK headquarters of the confectionary company). The lady may even have landed upon the roof of the building housing the pub. Whilst in this case the exact circumstances are still in need of verification, there does seem to be an interesting trend between some poltergeist cases and suicides, which we will delve into a little more later.

Adjacent The Kings Cellars pub this St George's House has long been rumoured to be the site of a suicide, who jumped from the top and may have landed on the buildings below. Can such incidents sometimes trigger poltergeist phenomena?

The bar had various names and styles over the years, depending on the trends and tastes in Croydon. It re-invented itself as 'Goodies Wine Bar' and then finally 'Bar Latino'. When I made enquiries to the management of Bar Latino in the late 1990s, they confirmed that phenomena were still continuing but on a lesser level. This did, however, include the unfortunate event of the then bar manager being mysteriously locked inside the premises on more than one occasion.

Sadly, however, the progress that Croydon has been making to shrug off that unfair 'Crap Town' reputation has ensured that this bar will now likely stay closed forever. The whole somewhat nondescript 1970s part of Park Street has been closed for some time due to City centre redevelopment which includes the Westfield and Hammerson mentioned in the *Croydon Advertiser* list of things to make our town great again.

Run-down and ready for demolition, this once vibrant pub put Croydon very much on the poltergeist map.

If it is finally to be demolished, would Croydon Council be as amenable to experimentation as Cambridge council was with my colleague Tony Cornell in the 1960s – sadly my suspicion is that health and safety has taken over such things but who can tell?

One of the main explanations of poltergeists is as a phenomenon centred on or around a particular person. We can see from the fact that phenomena continued after changes of management here that in this case that does not really quite fit the facts. But can a poltergeist continue to exist without any people at all, and is there something still lurking in the basement of that disused bar that just needs some kind of catalyst to ignite it?

So a quick exploration into a very untraditional paranormal domain such as Croydon has shown that with a small amount of research it seems poltergeist cases can quite easily be found – sometimes just in the next street. That they have been reported in local and national papers, investigated by well-known paranormal researchers and writers, and even in one case turned into a movie. Perhaps then poltergeists as not as rare as some would suggest?

What though if incidents described as poltergeist ones were only scratching the surface of the syndrome?

What if even more poltergeist incidents were happening around us and being simply misdiagnosed?

What if the whole of the Spiritualist Church was actually based around a misdiagnosed poltergeist incident?

Chapter 3

Is Poltergeist Phenomena Rare?

(Or is it simply misdiagnosed or given a different name?)

Two sisters, Maggie and Katie, who were aged 15 and 12 in 1848, were being disturbed by strange banging noises at night. Despite their initial shock they slowly discovered that if they clapped their hands the bangs answered back in a code that included the now familiar one rap for yes and two raps for no. The answers they received even had a ring of truth claiming to be from that of a murdered peddler, Charles Rosa, whose remains had been buried in the cellar of the house. Tantalisingly, some human teeth, hair and a few bones were later to be found in approximately the place they indicated.

Described in this way the above case has all of the hallmarks of a typical poltergeist one. The girls were in the same age range as Betsy Bell who was attacked by the Bell Witch (and an age range which seems to be a trend in many other poltergeist cases). Rapping and banging is (virtually) a compulsory poltergeist trend whilst signs of intelligent communication is not unusual either. Yet these events which happened to the impoverished Fox sisters of Hydesville, New York (a now non-existent district that would have been close to Newark, NY) occurred at a time when there was a thirst for new ideas, and were identified not like the Bell Witch as some kind of curse, nor even as simply something 'unexplained', as Major Moor had done when faced by those ringing bells in Great Bealings Hall!

When the sisters moved to stay with their older sister Leah in Rochester, Isaac and Amy Post, community leaders in this radically religious area, took an interest in the girls' talents which they found could be replicated outside of the Hydesville 'haunted' house. The confirmation bias of the Posts and their radical Quaker colleagues meant that this phenomenon was very much perceived as an important demonstration of religious faith. Through paid demonstrations, growing fame and growing use of the media, the Fox sisters soon became national and then international celebrities and poster girls for a newfound interest in the paranormal. This was not just to be a passing news story, as I fully explained in my previous book *Ghost Hunting: A Survivor's Guide*, in which I (slightly) light-heartedly compared the Fox sisters' media blitz to the well-hyped and publicised 1990s UK and worldwide pop sensation the Spice Girls.

> Where the Foxes had a greater lasting impact, however, was in the number of copycat incidents that seemed to come from their fame. Séances in the way that the term is now popularly understood (groups sitting in circles led by a medium that would produce phenomena or messages from the dead) became widespread, and by 1855 it was reported that the new 'religion' of Spiritualism, based around after-life communications, had over two million members worldwide.

Instead of the Fox sisters becoming known as just an interesting poltergeist case, they instead became known as the catalyst that set off the founding of Spiritualism, which in turn prompted interest from the scientific community to investigate the subject. This also prompted the founding of organisations such as the 'Ghost Club' (London) in 1864, the Society for Psychical Research (1882), and in the USA the American Society for Psychical Research (1885). It is therefore arguable that, without the Fox sisters, paranormal research in the way we know it may not exist today. With all the connotations that this famous case therefore has, the obvious poltergeist angle is often overlooked because it has become associated purely and simply as a direct communication with the afterlife. Our old friend 'confirmation bias' has clouded the issue again.

What if there are many other cases like that of the Fox sisters which, for reasons of the way that we perceive things or even for reasons of culture, are not identified as 'Poltergeist' cases – yet, when looked at clearly seem to have one or more of the key symptoms? If there are many such cases could it be claimed that it is possible that poltergeist type experiences could in fact be common occurrences? There are a few things more to say about the Fox sisters later, but for now, as another example of this, we will take a detour from New York to the remote countryside of the Isle of Man, an island just off the North West coast of England which is partially independent to the UK.

The Isle of Man is a strange and interesting place. On a recent visit in 2017 I took the regular bus service from the local airport which helpfully had an audio commentary as to which places we were coming to. The audio commentary became slightly different when crossing a small bridge on the A5 (Port Erin to Douglas Road), when it insisted that we should greet the fairies that own or inhabit the bridge, to ensure good luck while on the island. I think I remember doing just that in a spirit of good humour.

It is fair to say that not all take this superstition seriously but based on all the offerings and trinkets put on trees near to the bridge it is clear that some really do. The (London) Times reporter AA Gill was apparently aware of incidents where local taxi drivers stopped and refused to continue until their passengers made the greeting. The Isle of Man is also known for a series of historically dangerous annual motorcycle road races known as the TT (Tourist Trophy) race, and it has certainly become quite a tradition for many of the competitors to visit the bridge, to help avoid becoming one of the five competitors killed in 2016 or the 252 in total killed up to that date. When it comes to superstition and the paranormal, it is perhaps fair to say that the outlook of the Manx (residents of the Isle of Man) is perhaps still today a bit more open and accepting than most other folk. To quote its official tourist web page:

> *You'll also hear tales of giants, fairies, and brownies – which were said to intervene in the lives of ordinary people – and although times have changed, many of the original customs and superstitions live on.*

If such things still live on in a 2018 official publication it is abundantly clear that as far back as the 1930s and 1940s such beliefs would have been far more common. If giants, fairies and brownies can be claimed to have been spotted in the Isle of Man countryside, is it really such a leap of faith that a 'Talking Mongoose' might also reside in a remote house in the desolate Isle of Man hills?

James and Margaret Irving were not originally from the Isle of Man, though Margaret's mother was born there, which perhaps indicated she had both a knowledge and affinity for the place. Through much of the early 20th century James Irving ran a successful piano dealership in Liverpool, though when that business started to flounder he moved to a farm just outside a small Isle of Man village called Dalby, which he had previously bought as an investment, and decided to start afresh and try his hand at farming.

This was a brave decision as by then James Irving was already in his early forties, and his choice of farm even by Isle of Man standards was really quite unique. The farmhouse stood alone up on a hill about two miles outside the village at a place known as Cashen's Gap (or Doarlish Cashen to the Manx). Whilst still appearing on an ordinance survey map, this 'place' has no manageable road to approach it by, just two very rough tracks. One track approaches from Dalby partially through muddy fields and the other is hewn out of slippery slate from the other nearby village of Glen Maye – famous for its beautiful waterfall next to the local inn.

By then the Irvings had grown-up children. They also had a newborn child by the name of Voirrey, a Manx derivative of Mary. For a while, with the help of his son Gilbert and some local help, the farm was to make a reasonable living. Gilbert, however, moved out in 1928, perhaps bored of the isolation, leaving just the late middle-aged couple to try to eke out a living, and of course a lonely young girl called Voirrey just about to enter her teenage years. Whilst Voirrey did attend the local school in Dalby, the isolation of the farm gave her little other opportunity to mix with other children.

But was Voirrey totally isolated from companionship?

Christopher Josiffe, in his excellent 2017 book on the case,[13] quotes from the *Isle of Man Examiner* (19th February 1932) that:

When [Mr Irving] first heard queer and little tappings in the house... [he] put it down to the industries of a small mouse... then they began to hear peculiar animal noises such as the blowing of a stoat or ferret... These noises continued for some time... [he] made many efforts to trap the animal but without success... They began to hear noises similar to a baby child beginning to talk and before long heard definite words issuing from the walls... From that time on, this queer body has repeated parts of their conversations, has discussed their private lives with them and retailed gossip gleaned from outside.

When first glimpsed briefly by both James Irving and Voirrey, this 'entity' was described as having a long rat-like body with a long bushy tail and of a yellowish hue with brown tail speckles, and thought at first to more resemble a weasel. This was the ultimate view of the *Examiner's* reporter who came up with the theory that it was an actual weasel combined with subconscious ventriloquist skills of the by then teenage child. It was also identified by another local paper, the *Peel City Guardian and*

Chronicle, as being a 'Buggane' (a monster from Manx legend). It was suggested by others that the animal could in fact be a (real) mongoose, as a number of the species had been let loose nearby about twenty years before. The 'entity' at that point agreed deciding it wanted to be a mongoose and that his name was Gef and told the family this clearly. Who was going to really argue with a 'Talking Mongoose', so the mongoose became known as Gef.

Over the following years, the Irving household were to hear the regular voice of Gef, including its habit of singing at times, the occasional sighting as well, the throwing of stones and also noises such as crashes and bangs. There were witnesses other than the Irvings to the phenomena as well. The phenomena started to be reported by the media outside the Isle of Man. Initially by the Manchester *Daily Dispatch,* whose reporter stated that:

> *I have heard today a voice which I should never have imagined could issue from a human throat.*

The ultimate poltergeist friendly paper the *Daily Mirror* was to quote James Irving later as stating that:

> *It still speaks to us and we see it practically every day. This morning it killed a rabbit by strangling it and brought it back to the house just as it was.*

This was hardly typical mongoose behaviour but then again Gef had claimed amongst other things to be – "the fifth dimension" and "the eighth wonder of the world".

Now such a tale was sooner or later to get to the attention of Britain's most prolific paranormal investigator of that time, our 'old friend' Harry Price. As well as using some very up-to-date investigation techniques, it is fair to say that Price was also a man who enjoyed drumming up publicity both for himself and his subject.

This was admitted even amongst supporters of his work. For example even his literary editor and colleague Paul Tabori has stated that:

Few people had the courage to confess as freely as he did their innermost desires and ambitions.

When Price for example investigated the validity of fire walking (the act supposedly involving mind over matter of a person walking over burning embers), the initial experiments were not only conducted using the traditional charcoal, but also with 50 burnt copies of *The* (London) *Times* newspaper. *The Times* in return produced the important 'fuel' for Price of publicity for the experiment.

Criticisms of Price, however, included accusations that he went on 'unworthy' investigations just for the sake of courting publicity. He had already conducted what became known as The Brocken Experiment of 1932. Here Price went to Germany, with his colleague Professor Joad, to test an ancient ritual for transforming a goat into a youth of surpassing beauty. This actually gained Price much criticism with the scientific community, which took Price by surprise. After all his own National Laboratory had hinted at the light-heartedness of the affair telling its members that elaborate preparations were being made for the experiment and a most enjoyable evening will be the result.

So can a potential paranormal event simply be too far-fetched to investigate? It seems in the case of a 'Talking Mongoose', and following the debacle of the Brocken Experiment, even Price hesitated to act. The strange reports, however, continued and finally, in July 1935, Price was to find he had been persuaded to stay at The Waterfall Inn at Glen Maye, the other village close to Cashen's Gap. Here he based himself and visited the house along with journalist Richard Lambert, respected editor of the BBC magazine *The Listener*.

Price was not known for his physical prowess and likely took quite an effort to heave himself up that rocky track from Glen Maye to Cashen's Gap. However, when he finally arrived, despite the efforts of the Irvings to tempt Gef into making an appearance, Gef was to remain stubbornly elusive during the visit. (Gef was to later communicate a dislike of Price.) Price was somewhat sceptical – observing that double walls of wooden panelling covered the interior rooms of the home and noting that this unusual effect made the whole house one great speaking-tube. This was a potential explanation for either the family spooking themselves or possibly faking the phenomena. However, despite some doubts, he did not drop this case in the way he did with the Thornton Heath poltergeist, and published a book about it in 1936.[14]

Like the case in Thornton Heath, Price's visit of just two days was to be followed on by a longer one by Nandor Fodor who visited in 1937 for a week. Whilst he also did not experience any phenomena that was in anyway conclusive, he had enough time to interview locals outside the family unit who had also experienced the phenomena (this type of witness testimony is an invaluable source of record) and came away convinced that the phenomenon was not a deliberate hoax.

Apart from fleeting sightings, however, let us recap the main points of the phenomenon:

- Stone throwing
- Banging
- A voice coming from apparently nowhere, even singing at times
- A girl just about to enter her teens when the phenomenon started.

We refer back to the Bell Witch case which centred on Betsy Bell then aged 12 and had:

- Knocking and scratching
- The throwing of stones
- *And speaking sounds at a nerve-racking pitch when displeased, while at other times it spoke in low musical tones.*

Now assuming the world is not full of talking mongooses, what starts to be clear is that Gef is just a localised way that poltergeist phenomena might have been rationalised in those lonely hills far above Dalby village. In the world of superstition, and in the world of a young lonely child seeking excitement and drama, a magical 'Indian' mongoose was simply the way the phenomena presented itself to the Irvings. This becomes even clearer when remembering that in nearby Eary Cushlin (a farm a few miles away), mongooses had in fact been let loose about twenty years previously. Voirrey was likely to have been aware of this, and would therefore have had an 'exotic' animal with which she could identify the strange phenomenon through.

Desolate and lonely approach to what once was Cashen's Gap Farm, a place so remote that a young girl's subconscious mind might have summoned up a 'Poltergeist Mongoose' as a friend?

On my trip to the Isle of Man I was tempted to see how lonely and remote the site of the Cashen's Gap farmhouse actually was. The farmhouse itself had been demolished in 1971. There is speculation as to why it was demolished as many other ruined buildings in the area remain intact, and its remoteness must in itself have caused the demolition to be of some effort. It may have been a calculated act to put the legend to rest?

I stopped off first at Glen Maye, but was disappointed to find that though the beautiful waterfall remained, The Waterfall Inn where Price had stayed had recently been closed down. The Isle of Man used to be a tourist trap for those wishing to escape the big cities of Liverpool and Manchester, but with tastes in holidays changing that side of the island economy has sadly taken a turn for the worst in recent years.

I continued on to Dalby itself and found the church (dedicated to St James) a far more welcoming place. Whilst the building was deserted, there were cups of 'help-yourself' tea and biscuits with an honesty box provided. In the 1930s this would have also doubled up as the schoolhouse where Voirrey and just over a dozen other children would have attended. The lack of people around, though, made the atmosphere slightly eerie. I also found cuttings and a guide on the wall about Gef the mongoose which was known locally as the 'Dalby Spook', so it was clear that the incident had not been forgotten totally.

From the church, I decided to take the path from Dalby up to Cashen's Gap which started behind the old Ballacallin Hotel and bar. This hotel had been shut for years but I have been told it used to have a pub sign with a mongoose – long sold no doubt or taken as a unique souvenir? I have been 'silly' enough in the past to actually spend the night in an even more remote 'haunted' site – the beautiful and spectacular Sandwood Bay in Sutherland, Scotland. Four and a half miles from the nearest inhabitant and surrounded by potentially dangerous peat bogs – so this little two mile hike in the wilderness was taken very much in my stride.

I actually found I was in better shape than I thought when taking the clearly marked path up the steep hill but was surprised by the remoteness when I first lost sight of the road and the village below. I passed one and then another dead sheep carcass that had simply been left to rot – and apart from grazing animals not a (living) soul to be seen. The approach towards Cashen's Gap is certainly a place that has the ability to open the mind, and even possibly to unlock any hidden paranormal powers it has.

Other writers about poltergeists and the paranormal have also speculated if strange remote places or indeed sudden stressful events can bring such powers to life. Colin Wilson in his book *The Occult* (Grafton Books, 1979, pp. 73–74) has termed these possible hidden powers "Faculty X", a hidden part of the consciousness that contains:

latent powers that all human beings possess to reach beyond the present.

And which can:

Unite... the two halves of a man's mind conscious and subconscious.

That strange otherworldly feeling increased as I walked to what I believe was the site of the farmhouse. Previous visitors had identified the hole that used to be the well, but even that seemed to have disappeared amongst the long grass. However, the farmhouse site can be identified as being just down the hill from a more modern hay-stacking shed so I can be fairly sure that I passed through the domain of 'Gef'.

Feeling quite pleased with myself, I walked through a green field as a shortcut to get back, and then suddenly found that whilst the surface was green the greenery was actually hiding a fairly deep marsh. The further I continued the deeper it got, and soon I was right up to my knees. When I suddenly got cramp in one just for a moment, I immediately felt in genuine danger. I remember just briefly thinking that as I was wearing a yellow T-shirt I would have been very visible if a rescue helicopter had to be sent – assuming my phone had a signal.

Whether Faculty X exists in the way Colin Wilson describes, it is certainly still speculation rather than fact. What I do know, however, is that that momentary sense of danger made my senses far more alive and alert, and rather than continuing to the faraway gate, and quite possibly get even deeper into the marsh, I managed to sidestep through the marsh to what had seemed an impossibly-high barbed wire covered hedge which I surprised myself by being able to clamber over with ease. When I was back on the relative firmness of the dirt path, I remember smiling wryly to myself that of course I could not have been in any real danger; after all I had greeted the fairies when I had arrived at the Isle of Man and crossed the bridge into their domain!

As a postscript to the strange events at Cashen's Gap – Christopher Josiffe, when writing his very well researched book on the subject, discovered that there had been phenomena there prior to 1928. One such incident being in 1917 when two repairmen were staying overnight at the building and one said to the other:

> I can't sleep in that [bed]room. I have heard strange noises and there is something uncanny about the place.

He also found reference to an earlier event where:

> Some men unearthed a flat stone containing black ashes. They [re] buried it in the hedge bank.

And some time later a further gentleman:

pulled away the [same] stones and soil and while doing so he felt
something invisible pulling him back. When this happened a second
time a sudden fear overtook him and he ran down the hill side.

Luckily in his case I presume he missed the well-hidden marsh!

However, what becomes clearer to me in the cases I have studied is that many outbreaks of poltergeist phenomena seem to need a particular event to trigger them off, or possibly retrigger them again, as well as possibly the catalysis of someone in a particular state of mind. If we consider that Voirrey could well be the catalyst it is also quite possible that movement of what could have been a grave might have been the required trigger event?

A case of a 'Talking Mongoose' is a wonderful example of how a 'straightforward' poltergeist case can be hidden under the culture and the belief system of those who are involved. It is, however, a one-off event, and as such can only make us more curious as to how many more such one-off events are hidden 'Poltergeist Syndrome' cases. It also seems that the poltergeist seems to be a typical Western European and American concept which leads to two logical theories:

- That poltergeists only 'like' certain parts of the world (unlikely)?
- That the concept of poltergeist phenomena is 'revealed' by other cultures in an entirely different way?

Paranormal investigators have a 'thirst' for genuinely strange places and parts of the world where perceptions are so very different. As well as being paranormal investigators, I guess you could call many involved in the subject as 'romantics' to one extent or the other. We therefore have Harry Price looking silly to some by going to Germany for the casting of ancient spells or chasing after a mongoose – or myself for example spending the night in a ruined cottage in Sandwood Bay. This I did under the guise of an investigation but in many ways to just feel what it was like to spend a night in 'an otherworldly' place all alone.

That is likely why several members of the Ghost Club (including myself), in the late 1990s, decided to try to find contacts in Romania to discover if there was any truth in the mythology and folklore of vampires that of course inspired the writing of Bram Stoker's *Dracula*. This was at a time when the fall of communism was still fairly recent and Romania still had few main tourist trails.

When Bram Stoker wrote *Dracula* he undoubtedly took the name and some of the traits of the character from Vlad Dracula, a real life historical 15th century prince of one of the regions that is now Romania. Vlad also had the nickname of 'Vlad the Impaler' due to the fact that he was known to impale his enemies on wooden stakes. (It could be said that he actually invented psychological warfare, as this little trick of his kept far larger neighbouring kingdoms at bay for decades.) This was to become thought to also be a 'genuine' way of killing vampires and other 'restless souls' throughout much of Eastern Europe in medieval times. Even in England it was only as late as 1823 that a law was passed to prevent the act of driving stakes through the hearts of suicides.

Stoker therefore made a good choice in using the name of Dracula in his book. He had, however, never travelled to the region and took some imaginative choices on the detail of geography. Vlad Dracula had actually been the Prince of Wallachia, a neighbouring state to Transylvania, but perhaps because the folklore of vampires (known locally as Strigoi) was more prevalent in Transylvania, Dracula and his castle got well and truly moved! The craggy cliff face of Poenari Castle where Vlad had really lived became the non-existent castle on the Borgo Pass, seen only on a map by Stoker, which despite its foreboding name consists of impressive but rather more gently rolling hills.

This was Stoker's prerogative as it was only fiction after all.

When the Ghost Club's diligent trip organiser started to make choices of suitable guides she was offered a discounted price by an organisation known as the 'Transylvanian Society of Dracula', an organisation who it turns out had given us a discount as they were as intrigued by our name as we were by theirs. We accepted the discount and let them be our guides, and subsequently several of us were to cooperate with them closely in the future, as it could be said that we had found an organisation the truth behind which was far stranger than Bram Stoker's fiction.

This strange-sounding organisation was not the invention of underground folklorists or occultists, but quite surprisingly the brainchild of two former Communists fairly high up in the Romanian tourist ministry with the names of 'Baron' Alexander Misiuga and Nicolae Paduraru. On the Ghost Club 'expedition' they were to take the club on a fascinating mythological and paranormal tour, visiting the ancient UNESCO Heritage town of Sighisoara where Vlad Dracula was born, and the 1,200 steps to the top of his castle fortress at Poenari. Taken also to the fairy-tale Bran Castle often assumed to be Dracula's lair for no good reason other than it looks the part, and of course to the Borgo Pass itself. As much as the amazing sights captured the imagination, it was perhaps the people we met including Misiuga and Paduraru themselves who were to make the greatest impact.

The story of the Transylvania Society of Dracula starts in the 1980s when Misiuga and Paduraru both became fascinated by the increasing tendency of the trickle of foreign (currency) visitors, from outside the Soviet Bloc, to want to visit 'non-existent' places in their land. Those featured in Bram Stoker's *Dracula* book, such as a castle on the Borgo Pass and an equally non-existent inn in Bistrata called 'The Golden Crown', where Jonathan Harker, the hero of the novel, was meant to have stayed. Under the Communist regime of Ceaușescu, *Dracula* the novel was banned, and yet the enthusiasm and sincerity of these seekers into the unknown (and unreal) captured the imagination of both these men. There is a modern Transylvanian 'legend' that Misiuga caught the Communist dictator Ceaușescu in a mellow mood after a good day of hunting bears, and quietly and calmly suggested that a three tower hotel be built in the style of a ruined castle... on the sparsely inhabited but rarely visited Borgo Pass... and yes it needed dungeons as well! Not only did Misiuga remain a free man, he got a large part at least of what he requested. A single-towered, more civilised looking (Dracula) Castle Hotel was built in 1983... However, it did come with the dungeons that he requested. The tower came complete with the 'Moon Tower' bar allowing Dracula and his guest to have a panoramic view of the Transylvanian sunset. A lucky addition was a real graveyard, as private family graveyards are quite common in that fairly remote region, and the previous owners of the land had just happened to 'leave' one there. (When our group from the Ghost Club stayed at the Borgo Pass hotel we were fascinated by the lack of curtains in many of the rooms. Was there simply a shortage of material in the Bistrata region, or was this a plan to allow the count an easy way of viewing his prey at night?)

A 'Golden Crown' hotel was also built in Bistrata, despite the fact that names with 'Royal' connotations would have been frowned upon in a strict Communist society. Both buildings had enough success in tourist terms to keep Misiuga's credibility, and he was to use them to thrive on the wonderful kitsch of the novel, which he loved, for the next three decades till his death in 2009.

It was, however, the other man from the Romanian Tourist Ministry, Nicolae Paduraru, who has most relevance to our particular narrative. He truly immersed himself in the fascinating traits of people's fear of the unknown – those traits that came from both the real Vlad Dracula (something of a 'King Arthur' figure in Romania today), and his bloodsucking counterpart in the novel. He also took an interest in the real vampire folklore that continues in the more remote parts of Romania to this day, as well as more modern concepts of the paranormal.

Castle Dracula Hotel, Borgo Pass, Romania – perpetuating the myth of the vampire which in turn might provoke the reality of the poltergeist?

Nicolae was a fascinating man who I was to ultimately meet many times. As somebody immersed in Communism for most of his adult life, he did not give the impression of being deeply religious but definitely believed in something 'unknown'. He had a wonderful habit of calling stray dogs, "Sir". Whether this was part of his tour guide persona, or a genuine belief in reincarnation, we could never quite really be sure. Putting on his cultural and tourist hat, he gradually came to the conclusion that Dracula the vampire was better presented as a mysterious figure, rather than someone jumping out of a coffin with 'dripping tomato sauce' teeth. On arrival at any sites, he would in his quite commanding gruff voice invariably remind tourists that:

The Count may in fact be with us in disguise!

After a couple of glasses of underrated Romanian wine, you could well be studying strangers' faces and wondering if it were true.

Ceaușescu was overthrown in 1989 in a coup that caused much bloodshed and led to his execution. An interesting twist is that his initial escape by helicopter was to Vlad Dracula's legendary burial spot at Snagov Monastery – possibly one last desperate effort to revive his fortunes by associating with the 'vampire' Prince?

It was following the fall of communism that Nicolae Paduraru got the freedom to fully explore the subject of Dracula and his own beliefs. In 1991 he set up the Transylvanian Society of Dracula, consisting of writers, folklorists, paranormal researchers, historians, and romantics. The tours and seminars of the Society also started to have a genuine paranormal edge, visiting 'Wise Women' of the local peasantry, as well as organising seminars and talks with Romanian university-based scholars with sidelines in the investigation of Kirlian photography, UFOs and other aspects of the paranormal. Such open-mindedness to the paranormal by academics would put most UK and USA universities to shame.

The biggest achievement of the TSD came in 1995 when it created and organised the first World Dracula Congress, organising more than 300 delegates from all over the world, swapping ideas and thoughts on the real and the fictional Dracula. This set up a network of contacts worldwide. A second congress was also to follow in the year 2000, my main contribution to which was in negotiating the attendance of the cult horror movie actress Ingrid Pitt.[15]

But where is this apparent digression from poltergeists actually leading?

It was through these intercultural connections that I started to get an understanding that the culture of 'Poltergeists' was seriously missing from Romanian folklore, and for that matter recorded paranormal fact, and I decided to try and explore why that could possibly be.

Turning the question the other way round would be a useful place to start – do we in Western Europe and USA have any serious vampire folklore or cases? In a search for cases in the UK

I could find very few of any great note.

There is one exception to this, that of the Croglin Grange vampire.

The original source of this tale comes from the late 19th century writer Augustus Hare,[16] who describes how a house known as 'Croglin Grange' (in the little village of Croglin in Cumbria, UK) had been rented out to two brothers and a sister Michael, Edward and Amelia Cranswell between 1875–76. Sometime during the first summer there, Amelia was in bed when a brown-faced red-eyed creature appeared at her window – entering her room and biting her throat before being scared off by her brothers.

When the creature came back again it seems the brothers were more prepared. One shot it in the leg and it staggered off to the vault in the nearby cemetery. The next day they entered the vault, where they burned the vampire's body.

Now even this most famous of vampire stories has been proven to be controversial, but perhaps that controversy is actually for the wrong reasons. Much has been made as to the location of this happening, with Augustus Hare's near contemporary Charles Harper pointing out that no single-storey building of this description exists in Croglin village near to the churchyard. This has led to a wide range of later theories including the vampire story being of earlier origin, and an extra level being added to one of Croglin village's larger homes. Remnants of a disused graveyard have actually been found near the village which has led to further speculation on Croglin Grange's actual location. All of this is perhaps now missing the point!

When Hare's work was republished in the 1990s, Walter Kendrick of the *Voice Literary Supplement* had this to say:

Not only did Hare win dinner invitations from lords and ladies, poets and politicians; he also listened to stories told after too many glasses of wine. Hare delighted in those stories, which he tidied up and rendered coherent for inclusion in The Story of My Life.

Let us look at (as an example) one of Hare's other famous ghost tales... that of Ham House... thought to be haunted by Elizabeth, Countess of Dysart on the grounds that she murdered her husband at Ham House. Charles Harper, who appears to have been Hare's nemesis, again points out its nonsensical nature in his book *Haunted Houses* (1907). He refers to it as a "picturesque ghost story", on the grounds that the Countess' husband had actually died from natural causes in Paris.

It seems very likely then that Hare was basically a writer of fiction masquerading as fact, so it doesn't really matter if Croglin Hall existed or not; the chances of a vampire being there were slim to non-existent.

So what seems clear is that vampires are largely imported phenomena to English speaking nations (and much of Western Europe). These legends may have started as far afield as China, but in their current guise they are a derivative that came from the Slavic and other Eastern European countries. The dividing line in Europe seems to be almost the same as that of the original dividing line that emerged between the Catholic and Orthodox Christian Churches. This was potentially for a very good reason... the Orthodox Christian Church regards incorruptible bodies as being demonic, while Western-based Catholic countries regarded such 'incorruptible' corpses as being saints. Now saints of course should not be mixed up with 'demonic entities' that cause havoc and mayhem to unsuspecting peasants. So based on our Western belief system, there was never any point where the concept of a vampire could emerge. It is also worth noting that even today, the Romanian Orthodox Church is the second largest with the exception of their much larger Russian neighbours. With this sort of density of religious belief the potential for any strange events to be regarded as 'vampiric' was certainly there.

This separation of belief systems would of course have become even more distinct by the 40 years after World War

Two when an Iron Curtain also descended between countries of vampire mythology, and those in the West whose supernatural traditions were very much of a different nature. Here perhaps is the first connection as to what our strange tale of open-minded former fairly high-ranking Communists has to do with the form in which vampires may actually exist.

The clue perhaps here is the seamless way that the TSD studied both vampire folklore and also other supernatural things more accepted in the West. We in the West simply seem to think we have a monopoly on how and what we should depict the paranormal as being. If it's not a translucent figure in white sheets then it isn't a ghost. If it's not a hag with a cat and a broomstick then it isn't a witch!

If we look even further east than Romania we will find reference in Japan to a supernatural creature called the Mitama, a soul which returns from dead if not properly purified. Japanese tradition states that the Mitama has two souls. One of which is gentle (nigi-mitama), and the other violent (ara-mitama). Despite the strange terminology, what we have here I think are the basic fundamentals of the difference between a (gentle) apparition style ghost and a (more 'violent') poltergeist.

If this can be the case in Japan why might it also not apply closer to home? The same phenomena described in very different ways by the Orthodox East of Europe and the Catholic West?

The vampire from folklore of Eastern Europe is actually known as the Strigoi and comes in a variety of types:

The **strigoi viu** or the living Strigoi for example in many ways resembles our concept of a sorcerer or magician. Of far more interest to us, however, is the **strigoi mort** or 'Dead Strigoi' who emerges from his grave, returns to his family and behaves as in his lifetime.

Just like the Japanese, the Romanians also have a more benign supernatural concept. In the case of Romania this is known as the **Moroi** and is seen as being much more benign and 'quiet'. Though unfortunately for the mild mannered Moroi:

Both the undead [Moroi] and the vampire [Strigoi] are killed in the same way.[17]

So mild mannered or not the local peasantry were going to put that stake through your chest or remove your heart and burn it – or at the very least place a bit of garlic under your tongue.

The 'real' identity of the Strigoi Mort has become much more confused because of a spate of so-called real vampire incidents in 1725 and 1731 in Serbia, one of which resulted in the staking of the unfortunate recently buried Arnold Paole whose (original) death had seemed to trigger a series of strange deaths within his village. A future incident in 1731 needed the investigation of a specialist doctor called Glaser, who found the spate of deaths more likely to be caused by malnutrition combined with fasting that was then common in Orthodox Christians. Deaths that were far more unlikely to happen in Catholic or Protestant countries, but which were enough to feed vampire hysteria and lead to several bodies being exhumed.

However, malnutrition 'red herrings' put to one side let us try to look at what a more typical 'real vampire' incident in Eastern Orthodox Europe might have consisted of. Richard Sugg, a Lecturer in Renaissance Literature at Durham University, has researched numerous cases and come to interesting conclusions which with my knowledge of the region I believe are largely correct.

One particular case Sugg refers to is that of a dead man named Andilaveris who in 1890 was apparently revisiting his village and amongst other things would amuse himself by:

Smashing the plates and the glasses, by clattering the pots and the pans, howling horribly all the while like a mad werewolf.[18]

Very much the symptoms of a typical poltergeist, but as Sugg explains the villagers considered the entity to be a Vrykolakas, a Greek 'cousin' to the Romanian Strigoi or Vampire.

Sugg claims that all across what he describes as vampire territory (mainly the Christian Orthodox states), there were well authenticated 'vampire' incidents where the vampires behaved just like poltergeists making loud noises and smashing objects over a period of months. Sugg also believes that it might have been the extreme fear caused through misinterpretation of initial real events as a mythological Strigoi that may even have proved the starting incident that seems to often be necessary for an extended outbreak of Poltergeist Symptoms. Thus, much in the way that the blessing of a building by a priest or minister in Western Europe or the USA can cause phenomena to stop, the same effect could be had in the East by staking and decapitating – at least until such practices generally ceased.

Having contacted Richard Sugg, he was happy to confirm his views stating that:

> I certainly think that some big vampire panics have been substantially dominated by poltergeist phenomena; and may indeed have been purely that (allowing for difference between what they believed and what 'actually' happened). Ironically, given the variable attitudes to poltergeists and mystery of them, you might well say that blaming vampires was as good an explanation as any.

It is not only Sugg who has identified valid similarities. The paranormal investigator Geoff Holder, in his short e-book *What is a Poltergeist?* (David & Charles, 2012), dedicates the whole of Chapter 5 to the possible vampire connection, pointing out that the Bulgarian [shadow] vampires in particular behave very much like poltergeists and were:

> Comparatively harmless and only able to play... practical jokes.

Nor is this relationship just an ancient one. Holder refers to a *London Observer* article of as late as 1923 which:

> contained an account of a haunted house in Belgrade, Serbia [another Orthodox Christian country], [where] windows were smashed by bricks and stones and furniture was moved violently to the point of destruction. The inhabitants were of the opinion a vampire was at work.

All this very much reminded me of what my old Romanian colleague Nicolae Paduraru had said when putting his tour guide hat on – insisting as I previously mentioned that Count Dracula was likely to be around us in some kind of disguise. It was a good line that could scare tourists up in misty-covered Transylvanian hills, but strangely it was also much truer in a wider sense. It's our job as paranormal investigators to strip away these cultural disguises and look into the background of any myth. The more that these myths are looked into, the more that the facts of these cases emerge as those that are common to the 'Poltergeist Syndrome'. Through discovering this potential misdiagnosis we have phenomena that are surely not as rare as it originally seemed, and phenomena that seems to transcend most cultures, which in turn makes it far more likely to truly be something 'real' and not just the conformation of our own beliefs.

At the start of this chapter I discussed the case of the Fox sisters, whose outbreak of rappings was to bring about the whole new religion of 'Spiritualism'. There were many others who suddenly found they had similar talents to the Fox sisters, and this form of unexplained phenomena gradually expanded into a whole new world of physical mediums. I cited it as a possible example of misdiagnosed poltergeist activity, and it is quite possibly what is was. However, there is also a fairly strong possibility that the ladies were involved in nothing more than simple trickery. When the spirit of Benjamin Franklin (one of the founding fathers of the USA) starts to join in with the rapping communications of the sisters, and the greatest circus showman of all PT Barnum takes them to New York with a contract to 'perform', many suspicions are raised amongst their contemporaries.

Such suspicions were heightened in 1888, when Maggie Fox confessed that the whole thing had been a trick consisting of them training themselves to crack their toes in a loud and unseen manner.

Strangely Maggie was to recant her confession in 1891, and all the Fox sisters were to have died (or passed on) through either alcoholism or destitution by 1893.

Are potential fakes such as the Fox sisters a setback to those who wish to identify an unexplained cause to the symptoms of the poltergeist? If faking could be shown to be the predominant factor in most cases then this certainly would be a setback. One of the main premises of this book though is just how well the phenomena fits into either being (paranormal) 'fact' or 'faked', that is its neatness and testability when compared with other types of phenomena. The history of medicine is littered with quackery and frauds. From 'Cocaine Tooth Drops' to 'Snake Oil Liniment' (from which the definition of Snake Oil Salesman emerged), or even the everlasting pill – a metallic pill which 'apparently' was good for purging parasites and could be taken and then removed from one's stools and then taken again and again and again and again...!!! All these quack remedies were around at the time of the Fox sisters, and yet none by themselves undermine the great service that the study of medicine has ultimately done for mankind. Likewise some fraudulent cases do not necessarily undermine the case for a poltergeist.

What is true though is that, whilst most of us have a vague general concept of what a poltergeist is, when it comes to trying to find proof (or disproof) of the syndrome we need to be far more specific. If we are even to think of experimenting or observing for something – we surely first need to be sure what that something might be? Or with several symptoms to observe and test could the cause of poltergeist phenomena even turn out to be more than just one thing?

Chapter 4

One Phenomenon in Various Forms?

(Or is Poltergeist a word for several separate things?)

The 18th century philosopher Bishop George Berkeley (1685–1753) came up with the then unique notion that things did not exist in themselves but are only ideas in the minds of the perceivers – therefore a tree in the forest only exists when a man is in the forest to see it. He called this new philosophy 'immaterialism', overcoming the extensive theological concerns by stating that rather than god being the creator of all things he was instead the immediate cause of all our experiences, stating that:

> *Whatever power I may have over my own thoughts, I find the ideas actually perceived by Sense have not a like dependence on my will. When in broad daylight I open my eyes, it is not in my power to choose whether I shall see or not, or to determine what particular objects shall present themselves to my view; and so likewise as to the hearing and other senses; the ideas imprinted on them are not creatures of my will. There is therefore some other will or spirit that produces them.*[19]

This was important to a deeply religious man who was ultimately to become Dean of Derry in Ireland in 1724. However, by redefining the concept of 'existence' as something perceived by a perceiver, Berkeley rather admitted that in a day to day way his theory made little difference to the way we view the world and that:

> *The only thing whose existence we deny is that which philosophers call matter or corporeal substance. And in doing of this, there is*

no damage done to the rest of mankind, who, I dare say, will never miss it.

The fact that Berkeley's theory can be neither proved nor disproved (as all experimentation by its nature relies on perception) does indeed in a day to day way make his theory in some ways 'trivial'. It also goes against the grain of the 'common-sense' notion in which we all seem to view the world. His contemporary the diarist Samuel Johnson had little time for Berkeley's views and kicked a stone as a 'common-sense' way of showing its real existence with the words:

I refute it thus!

Whilst an interesting tale in itself, what has a likely flawed, centuries old view of the world from an Irish Bishop got to do with the way we view poltergeist phenomena? The answer to this is in some ways quite profound. We go through our everyday life rejecting Berkeley and assuming that things are there whether we see them or not – but when it comes to poltergeist phenomena generally speaking it is only the phenomena we observe that we even take time to consider the existence of. We all in a sense become 'little Berkeleys' not taking the time to consider any phenomena that might even happen when we are absent. If in fact poltergeist activity was a much more everyday event not simply dependant on witnesses, the last element of its so-called rareness (already largely explained away in previous chapters) would be finally cast aside for sure.

I will now ask the reader if you have ever had an experience where an object had disappeared from the place where you were certain you had put it – only some time later to find it again either in the very same place, or somewhere you could never have conceived it might have been? I suspect many if not most of you reading this paragraph would identify with this strange and irritating experience.

I myself had a particularly strange incident when travelling in Germany for the European Football (Soccer) Championships in 1988, and justifying my travels by taking a particularly expensive textbook I had out on loan for some financial exams I was taking in a few months. Did I get a chance to read it while trying to get accommodation in towns that were full to bursting point, during late night parties, trying to avoid the unfortunate odd incident of soccer violence – as well as watching the football matches themselves?

Let's just say I didn't pass these exams first time!

When I finally got home and unpacked my bag that particular unread book was simply nowhere to be found. I thoroughly searched on several occasions as to lose it would incur a rather painful fine from the lending institution. I extended the month's loan on at least a couple of occasions by phone to put off the day when I would have to admit the loss. After several months I had decided to 'come clean' but just before telephoning to declare it as lost I had one last look in the bag and there it was in a fairly obvious side pocket which I was sure I had checked several times before.

Such types of events happen all too often and are often summed up by a bemused shrug of the shoulders as **'just one of those things'**. Few have ever taken the time to consider just 'what type of thing' causes an item to apparently disappear and then reappear again. Are our brains somehow hardwired to miss things that are right in front of our eyes, or have the objects themselves had some kind of transformation or movement?

As such incidents are by their nature apparently 'one-offs', they are virtually impossible to investigate in the conventional sense of being there and waiting for a further incident to happen. Where they can be evidential are in the collection of witness testimony to look for patterns and to increase the strength of the 'similar fact' type of evidence which we discussed in Chapter 1.

Mary Rose Barrington has been a stalwart of the SPR council literally since before I was born. After joining the SPR in 1957 she was invited on to its ruling body in 1962. Apart from participating in many investigations, Mary Rose has perhaps almost single-handedly categorised the phenomena of 'JOTTs' on to the paranormal agenda. 'JOTTs' being a literal abbreviation for being **'Just One of Those ThingS'**, or as Barrington herself would put it:

Inexplicable happenings that are brushed aside as false perceptions, failures of observation, mistaken memories, or just things that could not happen and therefore did not happen (and are best forgotten).[20]

Far from there being just one type of JOTT, Barrington notes several varying classes of the phenomena which in turn may well have differing causes as well. These include:

The **Comeback JOTT** – which describes exactly what happened to me when I lost my expensive book. This is where an object disappears from a location and then reappears later in the very same place. It literally makes a comeback.

The **Walkabout JOTT** – where an object appears in a different location from where it was left. A good example of this being the experience of Alan Murdie mentioned in Chapter 1 when he entered the home of the recently deceased Lionel Gibson and found that the plastic watering can and a Perspex box containing a silver ornament of a flowering plant had appeared in the middle of the kitchen floor when previously put elsewhere.

The **Flyaway JOTT** – describes when an article which was known to have been in a particular location ceases to be there and never gets found. Here Barrington herself quotes a strange example of when a painter Raymond Bayless was giving a lesson to a student in a bare linoleum covered studio. In this incident Bayless dropped a rather large paintbrush and whilst he did hear it clatter on the linoleum despite a long search the paintbrush was never found again.

A final category of some interest is a **Windfall JOTT** where an unknown article is found to suddenly and inexplicably be present. The interesting twist here is the potential real 'windfall' as sometimes that article proves to be useful indeed. Barrington here gives an example that happened to the late John Styles who was a member of the SPR. Styles reported an incident to Barrington when his small motorbike had an oiled up (malfunctioning) spark plug and was in desperate need of a spare but when:

> *He wheeled the vehicle into a side road to consider his next move...*
> *He saw something bright lying in the gutter. It was a new clean*
> *spark plug of precisely the same make and size required. He installed*
> *it. It did not oil up and he rolled on to the garage.*

Barrington has several other categories of JOTT but the above I think give a good flavour of these types of incidents. What is definitely clear for now is that few of us who experience them should be calmly shrugging our shoulders and stating, "It's just one of those things." Most people's mental reactions are likely to be far more intense – more of a minimum entry level of **'WTHIGO'** (or 'What The Hell Is Going On' for those not familiar with text or urban slang). As if some mysterious entity or power is playing some kind of game. What sort of entity has such traits? Whilst no firm conclusions have as yet been agreed as to the cause of JOTTs, it seems in many ways that what we have described is a series of incidents that can sometimes fit very nicely within the concept of the 'Poltergeist Syndrome'.

Of all the types of JOTTs that exist Barrington notes that the Flyaway JOTT seems to be the most common, but as it involves only one unexplained action (the object disappearance) it may also be the least noticed going under the threshold that triggers that 'WTHIGO' in the brain. This may of course be for good reason as the mind may have simply forgotten where the object was put. Which is I guess by definition the natural explanation more commonly known as an item which is 'lost'. Whilst some Flyaway JOTTs such as the incident with Bayless' paintbrush can be intriguing, I would myself consider this type of JOTT on average as being fairly weak evidence of anything paranormal.

The Comeback JOTT is potentially rather more interesting as it takes a double unexplained action of an article going walkabout and then appearing back in the very same place – which assuming a thorough search in between makes it far less likely that it was lost in the conventional sense. It is good territory for a prankster as well, and as far as 'non-natural' pranksters go, a poltergeist is certainly high on the list of suspects. However, it is worth pointing out that the Comeback JOTT seems fairly uncommon in what are accepted as poltergeist cases. As evidence of the Poltergeist syndrome, whilst they are better than the 'Walkabout' JOTT, I feel there is likely a better example to come.

The Windfall JOTT I find particularly fascinating, as in the example given it conveys a feeling of 'something' being out there keeping an eye on you and giving life some meaning – perhaps when it is most required. However, with regards to potential poltergeist cases, this specific type of Windfall JOTT seems to be thin on the ground, and it seems far better fitting with the separate 'syndrome' known as synchronicity.

Synchronicity is a term invented by the pioneering psychologist Carl Jung to define what he termed as 'Meaningful Coincidences', two events that occur without causal relationship but appear to be meaningfully related. John Styles' moped sputtering to a halt just at the point where a necessary spark plug was lying in the gutter seems an excellent example of this. From a more personal point of view an even more 'WTHIGO' event was one that happened to me which I mention in my previous book *Ghost Hunting: A Survivor's Guide* when:

*I was travelling to Prague alone in 1992 shortly after the fall of
the Iron Curtain. I was having difficulty finding accommodation
at a reasonable price… when someone handed me a flyer for a new
'economy' hotel in the centre of town. It was clean, modern and
secure, next to a very large police station. I was happy to call my
fourth floor room home for the next couple of days. Like most lone
travellers I was travelling with a book to read. In my case it was
the fascinating* The Book of Laughter and Forgetting *by the
renowned Czech author Milan Kundera.*

I spent the first night there reading and came to a chapter
that dealt with Kundera's own experiences of Communist
oppression and how he was banned from publishing and likely
under surveillance. He explained ironically that he had a one-
room apartment on a short but famous Prague Street known as
Bartolomějská where ALL the buildings but two belonged to the
police and how he used to look down from his **FOURTH FLOOR**
window to the police station below.

It was at that point I put Kundera's book down and a strange
shiver went up my spine. I looked at the hotel flyer given to
me which did indeed have the address of Bartolomějská, and
was indeed one of two buildings which were not part of a large
police complex. Having recounted the floors I was satisfied
that I had somehow managed to end up reading Kundera's
book potentially in the same room he likely wrote it. Did the
book help me find suitable accommodation or did my liking
for Kundera take me subconsciously to his home? Hard-headed
'non-romantics' might claim that sooner or later, with all the
experiences we have, one of them is going to seem meaningful
even when there is no underlying meaning, and it is true to say I
had increased the chances by deliberately reading a Czech author
while travelling in the Czech Republic. But in a country with a
population of ten million people it is impressive nonetheless. I
suspect even in these days of sophisticated statistical models,

it is as yet impossible to say how often such meaningful events should happen if at all – how often for example a poverty-stricken man will find $100 bill flying down the street? So at least for now you can still be a romantic and look for real meaning in such events in the same way that Jung set out to do.

There are two little postscripts to this slightly diversionary tale. Firstly on returning to Prague just over twenty years after I could not even identify the hotel. My 'sensible' side assumes its existence was short-lived and it was likely turned into offices. My non-sensible side actually keeps remembering that there seemed to be few other guests. I did also more recently try to contact Kundera through his agent to ask if there was any specific reason he had gone into so much detail regarding where he stayed and whether he had a photo of his apartment to correctly locate it. Sadly his agent replied:

> *Thank you for your email, which my colleagues have passed to me as I assist with matters relating to Milan Kundera's work. In response to your queries, the author advises that he is not aware of a hotel on Bartolomějská Street and cannot offer an explanation for why he detailed the exact location of the apartment in the book. He does not own a photograph of the building.*

Perhaps this tale was a slight but enjoyable diversion for me (and hopefully for you the reader as well). What it does show in my opinion though is:

a) That the Windfall JOTT whilst fascinating in its own right does seem to quite possibly be a subcategory of Jung's synchronicity and that the 'Windfall' can be as diverse as a physical object or a cheap hotel room or even the windfall of a long-lost friend (who I once ran into in a foreign country shortly after discussing her with another mutual friend). This leaves the windfall JOTT quite distinct from

other JOTTs in that they seem unlikely to be directly
related to our poltergeist syndrome.

b) Our short exploration of the synchronicity syndrome
shows that most aspects of the paranormal still seem to
be at the stage of a series of loosely unexplained events.
It perhaps gives us some idea that we are as yet only
scratching at the surface as to what is truly happening!

Of all the categories of JOTTs it is the 'Walkabout' version that
with regards to the poltergeist interests me the most. Simply
because when it comes to recorded poltergeist cases, it is a key
phenomenon often found at the earlier stages. I previously
mentioned the incident of Alan Murdie finding the objects
moved at the apartment of the recently deceased Lionel Gibson.
This in fact is very much just the tip of the iceberg when it comes
to Walkabout JOTTs in poltergeist cases.

As we will see later, in a more in-depth study of the small
'haunted' house known as 'The Cage' in St Osyth, Essex, UK,
there were various incidents of Walkabout JOTTs that were
reported, particularly by one of the cousins of the owner
Vanessa Mitchell. Vanessa's cousin Kirstine Blackwall helpfully
sometimes came round to tidy up the house when Vanessa and
her lodgers were at work. She was therefore in a position where
she was the only (living) entity within those walls at the time,
but nevertheless experienced:

- Cushions being rearranged on the couch.
- Books that had previously been stacked in a corner being
  found in the middle of the floor.
- Items of clothes disappearing and being found in the
  most unexpected of places. (This was also a phenomena
  experienced by one of Vanessa's tenants and friends,
  Nicole Kirtley.)

Perhaps the most impressive and also the most controversial examples of JOTTs can be found during the time that Maurice Grosse and Guy Playfair were investigating the Enfield Poltergeist in the late 1970s. During the extended investigation Richard Grosse (Maurice's son) was communicating with an entity claiming to be a former resident called Bill but who was apparently speaking through the vocal chords of one of the current residents – an adolescent girl by the name of Janet Harper. After about an hour of what could have potentially been adolescent chit-chat in a deep gruff voice, Richard Grosse asked a surprise question about the whereabouts of some money that had been previously lost; the entity immediately claimed to have hidden it under the radio downstairs. At which point the three missing coins were found in the very same place.

Now whilst it is possible that the coins might have been hidden in advance by Janet, as she wasn't expecting the question, to what point would it have been? 'Bill' in any case went on to make further claims that were proved to have been largely correct, including the fact that he had gone blind and had a haemorrhage and died on a chair in the corner downstairs.

Subsequent research was to show that a William CL Wilkins did in fact die on the premises; a relative was to confirm the fact he was found in a chair and the cause of his death. I often wonder in such cases, as should any inquisitive reader, how much of the background research is solid fact and how much of it just passing hearsay. In this case I can vouch for the evidence being that of solid fact, having been shown a copy of William (Bill) Wilkins' death certificate registered in Edmonton, North London, 20th June 1963, and basically confirming the facts conveyed through the vocal chords of an adolescent child.

So if the entity calling himself 'Bill' was aware of how he died, and if he [Bill] also claimed to explain a JOTT by the fact he moved some money – it would be unscientific (and impolite) not to take 'his' claim seriously, and it starts to look as if walkabout

JOTTs and poltergeists are closely connected indeed.

Another JOTT incident at Enfield has provoked greater controversy by the fact that its strangeness goes far beyond what has become known as the 'Boggle Threshold', a term invented by the writer Renée Haynes (1906–1994), which she defines as the level above which the mind boggles when faced with some new fact or report or idea. 'Boggles' in this instance being when the implications go so far beyond the comfort zone of current belief as to immediately provoke scepticism – as if the brain is screaming, "WTHIGO," to use my previous terminology.

The JOTT in question was discovered by the neighbours of the Harpers, David and Peggy Nottingham, who after hearing what appeared to be a loud outbreak of poltergeist activity next door, discovered a child's book known to be owned by Janet was **on their own bedroom floor**. With the sense of mischief that some poltergeists have the book was called *Fun and Games for Children* – and the only 'obvious' solution to this possible 'game' would have been that fact that somehow this book did a walkabout through a stone wall from one property to the next!

In both the cases we discussed above, that of St Osyth and that of Enfield, as well as there being JOTT incidents, there were also the more widely accepted poltergeist incidents where objects were seen to move by themselves. In the case of St Osyth, one of the best was a Coke can sliding across a table in front of three witnesses.

The modest house in Enfield whose poltergeist has starred in UK docudrama and USA feature film. Also the site of a particularly strange 'JOTT' incident. (Photo Credit Lindsay Siviter)

In the case of Enfield quite honestly they are far too numerous to count.

Wanting at least one further case to prove my point, I went fumbling through some old letters I had been sent, and as if by magic (or perhaps a minor case of synchronicity) I very quickly found another suitable case. One which was sadly not followed up on at the time but which involved correspondence from a Mr J---- regarding H--- S---- farm which he had lived in between 1948 and 1967 in the north of England, the incident of which may have been triggered by the death of a small child there.

As our correspondent Mr J. describes the events unfolding they included:

> *Ghost lights that were seen on a number of occasions. There were footsteps heard on the landing and the front stairs. There is a door that did not like to be shut...* **Objects used to go missing and then turn up in odd places [walkabout JOTT] or even just vanish completely [Flyaway JOTT?]** *... My sister, seven years my senior, has told me fairly recently that she used to take off her watch at night and in the morning it would be gone. This happened on a number of occasions.*
>
> [Though he fails to explain whether it was with the same watch or different ones, and thus whether the watches were finally recovered later.]

This case does not only include particularly clear descriptions of JOTTs but, as we will see, a particularly clear description of many key aspects of the 'Poltergeist Syndrome'.

This brings us full circle all the way back to our 'old friend' Bishop Berkeley's attempts at a philosophically 'Immaterialist' view of the world. If you believe Berkeley, only the events we actually see could be counted as truly breaking what we perceive as our natural scientific laws. This would make the deduction of the paranormal through JOTTs very difficult indeed. However, many talented men of earlier times have had much insight but have ultimately been shown to be **totally wrong**. From Aristotle's belief that the elements of the world were simply earth, air, fire and water, or Sigmund Freud's belief that the Oedipus complex was the cause of most psychological disorders. This refers to a child's unconscious sexual desire for the opposite-sex parent and hatred for the same-sex parent (or vice versa in some cases). When geniuses such as Aristotle and Freud get things wrong when starting afresh, is it not safe to assume that clever men such as Berkeley got things equally wrong when in the earlier days of the renaissance of Western Philosophy. (There are also plenty of philosophical refutes but these are well beyond the scope of this book.)

Now on the assumption that Berkeley's view of the world is wrong, JOTTs – and especially walkabout JOTTs – with no other obvious or feasible explanation become nearly as strong a symptom of poltergeist phenomena as the witnessing of object movement itself. What is also important is that as many more mundane JOTTs do not always trigger that sense of 'WTHIGO' (and most unexplained moving objects do), it is quite possible that poltergeist phenomena are going on all around us and in many cases we are just shrugging our shoulders and ignoring it. Perhaps a more questioning attitude, a little less JOTT and a little more WTHIGO, would be useful in our search for truth. The more records we have the more truth is likely to emerge. It would also be the final nail in the coffin of those who claim that poltergeist phenomenon is somehow a very unusual and rare type of event.

Whilst 'Enfield' was Guy Playfair's most famous case in the UK, his interest in the paranormal and in particular in poltergeists was initiated in Brazil where he spent many years. In some ways it is perhaps even more useful to look at his earlier writings on this theme as these give further glimpses of how poltergeist phenomenon is viewed outside of British and North

American culture.

In Brazil he worked with the IBPP (Brazilian Institute for Psycho Biophysical Research) studying about twenty cases they were closely involved in investigating, and wrote about them in 1976 before the Enfield Poltergeist, in his book *The Indefinite Boundary* (Souvenir Press, 1976).

From this book he came to the conclusion that whilst no two cases seem to be identical six categories of poltergeist phenomena can be broadly defined.

This first is what he terms as **'Stone Throwing'** which he also states is common in initial stages sometimes within the affected premises, and sometimes also outside. Whilst I guess in some parts of the sparsely populated Brazilian countryside stones are a common object to be found, this is less likely to be the case in a London suburb. The stones of Brazil when it came to Enfield were replaced by an initial outbreak of flying toy marbles and pieces of Lego. These initial phenomena would be better described as a specific example of **Observed Object Movement**.

The next common event in these twenty Brazilian cases was **Poltergeist Rapping**. This is a common occurrence both at Enfield and many other poltergeist cases, to the extent that it will have a whole chapter to itself later. Though with careful training it can potentially be a conjuring trick (arguably with the Fox sisters), the spontaneous nature of such events makes it difficult to believe that this is the whole explanation. Of special interest were Playfair's observations that when he and his colleague Suzuko Hashizume tried to replicate the loud raps they recorded with such implements as broom handles and their own heels they:

> noticed that several sympathetic vibrations were set up as vases and small ornaments began to buzz and shake, an effect that we had not noticed at the time of the supposed PSI raps.
> (*The Indefinite Boundary*, p. 260)

These observations (of the uniqueness of poltergeist raps) were not measured at the time and as such are subjective but as we may find out later may in fact be something that might have a recordable acoustic difference.

The third category Playfair identified he referred to as **Displacement of Objects**, an example of which was when:

> *Suzuko's raincoat was transported from the back of a chair to the inside of a kitchen cupboard.*
> (*The Indefinite Boundary*, p. 260)

This is a typical Walkabout JOTT covered already in depth in this chapter.

The fourth common factor in the Brazil cases was spontaneous outbreaks of fire, which occurred in seven of the twenty cases he researched. This included clothes being burnt inside a plastic bag without the bag being burnt. This seems to be rarer in North American and British cases, but is hardly unheard of and was one of the minor phenomena at Enfield where small fires had started and then apparently extinguished themselves.

The fifth category of Playfair's is one that he calls 'Miscellaneous' which by its very nature is beyond any real comparison. It does, however, include voices and visualisations of more traditional ghost type phenomena, which seem often to be associated with poltergeist outbreaks as well. This interrelationship is so common that Gauld and Cornell coined the term **Intermediate Cases**, to cover such cases, and dedicated the whole chapter to it in their ground-breaking book *Poltergeists* (Routledge & Kegan Paul, 1979). Again we will hear more of this concept later.

Playfair's final category was one that he termed **'Black Magic'** where the casting of spells might be the trigger for some kind of poltergeist outbreak. This happened in six of the twenty cases involved. This would seem to be a very different type of factor to our typical cases but this can be explained by referring to the thoughts of Richard Sugg, Lecturer in Renaissance Literature at Durham University, who I stated in Chapter 3 believed that:

> ... *extreme fear caused through misinterpretation of initial real events as a mythological Strigoi [vampire] that may even have proved the starting incident that seems too often to be necessary for an extended outbreak of Poltergeist Symptoms.*

If this is the case in Eastern Europe when it comes to vampire incidents, surely the real fear in Brazilian society of 'Black Magic' might equally have produced poltergeist symptoms? If a curse is put on someone – might it unleash in panic certain mental powers?

The American paranormal researcher D. Scott Rogo mentions an interesting case known as the 'Tucson Rock Throwing' poltergeist,[21] which further encapsulates both the fact that poltergeists throw stones and rocks outside of Brazil, and that fear of an incident might actually trigger a poltergeist experience. In this case the phenomena consisted mainly of rocks being thrown in the house of a middle class family, the Berkbiglers. However, the anthropologist Patric Giesler pointed out to Rogo a possible trigger for the phenomenon. This was the fact that:

> *The rock throwing began when the Berkbiglers, already suspicious that a vagrant was living in their uncompleted structure, moved into their new home. He [Giesler] rightfully suspected that the family may have been suspecting some sort of trouble. The poltergeist then wreaked havoc for 10 weeks straight until a mysterious prowler was chased off their property. Thus alleviating the trigger for the fear.*

In a way it could be said that the Berkbiglers' phenomena had stopped because they managed in effect to 'stake' the equivalent of their own personal vampire.

When it comes to South America it is not only the cultural significance of black magic that seems to be either the trigger, or the way of articulating poltergeist phenomena. Alan Murdie has spent significant time there as well, not in Brazil but the neighbouring country of Columbia. Here, as Murdie points out, Columbian Spanish has no direct word for a poltergeist. Nevertheless he has researched some interesting cases which perhaps have gone under the radar of other serious researchers, due to the fact that they have been categorised as manifestations of 'Duende' which translates as manifestations of goblins or imps. Now let's be honest, even in the 'paranormal' community we don't tend to take goblins as being anything other than folklore.

However, Murdie spotted similarities between those stories of 'goblins' and those of poltergeists. One which greatly fascinated him was found in a book of old Columbian tales of folklore,[22] which in this case was very specific giving exact names and dates.

This story concerned an influential family who lived in the city of Poyan in 1837, where the home of a Dr Ospina was disturbed by stones and pebbles apparently falling from the sky – very much like Playfair's cases in Brazil. The source of these missiles could not be traced but Dr Ospina, suspecting his neighbours at first, used this influence to get the whole family arrested. However, this did not get the stones to stop flying, and despite Ospina getting no less than 12 soldiers to keep watch on his house, try as they might the source of the stones could not be identified.

The phenomena seemed to have the greatest effect on Ospina's wife – and perhaps predictably the more hysterical she got (and by implication the greater fear she received from the phenomena), the more intense it became. Senora Ospina soon after was to become gravely ill – though we are unable to say whether it was because of the direct effect of the phenomena, the effect caused by the stress, or something quite separate. However, following her death all phenomena ceased. If this was a poltergeist case I strongly suspect it was not the direct cause of death, as death or injuries by poltergeist are actually virtually unheard of – which is the first thing any investigator should tell a worried 'victim' when faced with a case. Nevertheless the other similarities are uncanny particularly to Playfair's research, and clearly show what a strange worldwide syndrome this is.

So when it comes to the Poltergeist, it starts to seem that the syndrome could well turn out to be a tree with many roots (and certainly not the 'immaterialist' tree defined by Berkeley at the start of this chapter). Some of the roots such as JOTTs might not even be identified, with this particular root brushed aside as we try to rationalise 'irrational' events in our busy and rather unspiritual modern lives. Other roots are simply ignored, as the language of differing cultures makes them seem beyond even an open-minded investigator's 'Boggle Threshold'.

To understand the true nature of the 'tree' it is first surely necessary to understand some of these roots far more deeply. With regards at least to object movement and raps I would hope that the following two chapters would go some way to achieving this!

Chapter 5

Object Movement – the Sign of an Active Poltergeist?

(Or just another 'boring' form of Psychokinesis?)

There have been two major flaws to date in the history of modern paranormal research since the latter half of the 19th century. The first one is the fact that it has been undoubtedly riddled with its fair share of frauds from the people who claim to have had paranormal abilities. Secondly it has been riddled by organisations with agendas when it comes to investigating the paranormal, and often by people more interested in their egos than sharing their findings in this ultimate search for truth.

This has created at times a situation akin to the famous Monty Python sketch in the controversial satirical 1979 film about the life of Christ, *The Life of Brian*. This had a well-known subplot about the 'People's Front of Judea', vehemently opposed to the Judean People's Front, in their Campaign for a free Galilee from Roman occupation. Both of which in turn were opposed to the Judean Popular People's Front (an organisation satirised by having just one member). In other words organisations with the same aim, becoming gradually more interested in fighting themselves which in turn did the Romans' own work and let them stay firmly in charge.

If the 'Romans' in this case were established science, then infighting within paranormal organisations has to a large extent ensured that after 150 years the bedrock of accepted science has not yet been undermined.

In 1929 Harry Price, the most famous and possibly the best British psychic investigator of his generation (and definitely with one of the biggest egos as well), nevertheless issued what he called a plea for better understanding in the *British Journal of Psychical Research*. In this plea Price analysed the mutual interrelationships of the main psychical research institutions and the principal personalities in the field. Price went on to say:

> *I wonder how many of my readers are aware of the number of squabbles, petty jealousies and open feuds that are taking place among those investigating psychic phenomena.*

By this time there were at least 15 institutions taking the investigation of psychic phenomena seriously. These were primarily based in Europe and the USA. Of these organisations some would take a sceptical position such as the SPR in London. Others would be primarily spiritualist organisations such as the London Spiritualist Alliance. Price's National Laboratory of Psychical Research perhaps came between the two organisations in its views, and Price recommended that all psychical research organisations should work closer together and possibly even merge.

In normal science investigative techniques and test data are shared openly by peer groups, and it is the repeatability of any experiments that creates progress and validates new theories. In the still newish 'science' of paranormal investigation that wasn't necessarily the case at all. Where this becomes important to us is that since the controversial phenomena of the Fox sisters gained worldwide publicity, more and more people made claims to have the same uncanny ability – to either produce poltergeist phenomena on demand or simply have it spontaneously occur around them. These phenomena in particular included the movement of objects, which when apparently occurring on demand was given the new name of Psychokinesis in 1914 by American author Henry Holt in his book *On the Cosmic Relations*. The term was not used by paranormal researchers until later. It was adopted in 1934 by the famous American parapsychologist

JB Rhine, who was perhaps the first researcher to truly work through an academic institution, in this case Duke University in North Carolina.

Of course if this key poltergeist phenomena (i.e. the movement of objects) can actually be done at will, this would mean that:

a) It is both scientifically testable and provable.
b) That the cause can be controlled either through the energy coming from a human – or that human being able to control or at least 'negotiate' with some kind of discarnate spirit or external energy source.

Those who made claims to have such powers at first also tended to imply that those powers were down to their interaction with spirits. The problem was not so much with this claim itself, but the fact that those who could apparently move objects more often than not made claims to be physical mediums. To assess the credibility of the 'poltergeist powers' of such people it is also fair to assess the other powers they claimed to have – primarily those of the physical materialisation of spirits, and sadly the evidence for the latter is tainted to say the least.

A prime example of this in the earlier days of physical mediums was the famous but controversial Eusapia Palladino (1854–1918), a medium reported as sometimes moody and difficult to work with who, however, was also on the face of it one of great talent. Such talents included her apparent ability to frequently move objects which were normally located inside a curtained spirit cabinet (with her outside but close to it) to nearby locations outside. These included such things as a sheet of paper, a little wooden sheep, and a mandolin. Even more impressive was her ability to levitate tables from the floor. However, several investigators were to catch her in fraudulent activity including the renowned American paranormal investigator Hereward Carrington who when testing her in Naples in 1908 saw her surreptitiously freeing a hand from the control of the investigators, and also observed her attempts to use a hair to create the appearance of an object moving.

Some see Palladino as a gifted psychic who had a tendency to play tricks when on one of her less 'psychic' days. However, such generosity is stretched too far when it comes to apparent examples of deliberate premeditated fraud.

The evidence of outright fraud was pretty clear when many such mediums were put under close inspection. A good example being the spirit forms of the medium Eva Carriére. Despite the fact that Carriére managed to convince the French immunologist and Nobel Prize winner Charles Richet of her talents in sittings in 1905, she was later after close inspection of photos found to have created spirit entities that at least partially consisted of cut-out paper faces from newspapers and magazines on which fold marks could sometimes be seen.

It could only get worse when photographs of Carriére taken from the back of the spirit face revealed it to be made from a magazine cut out with the letters *Le Miro*. The two-dimensional face had been clipped from the French magazine *Le Miroir*.

It was not only Carrière who fell short when it came to her fakery and poor ethics; the standards and ethics of those investigating could also fall dismally short of what was desired. When Carriére was 'investigated' by the German paranormal investigator Albert von Schrenck-Notzing, he insisted on the 'scientific' test of introducing his finger into Carrière's vagina to ensure nothing untoward was hidden there.

Such apparent premeditated frauds continued well into the 20th century and perhaps one of the best known later proponents was the medium Helen Duncan. Not investigated in this case by a Nobel Prize winner but that hard-headed self-taught self-publicising investigator Harry Price.

Despite his lack of formal training, Price had a reputation at the time for being thorough and sceptical. He arranged for a series of sittings with Duncan in 1931. Initially he allowed her to perform fairly unrestrictedly concluding through observation that Duncan had developed no less of a skill in regurgitation of cheesecloth which she claimed to be ectoplasm (a term for a supernatural substance that supposedly exudes from the body of a medium during a spiritualistic trance and forms the material for the manifestation of spirits). An example of Duncan's 'Ectoplasm' is still in the SPR archives complete with fine 'cheesecloth stitching'.

Just in case you were in any doubt, other samples of Duncan's ectoplasm consisted of:

- White of a new-laid egg
- Ferric Chloride
- Phosphoric Acid and stale urine mixed with gelatine
- Hot margaric acid from olive oil

An interesting further twist to this incident is that Price had actually 'stolen' Duncan from being tested at the London Spiritualist Alliance, who had requested that Duncan sign an exclusivity agreement. This gives his appeal two years earlier for greater cooperation between organisations a rather hollow ring.

Meanwhile back in the USA, JB Rhine claimed that he had observed the medium Mina Crandon faking phenomena by kicking over a megaphone. In doing so Rhine caused a split in the American Society for Psychical Research. It also caused Arthur Conan Doyle, the writer and great 'logical thinker' who invented Sherlock Holmes, to make the intellectual response of calling Rhine an "Ass" in the newspapers.

In the midst of all these egos puffing their feathers, was there actually any psychokinesis (PK) that wasn't explained away? There are certainly some practitioners that were more credible than the others I have so far mentioned. In the earlier days of paranormal investigation these would have included the object mover and self-levitator Daniel Dunglas Home (1833–1886), who despite some accusations was certainly never caught red-handed cheating.

It is a later case, however, that at least seems to hold out some hope, and also shows the rivalry of investigators in the field was increasing. This was the mediumship/PK of Karl, Willi and particularly Rudi Schneider, who were three apparently normal brothers from Braunau am Inn, a provincial Austrian town only otherwise famous for being the birthplace of Hitler.

Of the three brothers Karl was somewhat peripheral to events. Whilst he demonstrated his skills to some extent he was never subjected to any significant tests. More major manifestations started with Willi in 1912. Willi believed himself to be guided by a spirit guide going by the name of 'Olga'. These manifestations included levitations of his body, movements of objects, ringing of bells, billowing of curtains and manifestation of figures.

In 1919 a Captain J. Kogelnik was posted to Braunau am Inn as collector of customs and took a great interest in the unusual events that were unfolding. After attending séances at the home of the Schneiders he published a report which caught the interest of the German psychic investigator Baron Schrenck-Notzing. (Yes, this is the same Schrenck-Notzing (in)famous for his 'erotic' and unethical examinations of the psychic Eva Carrière!)

However, despite major ethical mistakes with Carrière, when it came to his follow-up investigation of the Schneider brothers many of Schrenck-Notzing's investigation techniques were sound and ahead of his time. He for example ensured that Willi was required to wear special tights covered with luminous pins and buttons to be visible in the dark. Harry Price, prior to the setting up of his National Laboratory, had been part of an SPR delegation (accompanying Eric Dingwall, the then SPR's investigations officer) invited to visit these séances. Whilst they both had a reputation for being sceptical, both Price and Dingwall signed statements that they witnessed genuine phenomena.

Willi then travelled to London at the invitation of the SPR, giving 12 sittings on the society's premises. Whilst there were still some impressive phenomena, it seemed his powers were slowly diminishing. Ultimately Willi's powers were to continue to gradually fade and he was to train as and become a dentist, and living relatively normally until his death in 1971.

In Willi's later years as a medium he operated through a new spirit guide known as Mina. When Willi retired, Mina was to transfer her abilities to his younger brother Rudi. This very much showed that the brothers' rationale was that the powers themselves came from an outside entity, and not just a case of hidden powers within.

Schrenck-Notzing had the same sort of success in testing Rudi in the early 1920s as he had earlier with Willi, but perhaps for the wrong reasons this didn't initially set the world of psychic research totally alight. Whilst Schrenck-Notzing was an experienced psychic investigator, he had proved controversial and seems not to have inspired much respect or liking from his peers. This was compounded by the fact that he was also:

> the champion of what must be the world's most unpopular cause — the physical phenomena of psychical research.[23]

Put another way, few had forgotten his championing of the 'papier mâché' spirit figures of Eva Carriére.

It did not help matters when the Vienna-based physicists Stefan Meyer and Karl Przibram assisted in the experiments with Rudi in 1923–24, and claimed they detected him evading control by freeing a hand, and claimed they noticed all PK phenomena ceased when Rudi's arms were made visible by luminous signs.

Harry Price, however, had respect for the modern electronic controls that had been introduced into Schrenck-Notzing séances, and following Schrenck-Notzing's death in 1929 with the assistance and initially also the premises of the London

Spiritualist Alliance (yes the same organisation he 'stole' Helen Duncan from later), Price was to invite Rudi Schneider to his National Laboratory of Psychical Research in London.

Price had been making improvements to the Schrenck-Notzing controls. Under Price's controls the sitters would sit hand in hand and foot to foot wearing electronically-wired gloves and socks connected to a red light indicator. This would signal if any limbs were freed which would in turn cause the circuit to be broken. Under these conditions Rudi's phenomena included impressive PK such as the levitation of a coffee table, the ringing of a handball, and the shaking of curtains. Price thought it impossible that anyone could recreate such phenomena by normal means, and offered £1,000 to any conjurer that could. The offer was not taken up but perhaps the point was simply to get Price in the papers again?

However, whilst the electronic controls that were added by Price looked very modern, scientific and high tech, Price may have led himself partially into the same pitfalls that many modern ghost hunters do today, and for that matter even the SPR members who built the 'S.P.I.D.E.R.' contraption discussed in our preface. Just because a contraption has bells and whistles, it does not make it 'scientific'.

Dr VJ Woolley of the SPR stated at the time that:

... The more apparatus and mechanical appliances are introduced, the more sources of error there must be, and the more opportunities for misdirection by anyone who aims at deception.[24]

Despite such doubts there is no denying that Schneider's demonstrations had been on the face of it impressive and Price handed Rudi a certificate, stating that:

Absolutely genuine phenomena had been produced!

Something Price might just later start to regret!

Rudi Schneider was subsequently tested in France by The Institut Métapsychique International led by Dr Eugene Osty, and whilst the phenomena was less spectacular there was enough of it to come out with positive reviews. Rudi had the potential to become a worldwide phenomenon but was still a provincial Austrian young man at heart who wanted to become a mechanic and had fallen in love with a girl called Mitzi who would ultimately be his wife.

Schneider's return to London for more (paid) experiments was quite possibly motivated by him to raise money for his forthcoming wedding. These further séances and experiments, though initially under the leadership of Price, were funded by the far deeper pockets of Lord Charles Hope, who took a great interest in the paranormal. It became clear that Hope's intention was to 'steal' Price's prodigy from him and experiment further with Schneider himself.

However, just as this further clash of egos approached, during one of Schneider's later sittings with Price, Price reported that a photograph taken at one of his sittings had revealed the fact that Rudi had managed to free his left arm and put it behind his back; this action having the apparent aim of moving a handkerchief by natural means, in a way that appeared paranormal. This information from Price was timed for release at the very time that Lord Charles Hope was investigating Schneider, and with that ended all chance of good will and cooperation in the community of paranormal investigators.

At this point the whole case for and against Rudi Schneider imploded into inconclusive farce with the counter accusation that Harry Price may have actually faked the photograph showing Schneider faking. The first and only potentially known case of faking phenomena being faked – to the best of my knowledge at least!

If, however, Rudi Schneider was in fact a fraud he must have kept his cards very close to his chest. It was clear that even his bride Mitzi believed in his power. Following his early death in 1957 she was reported to be regularly sitting by Rudi's old séance table begging Rudi's spirit guide for a sign that Rudi was still present. Sadly, however, the old séance table never again burst into life and no sign was ever to come!

Whilst the egos of the European paranormal researchers of the first half of the 20th century engaged in this form of one-upmanship, it was perhaps back at Duke University in North Carolina where the greater signs or real progress were being made. After some potentially encouraging results with testing ESP (Extrasensory Perception, more commonly termed telepathy or mind reading), Rhine turned his hand to testing for PK. He started speculative experiments in the early 1930s, mostly using dice thrown from a cup to see if a skilled operator could affect them to throw specific numbers above the possibility of chance. These were apparently based on the initial claims of a professional gambler who claimed to have these skills. Initial tests, however, were to prove inconclusive.

In 1942 when reviewing old tests a potential breakthrough was made. It was discovered that in most of the past tests the results at the start of the tests seemed to be considerably higher than those found towards the end. This would be very much in keeping with any theory that PK, if it exists, likely takes a great deal of mental effort, and therefore would diminish during a testing session. During the analysis of 18 previous testing sessions, Rhine found that the difference between the first quarter and last quarter of each individual test exceeded chance expectations by what he calculated to be a factor of about **ONE HUNDRED MILLION TO ONE**.

These results were positively peer reviewed by J. Gaither Pratt. Though Pratt was also at Duke and the review therefore not external, the results were nevertheless validated to some extent.

Assuming Rhine's findings were correct it leaves just two logical possibilities:

a) The one I guess we are all looking for, that under some circumstances there is a non-physical power that can actually have an effect on physical things (i.e. that PK exists and a key element of poltergeist phenomena might actually be real).

b) That there may actually be some physical skill in throwing dice from a cup which when done in a certain way can potentially give favourability to a particular result (i.e. that throwing dice is not a physical random event).

Scientifically speaking both possibilities are there. The necessity then became to produce a test where physical interference could be seen as rationally and totally inconceivable.

Whilst Rhine retired from Duke University in 1965 he continued his work by founding an independent organisation called the 'Foundation for Research on the Nature of Man', later to become known far more simply as the 'Rhine Research Center'. Helmut Schmidt, an experienced German parapsychologist, was appointed Research Director of the institute in 1969, and set about the task of producing a process that could be devoid of the possibility of any physical interference. His answer to this issue, in the days of still highly simplistic computers, was to produce a form of random number generating machines containing radioactive material which by emitting electrons at random intervals caused either a green or a red light to light up. Whilst the results over a large number of extended tests were only about 1–2% above chance, statistically speaking over a very large number of tests this is fairly impressive. However, even Schmidt admitted in 1993 that:

It has not yet been possible, however, to stabilize and strengthen the statistically weak effects so that they can be easily demonstrated on demand.[25]

There seems to be both strengths and weaknesses in this type of university- or institute-based research. The main strength being that it is done methodically and away from the immediate glare of publicity which had done our subject few favours. However, such research may also show a possible tendency to throw the proverbial baby out with the bathwater – as we will see.

In the UK, the first university-based parapsychology institution was the Koestler Parapsychology Unit founded as part of the University of Edinburgh in 1985, and financed by a legacy from the noted writer Arthur Koestler. Now despite the fact that full funding was on offer, initially this was seen as something of an academic 'hot potato' and something that Edinburgh I think were brave and far-sighted to take on. Thankfully as of 2018 the Parapsychology Association now lists 11 universities (including Edinburgh) in the UK which take part in this type of research to a greater or lesser extent.

In 2015 Professor Caroline Watt, the current Koestler Chair of Parapsychology, gave various talks and presentations as part of the unit celebrating its thirty years of existence. (They also hosted a rather nice party during a joint conference with the SPR as well.)

I attended one of Watt's talks on the Koestler Unit's achievements and got the impression that their achievements (this time more in the area of ESP) are somewhat like Schmidt's, statistically interesting without being 'paradigm shifting'.

It dawned on me during the talk that there was one essential thing missing from the experiments that were described, and I asked her during a question and answer session afterwards why the institute was testing 'normal' people and **NOT** those who claimed to have ESP skills. The impression I got was that, despite their otherwise stalwart efforts, there was a feeling that wider academia wasn't quite ready for the modern equivalent of the larger than life early 20th century mediums. That to have the modern equivalent of a Rudi Schneider (or even worse, a difficult to handle 'grumpy' Palladino equivalent) in their laboratories and likely all over the national press would take away the academic 'respectability' they felt they may have fought hard to gain.

This attitude is not unique to the Koestler Institute – with few exceptions it is the attitude of most of academic parapsychology past and present, both sides of the Atlantic. No modern equivalent of the Fox sisters was ever invited to North Carolina to be tested for PK by Rhine or his successors. Whilst it is clear that dealing with those who claim to be 'gifted' can be both risky and messy, not to deal with them seems to me to be trying to see if a four-minute mile could be run by using the average (slightly) out of condition (slightly) middle-aged man such as myself. Trust me, if that strategy had been taken we would still think running as far as a mile regardless of speed to be totally physically impossible.

So as things lie there is some evidence that shows the potential existence of the PK, though certainly not enough to say it is in any way 'proved'. The next key question is that if there is a controllable non-physical power able to move objects, is it likely to be a similar or identical power to the one seen in poltergeist phenomena? According to Gauld and Cornell in their *Poltergeists* book (p. 320):

The answer unfortunately seems to be a definite NO.

The logic of their conviction seems to boil down to two arguments:

a) That whatever the value of PK experiments – "They have yielded no clear or certain evidence as to the nature of PK."

b) That – "There is no obvious similarity in the fall of dice or in the outcome of binary number generators, and the sorts of happenings which are reported in poltergeist cases."

Here I think, despite their excellent book, Gauld and Cornell have possibly missed the point. As neither the 'Poltergeist Syndrome' nor PK are fully understood, the first steps by definition are to prove their existence, not understand their nature. By gaining evidence as to the occurrence of both effects, the simplest theory at least to begin with is that these effects are connected in some way. A feather falls in a slightly different way to a brick, but they both are caused by the same basic law of gravity. Even if we hadn't yet discovered the subtle aerodynamic twist that makes the feather fall somewhat slower, it would have been clumsy of Newton (who discovered gravity) if he'd dismissed its effect on a feather just because it acted in a way that as yet wasn't fully understood.

They also, I think, failed to note that the PK tests of Rhine and Schmidt were a deliberate attempt to measure and quantify what had until then been seen as a spontaneous effect. So by the nature of their aims the apparatus used was always going to be very different from flying marbles and stones. Whilst the latter could also be tested for movement under control conditions, it would not have given them the type of data they wanted to try to prove their point through statistical analysis.

In defence of my opinion on this, I would also call on the opinion of William G. Roll who also worked with Rhine at Duke University, but was one of the few researchers who actually left his laboratory in search of the spontaneous poltergeist object movement. This culminated in him, like Playfair and Grosse, virtually moving into the home of a family called Resch – for some weeks in 1984. His purpose was to observe the phenomena of the controversial case that become known as the Columbus Poltergeist, taking place as it did in Columbus, Ohio, USA.

This case itself is controversial as the main 'victim' of events,

14-year-old Tina Resch, was once caught fabricating the apparent poltergeist effect of a falling lampshade on camera, and some years later was implicated in the death of her three-year-old child who was murdered by her then husband in 1992. However, Roll was adamant in his support of the reality of at least most of the phenomena (which included picture frames falling down from the wall and a host of other objects apparently moving), and was ultimately to write a book called *Unleashed*, putting his side of the case on record.

Whatever the truth of the events, Roll's best contribution to our understanding of poltergeist phenomena was neither this particular case nor the many others he was involved in. It was the fact that he was one of the few people that went from PK research to poltergeist investigation and saw the connection between the two to such an extent that he re-termed poltergeist object movement as 'Recurrent Spontaneous Psychokinesis' – RSPK. It is clear from this that he thought of them to be two roots of the very same 'tree', or to re-explore my earlier analogy – PK as the subtle floating feather, RSPK as the rather unsubtle falling brick. Both, however, caused by the very same force.

He also showed through the Columbus case the difficulty of keeping an academic reputation intact when a case becomes so controversial. Now personally speaking I think the search for truth is worth that risk, but then again I have no formal academic reputation to protect!

Whilst I think like Roll that there is a prima facie case for connecting PK and poltergeist movement events, the differences between the two in many instances are enough to ensure the debate goes on. Many poltergeists seem to be place-centred things not quite acting in the same way as Rudi Schneider who could apparently travel the world and still show the same powers. To make the connection still more persuasive it would be interesting if some cases could be found that seem to link the two types of phenomena. Perhaps if a poltergeist case could be entirely person-centred and not place-centred, and go on for a good length of time that was similar to those who had ongoing skills in the use of PK – that would surely bridge the gap between poltergeist phenomena and PK?

The question is whether such hybrid cases exist?

To discover that, we need to go back in time again to the first half of the twentieth century – that flawed but occasionally 'brilliant' time of research. The case in question also further demonstrates that the concept of ethics in investigating poltergeist cases was at a very early stage – and we will say more about ethics later. The subject under investigation was not a grown-up medium, but a poltergeist-evoking child of 12 by the name of Eleonore Zugun. Zugun was nevertheless to find herself on the well-trodden European experimental circuit (or circus?). That similar circuit which Palladino and Carrière – fully grown, fully understanding, and fully consenting adults – had found themselves on as well.

Eleonore Zugun was born in a small village called Talpa in Romania in 1913. At the age of 12 she went to live with her grandparents, and possibly this upheaval caused a typical poltergeist outbreak. This included showers of stones entering her grandparents' cottage, similar to those poltergeist cases reported by Playfair from small villages in Brazil. Amongst other things an iron ring fell off a stove and a small mug off the dresser. She quickly outstayed her grandparents' welcome and was promptly sent back home. However, the phenomena followed her there first in the form of stones and then later large potatoes were also thrown. Being Romanian peasants there was talk of her being taken over by Dracu or the Devil, and ultimately her parents felt they had no other option than to send her to a nearby convent. But despite masses being read out by priests and even the intervention of psychiatrists, the phenomena still occurred. Poor Zugun was declared insane and put into the local asylum.

While she was there, the press found out about the controversy which in turn increased the awareness of these incidents around all of Europe, and instigated a visit by the German paranormal investigator Fritz Grunewald. At this stage Grunewald's investigation appeared both thorough and ethical, and included the interviewing of hundreds of witnesses (it's as if he had been listening to Murdie's theory of similar fact evidence, as such in-depth interviewing is rare). He took her back to the convent where he simply observed her for a few weeks and confirmed the phenomena as being active and unexplained.

He agreed to help her further and seemed a man of good faith then returned back to Berlin, Germany to make some arrangements and:

Almost instantly dropped down dead!!

After that, the Countess Wassilko-Sereki stepped in. Also interested in the paranormal but hopefully as a Romanian national, living in Austria, she felt some sympathy for this child that the local peasants had no idea what to do with. When Zugun arrived in Vienna to visit the Countess in September 1925, far from the phenomena diminishing, it actually grew stronger. It would not be long before reports got back to Harry Price in England who visited the Countess and Zugun in April 1926. Within a day he had reported the throwing of a letter opener by an unseen force, when both the Countess and Zugun were at least ten feet away from where it was thrown. By the end of the visit he was so impressed that, in Price's own words (*Poltergeist Over England*, p. 260), he:

> decided to import both the 'Poltergeist Girl' and her benefactress – and I hoped the phenomena – to London.

Now perhaps it is just Price's writing style but the talk of 'importing' seems flippant in the extreme, and indicative that everyone seemed to be forgetting that this wasn't a walking, talking paranormal experiment but a girl who has as yet not quite turned thirteen.

Perhaps it was the stress of all the travelling and testing that seemed to make the powers greater to the extent that Zugun didn't only move objects but started to get strange stigmata scratches and bite marks – after all in her mind all this 'evil' was caused by Dracu – the Romanian devil. Yes, another example of the hypothesis of 'Sugg' that fear in itself and of vampires in particular can bring on poltergeist phenomena. The bites and scratches happened on numerous occasions – but before she could get any further on the 'European Testing' circuit, she began menstruation and her powers were suddenly gone.

It also thankfully turned out that Countess Wassilko-Sereki finally acted with the best of intentions training Zugun successfully as a hairdressing apprentice which she apparently thrived at, and ultimately opened her own shop back in her native Romania.

We will hear more about poltergeist scratching in later chapters. They are not the most common factor in poltergeist cases but definitely are a symptom. This chapter, however, is very much about object movement. Zugun apparently moved objects as well as any medium could. It was not in any way connected with the place she was in. It went on for a long period until only her development and menstruation intervened. Every important factor between Zugun and a medium's experiences seem the same, apart from the fact that mediums, when tested, often show signs of PK, whilst the involuntary nature of Zugun's phenomena would make it by Schmidt's definition RSPK. Zugun's case fits perfectly between poltergeist cases and those whose powers were ongoing and simply tested in laboratories. In many ways that 'missing link' between the two.

As Zugun lost her powers early when her menstrual cycle began, in some ways it was difficult for her to accurately articulate, as a grown-up could, the processes that were going on within her. Was she actually possessed and manipulated by Dracu? This seems an easy rationale for a Romanian peasant girl to take, but as a literal reality of the phenomena it seems rather unlikely. This leaves us with three possibilities, assuming of course the phenomena itself was real.

a) That she was in communication with one or more external intelligent beings – for want of a better word let's call them 'spirits' – who were not geographically fixed to a particular spot, and who happened to unleash their powers each time wherever she was.

b) That she had, during that period, her own personal psychic energies, that her own subconscious mind triggered, and that these triggered – possibly at times of stress or excitement due to her travels. This of course is the option that has the closest link to what Schmidt would have referred to as RSPK.

c) That both options a) and b) are partially correct. That Zugun's phenomenon was caused by powers within her own mind but those powers were manipulated by some kind of spirit or spirits.

In essence that sums up the three options we have when it comes to the poltergeist syndrome. I can think of no other 'paranormal' options that, once the cultural terminology of Devils, Vampires and Duende are brushed to one side, the phenomena could possibly have. It is within the context of these three options that we should ultimately try to fit the phenomena. There is of course a fourth option, that of conscious or subconscious fraud, which we will also say more about later.

Whilst Zugun was not in the position to really indicate which of these options would have best fitted what was happening to her, a person whose apparent paranormal abilities continued long into adulthood would not have a similar problem. For a good example of this we would need to fast forward about just over half a century to 1970s UK, when the phenomena surrounding Matthew Manning ultimately earned him the nickname of 'Poltergeist Boy'. The key main difference between the 'Poltergeist Girl' Zugun and her male 'equivalent' Manning was that there was no trigger that cut off his powers (as there was with the coming of Zugun's menstrual cycle), and they actually continue till this day. So unlike Zugun who was never in a position to articulate her experiences, Manning was articulate enough to write a 'one million best-seller' about his powers at the age of only 19.[26]

It is interesting that the phenomena involving Manning began quite simply with what is in effect a 'Walkabout JOTT'. When Manning was only 11 his father came down to find a silver tankard – normally kept on a shelf – lying on the floor. After replacing the tankard three days later it was found back on the floor again – with careful examination there was no obvious explanation such as the shelf having buckled. By then Manning's father was curious enough to place talcum powder on the floor around the area where the tankard was kept, so as to look for disturbances and perhaps suspicious that one of his three children might have been playing tricks. However, the tankard was found on the floor the very next day – not only without footprints in the powder but without any disturbance caused by it rolling after falling. In effect it must have rose up in the air and then came down on exactly the spot it was found – and other objects were beginning to move as well.

Concern for these strange incidents caused Manning's father to contact both the police and his doctor, both of whom were of little help. He then contacted Dr George Owen a fellow of Trinity College, Cambridge, lecturing in genetics, who had more than a passing interest in poltergeist phenomena. Owen had already published a book, *Can We Explain the Poltergeist?*, and had received the Duke University prize for distinguished work in parapsychology in 1964. When later moving to Canada, Owen was to be involved in a unique exercise to 'create' a poltergeist that become known as the Philip Experiment – of which we will hear more later.

With Matthew being the oldest of the three Manning children at 11, there could have been a suspicion that he may have been, in a paranormal sense, responsible for the phenomena. The traditional theory of poltergeists being that they in some way use, or actually are, the energy of children about to enter puberty. Whilst there seems to be some correlation, there are so many cases that don't fit this theory as to make it sound like a simplistic stab in the dark.

Whatever Owen may have thought was causing the phenomena, he was eager to investigate further. Now I would always recommend that anyone experiencing unexplained events, especially those of a poltergeist, is (correctly) reassured as to the lack of physical risk. Owen gave slightly more unorthodox reassurance – which was recorded in Manning's book *The Link* as being:

The scientific interest outweighed the inconveniences these events occasioned.
(*The Link*, p. 29)

It also seemed that, during his time of investigating, both the scientific interest and the 'inconvenience' increased.

The phenomena seemed to become more intense and with it came according to Manning's book *The Link*:

erratic and unsuspected taps and creaks. The noises would vary from a dull knocking to a sound like a small stone being thrown at the window.
(*The Link*, p. 35)

The phenomena hit a possible peak when the children returned from a short stay away and on returning nine objects moved within half an hour. The objects also increased in size, so that an upholstered chair moved about six feet, a dining chair was upturned, and a candlestick was placed in the middle of a vase of flowers.

Within a few days though it started to diminish, and within about three months of them starting the initial outbreak ceased completely – with all the hallmarks so far of a very typical short-lived poltergeist case. Things for a time returned to normal and Manning, on passing the entrance exam, started attending Oakham School – a top class boarding school. (Current annual fees of £32,520 – approximately US$43,000.)

However, after a cessation of about three years, the phenomena began again in 1970 – firstly at the new home of the Mannings in Linton, Cambridgeshire, England – where the doors on a heavy wardrobe in Manning's room began opening of their own accord. Ornaments also began to be moved around again along with larger objects such as tables and chairs. The phenomena extended in scope with scribbles starting to appear on the walls of the house.

Any doubt that the 'source' of the phenomena was Manning was also removed when similar events started to happen at his boarding school as well. This had such an effect that on two occasions he nearly found himself expelled. For the first time as well there appeared to be evidence of 'outside' entities involved including a Henrietta Webb who had apparently lived in their historic Linton home during the 17th century. Webb and others started communicating with Manning, who also started experiencing bouts of automatic writing and drawings (writing that seems to come not from one's own conscious mind) in languages completely unknown to him, such as Greek and Arabic. He claimed to be communicating with dead people including Frederic W. Myers, pioneer psychical researcher and one of the founders of my own society, the Society for Psychical Research.

From poltergeist boy he seemed to gradually become what would be regarded as more of a conventional medium – from there he was to engage in a bout of metal bending and ultimately to become a spiritual healer which is what he remains today.

Over and above the apparently impressive set of poltergeist and other paranormal type incidents, what are we to make of the longevity and duration of Manning's phenomena, which whilst at first poltergeist in style turned in the end to more of a conventional psychic able to produce phenomena on demand? To look for some conclusions we can do no better than to look at what Manning has to say about the process itself. When asked about his automatic drawing and asked how he knew he was being guided by a particular artist Manning stated that:

I empty my mind as completely as possible and in that state I think of the person I am trying to contact – sending all my energy out to this person who then writes or draws through my hand.

Using:

What would be called kinetic energy associated, I think, with my subconscious?
(*The Link*, p. 125)

He states when asked if he actually communicated with the artists in question that:

Mediums seem to receive strong impressions concerning their communicators; some even see them. However, I get no such impressions, although I can gauge the strength of the person by the pressure applied to the paper by my hand.
(*The Link*, p. 140)

It would seem, based on this, that Manning has a very powerful and active subconscious mind. Not necessarily communicating with the afterlife but giving him the untapped ability to draw in various styles when otherwise a very poor artist.

Colin Wilson speculates frequently throughout his book *The Occult* that it takes such acts of focus to truly unleash or at least to control such ancient powers which have been dulled with consciousness and oncoming civilisation. When talking about the sixth sense he suggests:

> *There is even more reason for supposing that man once possessed an unusually developed sense of impending danger, for our primitive ancestors would otherwise have become extinct in the great droughts of the Pliocene era, more than five million years ago... Man no longer has a great deal of use for... a highly developed premonition of danger. These facilities have fallen into disuse – **but they have not vanished**.*

This seems to sum up nicely the processes that Manning went through. When Manning concentrated he could control his hidden powers – whether automatic drawing is 'supernatural' or not the process is certainly impressive. Stranger still, when Manning was not channelling those powers, they seem to channel themselves in different ways. As he puts it himself.

> *If I do no writing or drawing for two weeks or more, I become subjected to poltergeist activity. After I have been writing or drawing for much more than an hour, I begin to 'run out' and feel tired. The messages become fainter until they fade away or become incomprehensible. It then takes some hours to recharge.*
>
> (*The Link*, p. 115)

Manning was tested several times during the 1970s, including by an SPR team which included the previously mentioned

Mary Rose Barrington in 1978. These particular results were not wholly conclusive with regards to his powers. He had, however, previously been tested in Toronto, with his brain patterns being measured, and most interestingly, where the results were found to be impressive, it was also found that:

> The origin of... the source of... psychic energy in Matthew... was found to be in the oldest part of the human brain; [and] ... therefore suggests that psychic ability or energy is not a 'random gift' or a 'space-age ability', but an innate function and ability in homo sapiens that probably goes back to the earliest history of man; it may be a function that became lost or defunct in most people many thousands of years ago.
> (The Link, Preface)

It is interesting... I would say very interesting indeed... that the whole speculation and subplot of Wilson's book The Occult – of man's latent powers – seemed at least on this occasion to stand up to scientific testing. It would also possibly explain Rhine's observations when testing PK that when the immediate excitement of being a test subject and throwing the dice diminished, the everyday conscious brain took over and the results became normal as well.

Could it possibly be that we all once had the potential to be 'Poltergeist Boys' or 'Poltergeist Girls', and that PK is simply a more mature and controlled sourcing of these natural powers from inside the mind?

Surely when discussing the poltergeist nothing could be quite as simple as that – or is the simplest solution the one that is always missed?

Chapter 6

Is Rapping Phenomena Communication with Something Intelligent?

(More than simply a variation of old Victorian party tricks?)

"Is there anybody there? One rap for yes, two raps for no?"

This phrase is perhaps the most overused cliché in a paranormal investigation, even setting aside the fact that if no one is there, there would be no one to make the two raps for no either.

It starts to sound even more of a cliché when one remembers that this type of 'communication' was brought to prominence by the Fox sisters whom we have discussed earlier. Sisters who were the catalysts of the whole spiritualist religion, but also who were suspected of and at one point admitted to fraud.

However, rapping or knocking in poltergeist cases comfortably precedes the Fox sisters, a good example being that of the drummer of Tedworth which we reviewed in Chapter 2. If we also look at Gauld and Cornell's very thorough analysis of poltergeist cases, as many as 48% had rapping or knocking noises, a clear second to object movement which had 64%. Of these cases where rapping appeared, in about one-third of them the raps appeared to have some 'intelligence'. Where enough 'intelligence' is shown to discount a random natural noise you are again left with the fact or fraud scenario. Either there is trickery involved or else there are supernatural forces – no middle ground. This is what continues to make poltergeist 'symptoms' so very fascinating.

There is a case for poltergeist rapping being potentially the most fascinating and potentially testable symptom of the poltergeist, as not only does it fit in to the 'fact or fraud' analysis, but there is also a potential working hypothesis that may distinguish poltergeist rapping from ordinary knocks and sounds.

The credibility of any hypothesis partly rests with the person who makes it – so a bit of background to the person helps put it nicely in context. The person in question is also a colleague of mine but about whom I would hope to speak objectively and without favour – to quote from the PSI online encyclopaedia:

Dr Barrie Colvin is a specialist in the chemistry and physics of polymers, having graduated with a doctorate degree from the University of Manchester. He worked as a senior research scientist for Shell Chemicals, and now runs his own company. Barrie has been involved with the physical aspects of psychical research for over forty years.

Colvin joined the SPR in 1973 and was co-opted to Council in 2007. He also became an active member of the Spontaneous Cases Committee, where despite his impressive academic and business credentials he has always come over as approachable and friendly as well – a good person to share a pint with at the end of the day at an SPR conference – an 'experiment' in which I have participated with Colvin on more than one occasion with some success. He is also a qualified pilot and owns a private light aircraft. On several occasions when we were discussing the possibility of investigating a case in a more remote area, he also mooted the possibility of finding a private airfield nearby as a perfectly feasible means of getting there. I believe this idea never quite 'got off the ground' so to speak, but in the days when paranormal investigation teams wear uniforms and even have customised vehicles in an attempt to appear 'professional' and corporate, it was an amusing thought that a literal flying visit to a paranormal location would rather impress those who follow this emerging 'style over substance' trend.

Although only on the SPR council for just over a decade, Colvin's experiences in investigating the paranormal go back a long way further than that. It was perhaps a case in 1974 in Andover, Hampshire, UK, that began his fascination in the rapping noises that were so common in poltergeist cases.

The Andover case like so many others began not in an old spooky mansion but in a rather mundane 1960s-built council-owned house, occupied by no less than eight members of the Andrews family, who had lived there quietly for the five years up to 1974 if quietly can ever be a description for such a large household.

However, in April 1974 news of strange events got reported in the local paper. The article described peculiar rapping sounds that were causing the family anxiety. The noises did not seem just to occur to one person as they had been experienced both by Mr and Mrs Andrews, and all of their children whose ages ranged between ten and twenty. There also seems to be a rather mundane intelligence behind the rapping, as it was reported the raps had told some of the children their ages, as well as predicting the results of some important soccer matches.

Colvin visited the family, and after carefully explaining to them his interest they were willing to cooperate in further research. They explained that the noises had first been heard by their eldest child Maria (twenty) and her younger sister Theresa (12) who became convinced they were not random when they started to get answers to questions said in a whispered voice so no one outside the room could hear.

Initially the rapping answered questions in that rather clichéd paranormal code mentioned earlier... One knock for yes... two knocks for no. An alternative but rather cumbersome code was later followed, with the number of consecutive knocks equalling the consecutive letters in the alphabet. Quite often the final knock was loudest as if to indicate which letter had been reached. In this way the intelligence was identified as being called Eric Waters.

As for the football predictions there were enough inaccurate ones as well to show that whatever powers 'Eric' had, the power of premonition was not necessarily top of the list.

Colvin noted during his first visit the appearance of a happy family who were not unduly concerned by the events. However, this perception somewhat changed after the unhelpful visit of a member of the local spiritualist church who explained that the house had a spirit who was trying to take over the personality of Theresa – and even more melodramatically it was the spirit of a young boy who was buried under the floorboards – in a house that had only been built a decade before! If you refer back to Chapter 3, the similarities of this macabre claim to the claims of the Fox sisters having the peddler Charles Rosa buried in the basement are all too apparent, which shows how unhelpful 'belief-led' interventions can be. It is also further evidence that a fear factor can feed phenomena. Subsequently the family reported to Colvin that since that point, communications with the intelligence had become tenser, to the extent that by the end of April 1974 they were kept up all night by what was much louder knocking. When Colvin revisited the family the very next day he managed to witness loud unexplained bangs as well as frequent rapping sounds. The raps emanated from the side wall of the final bedroom in the house, so any fraud could only have been caused by collusion with the Andrews' neighbours with the rapping coming from the shared party wall. This is of course an explanation that, whilst there is no apparent motive for, cannot be discounted. We are back again to that fact or fraud scenario.

In any case there were also to be occasions when 'Eric' rapped on different walls and even on the bedhead. The latter incident is very interesting indeed as when Colvin took hold of the bedhead he noted that:

On each occasion the onset of vibrations seemed to be slightly before the moment when we heard the rapping sound.[27]

Whilst Colvin accepted at the time that this impression, though distinct, could have been subjective, it was perhaps to have a real effect in his thought process, when he did further experimentation into rapping phenomena over three decades later.

There was a period when the rapping became even louder and more aggressive, perhaps prompted by provocative questions by one of the children accusing Eric of "never existing". However, when things calmed down Colvin tried an interesting experiment. This consisted of picking a random playing card when Theresa was facing the other way and asking Eric to tap out the number it was. This experiment was on the whole a success, thus significantly diminishing the possibility of either trickery by Theresa, or by someone outside of the room.

During one of his final visits Colvin was accompanied by Dr Reinhardt Schiffauer, a scientist at Egham Research Laboratory in Egham, Surrey, UK. Though describing himself as an open-minded sceptic, Schiffauer could find no obvious explanation for the phenomena he experienced. By June 1974, like many poltergeist cases, the phenomena were to finally die down and apparently stop.

Whilst the family believed Eric was an intelligence of a past life and, due to the influence of the medium, also believed his bones would be found under the floorboards someday, Colvin's thoughts on the matter were rather different. After extensive research he could find no reference to any Eric Waters in the area and pointed out in his report that:

No verifiable information was derived from Eric to suggest the existence of a personality outside of Theresa's mind.

And that:

There is no reason to assume that if intelligent communication is witnessed by means of rapping sounds, then the source of that intelligence must be from a discarnate entity. Overall the evidence suggests to me that the 'living person' hypothesis is a more probable interpretation in this case.[28]

He also found distinct connections between Andover and other cases, such as a well-known case in Cideville, Normandy, France which took place in 1850. This particular case included multiple raps, which also showed they had ended in a much louder rap. Further similarities were found to a case in County Fermanagh, Northern Ireland, which was investigated by a Professor Barrett in 1911. Here Barrett used a similar experiment to when Colvin held up cards to test the poltergeist's communication skills. Whilst with Barrett's test, the number of fingers he had open in his pocket was a little more subjective and difficult to observe than Colvin's, the fact that 63 years earlier a similar test got similar positive results is nevertheless of interest in our search for 'Similar Facts'.

Since Andover, Colvin has been involved in numerous areas of investigations, from physical mediums to auras and more straightforward cases of hauntings. My suspicion is that elements of the Andover case have always stuck in his mind especially with regards to the nature of the raps, and the fact that he could feel vibrations on the bedhead before any noise appeared. The main difference between poltergeist raps and other elements of poltergeist phenomena is that, whilst for example there are very few credible video recordings of object movements, there are numerous examples of audio recordings of unexplained rapping sounds. However, if an object is videoed flying across a room of its own volition, it is immediately very good evidence for the paranormal. The problem with recordings of raps is that without evidence of the whole context of how they were gained, they are simply recorded noises that could be caused by numerous natural means.

Or are they?

Colvin became curious as to whether a paranormal sound could by its paranormal nature be shown to be different in some ways to normal sounds, and more than thirty years after Andover he began to collect different examples of 'apparent' poltergeist raps. As the paranormal community in itself has no central database of information, this by itself is quite a task, but by hard work and persuasion of his peers Colvin managed to collect rapping recordings relevant to the following cases:

*Schleswig, Switzerland (1968) – A case involving mainly rapping phenomena centred on a 13-year-old boy.

*Ipiranga, Brazil (1973) – One of the series of previously mentioned poltergeist investigations carried out by Guy Playfair and the Brazilian Institute for Psycho Biophysical Research.

*La Machine, France (1973) – Where in this old mining town an 11-year-old boy asked an unseen entity questions and got 'intelligent' raps in return.

*Enfield (1977) – Thankfully Grosse and Playfair had extensive tapes of communicative raps that occurred here and were happy to share the results.

*Santa Rosa, Brazil (1988) – Where rappings on a young girl's bedroom were captured on TV.

*Euston Square, London, England (2000) – A case investigated by Maurice Grosse and Mary Rose Barrington involving rappings near the bed of a boy called Edwin.

*Suachie, Scotland (1960) – Where an 11-year-old girl seemed to be the catalyst for the recorded rapping phenomena.

*Thun, Switzerland (1967) – This was different from the stereotypical case involving a child around the time of puberty. This case involved a lady who had been recently treated for both depression and addiction.

*Pursruck, Germany (1971) – A case investigated by the famous German paranormal researcher Hans Bender, where there were two apparent triggers for the phenomena, sisters aged 11 and 13.

He had also become aware of some tests on recordings of poltergeist raps previously. These included raps recorded by those familiar names Gauld and Cornell in 1959, which when analysed at Nottingham University were found to have:

> *a curious feature in the lower frequency ranges. The amplitude of the sound wave of each rap, instead of beginning to peak and then dying away... worked up to a peak over a brief period of time.*[29]

Colvin put the entire above list of examples of recorded poltergeist rappings through a similar process and found that, virtually without exception, they had the same unusual 'sound envelope' which he described as:

> *a relative gradual increase in amplitude, sometimes exhibiting several wave cycles before reaching a maximum.*[30]

This is entirely counter-intuitive – for example imagine a hammer hitting a piece of wood and the sound increasing after the initial impact – but of course counter-intuitive and supernatural are both very different things.

Colvin's next step in the process was to see if normal raps could under certain circumstances behave in the very same way. To test this he tried the following combinations of natural raps:

- Knuckle tapped on both brick and plasterboard wall.
- Teaspoon tapped on crystal glass.
- The sound of middle C on a piano (in effect the sound of a padded hammer hitting stretched wire).
- The sound of a rubber mallet hitting a wooden desk.
- The same rubber mallet this time striking rubber – to see

if the impact of two flexible surfaces could change the normal sound pattern.

In all cases, however, Colvin found that the peak in sound was virtually immediate and then died down at different speeds depending on the material.

Could it be that paranormal raps are an entirely different type of sound – that a poltergeist in effect has a sound signature?

Could it possibly even be that the 'poltergeist' energy in some way causes the sound to emanate out of the material itself? That would account for Colvin's experiences at Andover, when the bedhead seemed to vibrate before any noises were heard.

The implications of such a hypothesis are of course immense. If a feature of the poltergeist syndrome is very difficult or impossible to replicate in everyday life, this would be indicative of a phenomena at least currently not fully understood by science. An important secondary implication would be that any rappings claimed to come from a poltergeist which didn't fit the 'delayed peak' sound pattern would be prima facie caused by natural causes or fraud.

In 2010 Colvin published his paper "The Acoustic Properties of Unexplained Rapping Sounds", giving a presentation to the SPR in Kensington, London. Such speakers meetings normally get about 40 people attending, but such was the initial interest that I understand attendance was well over 100.

You would have hoped at that point that someone would have tried to replicate Colvin's experiments or that even a sceptic would have set out to find a much more natural explanation for the differences. Initiatives in investigating the paranormal have become such voluntary ad hoc efforts in recent times sadly – to the extent that:

Nothing really happened at all!

Theories were shared in paranormal social media but no one thought to 'get off their butt' and actually try to replicate Colvin's experiments for themselves.

So a potentially important breakthrough was left to gather dust for several years!

In late 2016 I attended a monthly speakers meeting of 'The Ghost Club' which meets at the Victory Services Club, near Marble Arch in London. I had no real knowledge about the speaker and in reality simply wished to meet up with some old friends. Several of my earlier investigations were done whilst Vice Chair of the Ghost Club before I became more active in the SPR and it still has excellent social function in bringing like-minded people together.

As a 'bonus' the speaker, Rachel Hayward, turned out to be very interesting. She explained her experiences of being brought up in an apparently haunted house, which fascinated her so much she subsequently helped set up an investigatory organisation called 'Researchers of Paranormal Events' (R.O.P.E.).

There are now many local paranormal groups in the UK – one estimate states as many as 1,200. These groups vary enormously in quality – some simply wish to prove their own preconceived ideas and should not be let within a mile of any potentially haunted home. We will say more about that in a discussion about ethics later. However, when Hayward explained her group's investigation techniques, I must admit to being rather impressed. She also mentioned a case her group had investigated recently, that of Hereford Shire Hall in Hereford, England, in which poltergeist rappings had featured, and though I didn't get a chance to talk to her after the meeting I later sent her an email out of curiosity enquiring about the quality of these rappings.

Hereford Shire Hall is one of those places which, whilst it undoubtedly has a strange past, currently encourages Ghost Hunters to 'experiment' there for a fee. This doesn't of course mean there are not phenomena there – but the extent of it in such places can be prone to exaggeration. To quote the website of Dusk Till Dawn, who promotes such events in the hall:

> *Built in the early 1800s and Grade II listed the Shire hall in Hereford has a gruesome and chilling past. Reputedly haunted and built on the site of the original Herefordshire prison – the Shire hall consists of eerie court rooms, dark and creepy cellars and the original scary prison cells...*
>
> *Much ghostly activity has been reported here such as loud bangs and knocks – whereupon further investigation no living person was present at the time along with reported sounds of heavy footsteps walking down stairways.*

My sceptical side, when listening to the tape, was perhaps half-expecting one or two creaking floorboards or very quiet tapping sounds. What I actually got were very distinct noises that seemed to be attempting to hold a basic conversation for over five minutes.

The first thing to do was to make a written transcript of events and to see to what sense real communication has been made. A copy of which is below:

1) 6 seconds: Two faint taps.

2) 20 seconds: One further tap.

3) 48 seconds: One further tap on demand by the investigators.

(Investigators then start trying to communicate via the code of silence for no and one tap for yes.)

4) 1.02 minutes: Asked if communicator was the jailer – silence.

5) 1.16 minutes: Asked if communicator had been in custody

there – one tap response.

6) 1.37 minutes: Asked if communicator was female – one tap response.

7) 1.48 minutes: Asked if communicator had died at the jail – no response.

8) 2.03 minutes: Asked if the communicator had been hanged – one tap response.

9) 2.14 minutes: Asked if the communicator had been accused of the crime of murder – one tap response.

10) 2.26 minutes: Asked if the communicator was guilty – one **very** faint tap.

11) 2.37 minutes: Asked to confirm guilty to murder – silence.

12) 2.53 minutes: Asked if communicator was innocent – one tap response.

(N.B.) This was the one clear case of inconsistency in the communications.
13) 3.12 minutes: Asked if the communicator was under 25 – silence.

14) 3.30 minutes: Asked if the communicator was over 25 – silence.

15) 3.40 minutes: Asked if communicator was over 50 – silence.

16) 3.53 minutes: Asked if communicator was 25–50 – one tap response.

17) 4.10 minutes: Asked if buried in the Shire Hall – silence.

18) 4.29 minutes: Asked if buried in churchyard – silence.

19) 4.35 minutes: Asked if buried by a road – silence.

20) 4.40 minutes: Asked if communicator was not buried – one tap.

21) 4.50 minutes: Communicator was asked if he could speak – no response.

There were no subsequent responses including when the R.O.P.E. investigators asked if the communicator was still there and then thanked the communicator for her efforts.

Whilst there was not enough information gained to imply 'who' had made the rappings, their timing definitely appeared to go beyond simply random creaks in a fairly old building, and had in any case a very definite resonance of being very deliberate. So we are left again with that much simpler analysis that comes with poltergeist phenomena, when compared with fleeting sightings of a ghost. Were the rappings supernatural 'fact' or natural 'fraud' (be it conscious or subconscious)? The next stage then was to ask who was where in Hereford Shire Hall at the time and get some idea of how easily an outside (living) party could intervene.

Hayward came back to me explaining that there were only two people involved, in the impromptu communication session, including herself, and that they were both:

seated at the Custody Sergeant's Desk by the cells… The cells are located directly under the main courtroom. The tapping is coming from the table itself and whilst we are talking/communicating we are checking each other and the table to find the source of the noise. Both [of us] can confirm that not only was it not us tapping but there was nothing in the vicinity that could cause the noise. There was no heating on and no heating implement anywhere near us. The cells have been upgraded in recent years but the main structure of the building including the walls that hold the cells were built in 1815 and are very, very thick.

There were other people on the upper floors of the building that night when they were in the basement but in response she went on to say that:

We have investigated the possibility that we could hear people above us (unless there is a crowd of people yelling you can't) but could also confirm that there was no one in the courtroom [directly above where they were] whilst we were downstairs.

With regards to the location of the recording equipment she identified it as a Philips DVT1110 Digital Voice Tracer Audio Recorder and stated that:

The voice recorder was on the table. The tapping seemed to come from both under the table top and on top of it. Kim and I were seated opposite but away from the table and we could both see each other's hands, feet, and legs.

Based on Hayward's further remarks the scope for outside fraud appeared limited. Now theoretically speaking of course, collusion by the two people in the room is a possibility.

If we look at the context, however – the fact that I asked for the recording (it was not offered to the SPR to prove any point), and the fact that she took a few weeks to dig it out of her archives, and add to that the fact that there was no evidence that they were in any other way trying to publish the tape, and the theory of fraud becomes meaningless in that there was no one they were actively trying to trick. Whilst Bishop Berkeley's unseen tree (discussed in Chapter 4) may well actually exist, fraud is something that definitely needs a third party to give it some meaning.

By coincidence, I had a colleague in the Spontaneous Cases Committee of the SPR who was taking a particular interest in the previous work by Colvin. Like Colvin, James Tacchi is also a pilot but a commercial one of far bigger planes. He studied Theoretical Physics & Applied Mathematics at degree level, and holds the position of Training Captain with a major UK airline. James is a Council member of the Ghost Club in the role of Science & Technical Officer, and a member of the SPR where he sits on the Spontaneous Cases Committee. He is also very experienced dealing with the acoustic side of paranormal phenomena, through his involvement in a long-running group called 'Para.Science' who are renowned in the UK for being the most thorough of investigators. This included (prior to Tacchi joining the group) an investigation in Cammell Laird shipyard, near Liverpool, UK, for an astonishing 750 hours over a period of time.

Tacchi was enthusiastic to both test the Hereford Shire Hall tapes and also to see to what extent Colvin's work could be replicated. I have further thoughts on the matter myself, but for those more interested in the science of sound or those who simply like an interesting but accessible report, Tacchi was happy to allow it to be used in full.

Report into Acoustic Analysis of Anomalous Raps
By James A. Tacchi

Abstract

In February 2017 I was sent by Mr John Fraser a recording made during an investigation that appears to contain evidence, through a series of rapping sounds, of communication between the investigators & an unknown intelligence. I was asked to carry out a preliminary acoustic analysis similar to that described by Dr Barrie Colvin (2010). Initial analysis of the waveforms appears to show characteristics similar to those described by Colvin; however, I was able to produce, through conventional means, 'control' rapping sounds which when subjected to the same analysis revealed very similar qualities. Thus since little is known about the details of the recording, it is impossible to make any conclusions regarding the nature of the alleged anomalous rapping.

Introduction

Colvin (2010) subjected a series of alleged anomalous raps to detailed analysis & the results indicated that the acoustic properties differed to those of raps produced by conventional means. In particular, it was noted that the 'attack' time of an anomalous rap (that is, the time taken for the rap to reach its maximum amplitude, or volume) showed a steady increase to maximum, in contrast to a conventionally produced rap in which the maximum amplitude was reached almost immediately.

This was despite both types of rap sounding identical (as heard by a human ear). Importantly, some of the examples included contained both anomalous & conventional raps recorded at the same time & with the same recording equipment, hence providing a useful control by which any results obtained could be compared.

My aim here was to subject the raps submitted to a similar analysis & to see whether any conclusions could be drawn.

The Recording

The recording was sent as a CD which had been burned from a recording made by a Philips DVT1110 Digital Voice Recorder. A detailed description of the methods & equipment used for audio recording is outside the scope of this report, neither is it required here, however, it is useful to cover a basic overview.

Having downloaded the user manual, it appears that all files are recorded in a 'lossless' WAV format at one of two quality settings. The 'bit rate' (effectively how much data is recorded per second) is quoted although there is no mention of 'sample rate' or 'bit depth'. The sample rate determines the frequency of sound recorded (half of the sample rate) & the bit depth determines how much data is recorded per sample. Multiplying these two numbers together gives the bit rate per channel (one for mono, two for stereo) – since this is a voice recorder (& due to the physical appearance of the device) it is reasonable to assume that it is a mono recorder.

It is not clear from the recording as submitted which quality setting was used; however, we will assume here the highest was used of 384 kbps. It is normal for modern devices to record with a bit depth of 16-bit; hence this gives the sample rate of 24 kHz. This sample rate would allow recording of sound up to a frequency of 12 kHz, which as we will see later is consistent with the audio analysis.

That said, the recording was then converted to a stereo CD file which I then converted to a WAV file to allow the acoustic analysis. This has resulted in the final recording used for analysis being recognised by the analysis software as being a stereo file, with 16-bit bit depth & 44.1 kHz file sample rate, giving a bit rate of 1411 kHz. As described above, this is not consistent with the manufacturer's specification.

Hence some assumptions have been made regarding the original recording, plus it has undergone some processing. This in itself presents problems when attempting to draw any conclusions.

Analysis
Adobe Audition software was used to analyse the waveforms.

This is the same package used by Colvin (2010) & allows full acoustic analysis.

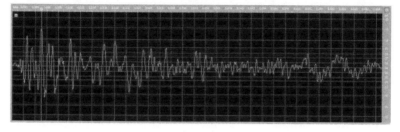

Figure 1

Figure 1 shows one of the anomalous raps. It can be seen that there is a steady rise to maximum amplitude (where the waveform has its largest vertical extent), reached after 5 or 6 cycles have occurred.

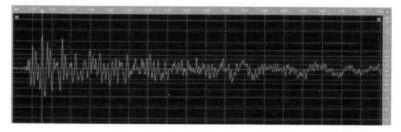

Figure 2

Figure 2 shows another example of an anomalous rap. It is now worth comparing these to raps that I created using conventional means. In all cases an Olympus LS-11 Linear PCM Stereo Sound Recorder, recording at 96 kHz & 24 bit into a WAV file, was used. I then separated the resulting file into left & right channels & the figures represent the left channel only. This was a purely arbitrary choice as both channels exhibited almost identical properties.

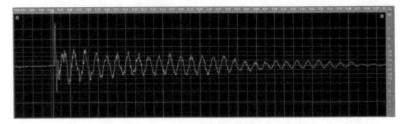

Figure 3

Figure 3 shows the waveform of a knuckle on a wooden table. An instant rise to maximum amplitude is evident.

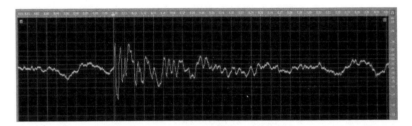

Figure 4

Figure 4 is a rap produced by a knuckle on a plasterboard wall. This was a 'quiet' rap, almost inaudible to make any maximum amplitude less obvious but again the expected waveform pattern is evident.

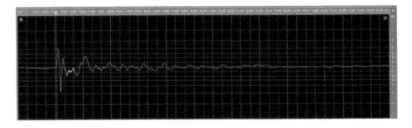

Figure 5

Finally, Figure 5 was an attempt to produce a waveform with a slower build-up to maximum amplitude by using a rubber mallet on a carpet. Despite this, an instantaneous rise to maximum amplitude is clear to see.

However, for my last few attempts at producing conventional raps, I used a slightly different approach. The previous three examples all involved positioning the recorder near (within 10–20 cm) the source but in this case I positioned the recorder approximately 5 m from the source, in direct 'line of sight'.

Figures 6 & 7 show the resulting waveforms of these two knocks on a plasterboard wall (as per Figure 4, although with a little more force).

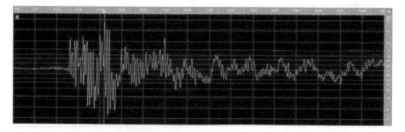

Figure 6

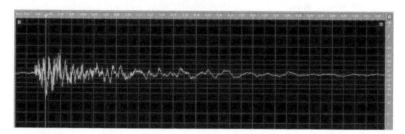

Figure 7

As can be seen in Figures 6 & 7, a clear maximum amplitude is not as obvious as in the previous raps & the waveforms do contain some marked similarities with the anomalous raps, particularly the slow apparent build-up to maximum amplitude.

Discussion

From the analysis performed, it seemed superficially that the anomalous raps submitted for analysis did indeed conform to the conclusions made by Colvin (2010), that is, these raps did appear to have markedly different acoustic properties to those produced by conventional means.

Unfortunately, I was then able to demonstrate, through conventional means, rapping sounds that mimicked the acoustic properties of the anomalous raps submitted, thus I am unable to conclude that the raps submitted were either normal in origin or indeed were produced by some as yet unknown method.

From the analysis performed, it appears that the distance from the recorder to the source of the raps has a significant effect on the waveform characteristics. A discussion of why this may be the case is outside the scope of this report, however, very briefly, one may assume that the acoustic properties of the surrounding environment (objects, furniture, walls etc.) play an important role with reflections & absorption affecting the sound when it reaches the recorder.

It is unfortunate that the submitted recording contained no examples of 'control' raps to which they could be compared, nor details of the position of the recorder. In addition, even if recorder position was available, it may not have been obvious where the source of the anomalous raps was, making any assessment of their distance from the recorder meaningless.

Recommendation

It is the author's belief that this area would benefit from further research, as suggested by Colvin (2010), one area to be looked at in particular would be a more robust & standardised methodology of recording anomalous rapping sounds. This would encompass many areas, not least the recording equipment used, format of the recording & the effect of any subsequent processing. Perhaps it could also include a recommendation to produce some 'control' raps at the time of the anomalous raps in order to make any comparisons meaningful.

This analysis has been hampered by many uncertainties surrounding the origin of the recordings & it is hoped that going forward, any future investigations into this subject will have access to high quality data whose integrity is not in doubt.

This was an excellent report, which was as much a reanalysis of Colvin's work as an analysis of the Hereford Shire Hall case. It is worth looking at analysing the more interesting conclusions that Tacchi makes.

In his report summary Tacchi notes that:

Since little is known about the details of the recording, it is impossible to make any conclusions regarding the nature of the alleged anomalous rapping.

Now it is unusual and potentially foolhardy to say anything unusual is by its nature paranormal, and Tacchi is quite correct not to make definitive conclusions. In fact the only time I remember this happening is when Harry Price in effect gave Rudi Schneider a certificate of paranormal authenticity – fully discussed in Chapter 5. As Price was later rightly or wrongly to accuse him of fraud such actions are definitely not wise.

What is also fair to say is that I was the only one having an ongoing 'conversation' with Rachel Hayward during the time Tacchi was doing the analysis, and had basically asked him to carry out the analysis without any real back-up information. So he was correct to say little was known to him of the details of the recordings, but as we have seen from our earlier discussion this is not necessarily true in the wider sense.

Tacchi then went on to replicate natural rapping sounds in the same way as Colvin did including very quiet raps and using more flexible surfaces such as a rubber mallet on a carpeted floor and got the same instant peak effects as under Colvin's experiments. As with Colvin's poltergeist cases, when Tacchi analyses the Hereford Shire Hall recording he finds the slow build-up to amplitude peak as well.

However, there are a couple of very important provisos that Tacchi notes, the principal one being his experimentation when he:

Positioned the recorder approximately 5 m [about 15 feet, 5 inches] from the source, in direct 'line of sight'.

In this case he found that conventional rapping can have the same build-up of amplitude as the paranormal ones when in effect the recording equipment was on the other side of a fairly large room.

This proviso is of course very important as it both refines Colvin's hypothesis and restrains its use to when the recording equipment is in the immediate vicinity of the rapping source. It does not though directly affect the finding with regards to the Hereford Shire Hall case, especially so as the source of the equipment was established as being close before it was known to be relevant. With regards to the other cases investigated by Colvin, the location of the equipment after such a gap of time would likely be an open question of course. An investigator's instinct I think would be to record as close as possible to a strange event, but as it was not then thought to be a scientifically relevant point it is likely the exact locations were neither recorded nor necessarily even remembered.

Now that one important proviso has been created, it is possible there may be others, for example to test how quickly peak amplitude is reached when the recording equipment is close to the source of the rap, but the rap itself whilst close is made through a wall in the next room – which of course might well occur in a case of fraud.

Tacchi also noted how useful it would have been if a normal rap had been made at Hereford Shire Hall to compare with the unexplained ones. This if you remember was carried out in one of Guy Playfair's Brazilian cases, and a recommendation which Rachel Hayward and her colleagues were happy to take on board, if 'lucky' enough to experience such distinct noises in the future.

So where does this all leave us? Personally I would say that it leaves us in a very interesting place. There is no obvious explanation why the Hereford Shire Hall case raps should have built up slowly – with the recording equipment close to source, and unlikely that in most of the other cases the equipment was placed far away. Even more importantly it gives good guidance notes for ways to progress in the future:

a) Always keep recording equipment close to source – and always keep current notes as to the recording equipment's location.
b) Always rap the apparent source of the unexplained raps (table, bedhead, wall etc.) in a natural way with the knuckle to allow comparison.
c) If any acoustic expert has a couple of days to spare they should explore how amplitudes peak when a rap comes from the outer side of a wall to where the recording equipment is.

These are excellent ways to experiment and to avoid one-off incidents simply remaining 'one-off anomalies' – by building up a worldwide case file that could look to either prove or disprove the hypothesis. That is the way a hypothesis becomes a theory and then a fact in science – if we wish to make further progress we should surely learn from that!

Let's assume though, for argument's sake, that poltergeist raps are in some way paranormal, we are left again with questioning whether they are caused by a spirit of a dead person, or a spirit that never lived such as a demon/vampire/imp – take your choice of words – or whether instead they are caused by a subconscious power within us. My suspicion is that in most cases people who are catalysts for poltergeist activity opt for an outside entity. It is nearly counter-intuitive to put the cause of something on to yourself of which you have no awareness of doing. What though if it was possible not only not to find any evidence for that outside entity existing (as was the case with Eric Waters in the Andover Poltergeist), but actually to show that the outside entity **definitely** never existed at all?

As mentioned in Chapter 5, George Owen, who had spent time investigating the 'Poltergeist Boy' Matthew Manning, was later to emigrate to Canada where he helped set up the Toronto Society for Paranormal Research (TSPR). In 1972 in an experiment to prove whether a paranormal phenomenon was an extension of the human mind, he decided to literally try to 'invent' a ghost.

With the assistance of psychiatrist Dr Joel Whitton, he got a group of eight people together from diverse walks of life – from engineers to an accountant, a nurse and a student. The (retired) nurse, a lady called Sue, was given the task of inventing in effect the ultimate archetypical ghost story, and created an absolutely totally fictional character named Philip Aylesford, a nobleman and supporter of the Royalists at the time of the 17th century English Civil War. Philip, she decided, had an unhappy marriage to a lady called Dorothea along with a passionate affair with a gypsy girl called Margo, who was ultimately to be falsely charged of witchcraft. Due to Philip not intervening in her defence she was found guilty and burnt at the stake. The cowardly Philip, full of remorse, was to throw himself off his own battlements and commit suicide. His (non-existent) spirit could surely not rest in peace.

All the participants in the group were aware of the fact that this story had been made up but were told to visualise Philip as if he were real. A picture was drawn of him to make the process more authentic, weekly meditations ensued and details were added to his character, but at first there were limited actual results. It was only when the solemnness of the proceedings was lifted, and the weekly sessions started to resemble a more light-hearted impromptu séance of the type that had existed in the 19th century, that strange things started to happen. Lights went off, objects were moved by unseen hands and even the table started to levitate. Most interesting to our current discussion was the fact that Philip started trying to communicate through rapping... using that tried and tested formula one rap for yes and two raps for no! This way the group got yet more information about the non-existent life of Philip Aylesford. Subsequently they were also to create an entity called Lilith who died working for the French resistance during the Second World War.

Creating in effect an active 'thought form' might have been unique in 20th century Canada, but is a tradition of ancient Indian and Tibetan Buddhists that was also taken on by some Western occult groups in the 19th century. Such thought forms are known as Tulpas and defined as an entity created in the mind, acting independently of and parallel to your own consciousness. Like a sentient person living in your head, separate from you. It seems to me that this definition comes so very close to an active and wilful subconscious mind, which can independently play tricks, move objects and even communicate with others.

Even if sceptically inclined it is difficult to write the Philip experiment off as a hoax, as the group became more famous, media became interested and full table levitation was filmed on Canadian TV, during which one sceptical observer from Kent State University had the table hurled towards him when he made some negative comments.

There are two last and very relevant twists to the 'Philip' experiment. The participants specifically reported that the initial raps were not heard but felt to be vibrating through the table before there was any noise. This is a very similar experience to the one Colvin had at Andover, and gives further credibility to poltergeist rapping having a specific sound 'envelope'.

The second interesting twist was that the intention was at first to try to create a visual entity. It seems it was possible to summon up a poltergeist but far more difficult with regards to a conventional ghost. This furthers the argument that supernatural proof, if it is to be found, is far more likely to be found in this type of phenomena – though as we will see in the next chapter the two can become very mixed up indeed!

The implications of the Philip experiment are very far reaching. If an entity can be created it either means that that entity is:

Created from some power within ourselves.

Or

Created by some malevolent demon who has a compulsive bad habit of impersonating fictional characters just for a bit of 'fun'.

Both are logically possible and both are 'supernatural'. It's simply that one of these theories seems just a little beyond our current understanding, while the other seems unnecessarily complex and has a 'feeling' that it would not be out of place in a book of Grimm's fairy tales. I will let you decide which of these theories is which!

Chapter 7

The Mixed-Up World of the 'Intermediate' Case!

(Not everything fits perfectly when the subject matter is both 'mischievous' and unexplained.)

Up until now it could be claimed that this book has had the slant of our two main phenomena battling for superiority. A situation that could be parodied as Poltergeists versus Ghosts – like one of those B Movies such as *King Kong vs. Godzilla* in which (if I remember correctly) King Kong came out on top?

There has certainly been a claim that poltergeist phenomena are the more spectacular and testable of the two. I have made particular emphasis of this partly because it seems that compared with the effort put into investigating 'ghostly' phenomena in traditional 'haunted sites', so little comparable effort is put into discovering and investigating active poltergeist cases.

If the poltergeist is indeed the 'King Kong' of paranormal phenomena, this is not to underestimate its partner in crime 'Godzilla', that mutated dinosaur lizard with 'atomic' breath, who has made appearances in about thirty movies to date, and who was never definitely killed off by the great 'Kong', simply disappearing into the Pacific Ocean until a likely sequel was made.

This analogy is an amusing one with which to start a chapter, but also shows, with regards to poltergeists and ghosts, that if either phenomenon exists we are discussing strong paranormal powers in each instance. The analogy also has one big weakness, however. Rather than poltergeists and ghosts being involved in an epic struggle they have a surprising tendency to team up and work together.

To see how surprising this tendency is, we have to look again to the encyclopaedic efforts of Gauld and Cornell, who noted from the 500 cases they studied for their book *Poltergeists* that in 29% the appearance of phantoms was also a significant feature, whilst 26% included audible human-sounding ghostly-like voices. Gauld and Cornell termed these "Intermediate Cases" – a strange hybrid of poltergeist and ghost.

Whilst I know of no survey done the other way round, to find out how many haunted houses have also had poltergeist phenomena, I would expect that to be very significant as well and possibly significantly higher than the 29% the other way round. My supposition is based on the fact that due to the nature of the way the subject of hauntings is presented by authors, there is a whole subcategory of 'haunted places' that are not really haunted at all. Take away these cases and it might just be possible that what you are left with is a core of mainly such hybrid 'intermediate' cases. This is a point that needs some further explanation to fully understand the concept, and the implications behind it as well.

In the UK the first real modern guide to hauntings came in 1971 when the late Peter Underwood, one-time colleague of mine in the Ghost Club, wrote his *A Gazetteer of British Ghosts*. Though some of the cases were well researched, others were based on folklore – wonderful to read but ultimately tales likely unfounded in fact. Such tales included those of children starved and in rags being seen outside of Bramber Castle in Sussex, UK, always apparently at Christmas – or a coach and headless horses galloping across a road on Dartmoor, Devon, possibly ridden by the ghost of the beheaded Sir Francis Drake. Other tales included a bloodcurdling tale of the poor ill-fated Dame Dorothy Selby, walled up in her own ancient home of Ightham Mote in Kent, for apparently betraying her fellow Catholics and foiling the 'Gunpowder Plot' – that ill-fated attempt to blow up the largely Protestant Parliament in 1605. However, there is an inconvenient problem in that Selby's mausoleum and burial place is in the nearby church, and the fact she didn't pass on until near forty years later – likely from septicaemia (blood poisoning). This is in effect a ghost story that simply could not exist.

Romantic ruins of Bramber give a traditional ghost story of child ghosts whose basis is likely just myth – more recently 'active' cases tend to be of the 'intermediate' type.

The book includes more recent cases such as one I have myself researched in some depth – that of Sandford Orcas, a wonderfully authentic Tudor manor house built of Golden Ham Hill stone and dating back to around the 1550s.

Whilst Sandford Orcas has been in the ownership of the Medlycott family since 1976, it was leased and occupied for a long period between 1967 and 1979 by Colonel Francis Claridge who claimed that he and his family had experienced at least 14 ghosts. It was Underwood amongst others that publicised the Colonel's claim to have the most haunted house in England and basing it on the reported numbers it might have been a reasonable assumption to make at the time.

However, when I contacted the house as a possible prelude to an investigation in 1999 I got a very robust response from Mervyn Medlycott, claiming that whilst he was not a disbeliever of psychic phenomena, nothing had been seen in the house for the 21 years since Claridge had left. Medlycott thought that the stories had been simply made up in an effort to bring in more paying visitors.

Some of the manifestations claimed by Claridge had quite a detailed description. These included a young sea cadet who committed murder whilst at sea and was incarcerated in a room to avoid a public scandal, and a seven-foot-tall footman who was jailed after accosting a girl from the village. Based on the fact that Claridge would have not got this information from the Medlycott family – one would then have to ask, where else would he have got such detail and how could he be so sure what phenomena was caused by what entity? Outside Claridge's experiences there is only a very small amount of other witness testimony, so when we combine this narrowness of the witness pool (to largely just one family) with the whimsical and uncorroborated nature of the ghosts themselves, we are left with a case of very little use in the evidential sense.

Whilst I have every respect for Underwood as a ghost hunter, by including uncorroborated or poorly corroborated folklore in his book, he rather started a trend – to mix our country's wonderful folklore up with more recent well-authenticated cases. I would be interested in discovering whether such a trend is present in other countries with similar cultures of ghosts such as the USA, Canada and also parts of Scandinavia!

In the UK many factual ghost books have been something of a rehash of much of this wonderful whimsy. However, the other main UK ghost hunter of that period Andrew Green at least made an effort to buck this trend in his first major volume in 1973 *Our Haunted Kingdom*, where he made sure he only included cases that had at least some witness statements from the previous 25 years. We should not be overcritical though of Underwood or those who came after; a good readable book on ghosts or poltergeists has to follow an interesting narrative. They are meant to make people think and provoke the mind to new possibilities. They are certainly not meant to be a dry 'scientific' journal as I fully admit this book neither sets out to be. In fact I found recently there is now a likely error in one of my earlier chapters, that I wrote in good faith at the time, but which I now think of a good example to keep in – to discuss in a later chapter when the 'fact' or 'fraud' scenario is more fully discussed.

Within Underwood's book there are of course also examples of far more recent cases, an example being of Kenton Theatre in Henley-on-Thames, Oxfordshire, where to quote Underwood:

In 1969... [the play] The Hanging Wood based on a story of a local girl, Mary Blandy, who was hanged in 1752 for poisoning her father, was produced here. As soon as rehearsals began unusual incidents took place. A large mirror 'jumped' off a wall, lights were switched on and off, doors were mysteriously opened and closed. A figure of a girl was reported at the back of the theatre...

This case happened only two years from the book's publication so is likely reported with accuracy. It is interesting to note that it includes elements of hauntings such as apparitions and those of poltergeists all mixed into one. Both 'King Kong' and 'Godzilla' were clearly on the premises.

There was also of course a large section on the haunting of Borley Rectory – which with numerous books written about it to date is perhaps the UK's most famous recent haunting of all. Borley despite some controversies and accusations of fraud has witness statements regarding the haunting starting from Victorian times and continuing to this day. This included visual phenomena such as the sighting of a phantom nun in the garden but also flying bricks or stones far more suited to the poltergeist genre. At one stage it included possible poltergeist wall writing as well – similar to those that may have occurred in the Matthew Manning case.

In 1940 its long-time investigator Harry Price (of whom we have heard so much about before) had the first book published about Borley unabashedly titled *The Most Haunted House in England*. As you have gathered by now such 'downplaying' of his cases was very much Price's style. However, the Borley case has an even more interesting factor with regards to good paranormal research. It initially had only one family, the Bulls, resident in the Rectory from when it was built in 1863 for 65 years until 1928, but then had a fairly fast succession of Rectors.

Guy Eric Smith and his wife moved to Borley on 2nd October 1928 for only two years.

In October 1930, Reverend Lionel Foyster, his wife Marianne, and their adopted daughter Adelaide moved in – they lasted a little longer moving out after five years.

The Rectory remained empty for a while until in 1937–38, when it was rented out by Price himself for a year.

Captain William Gregson and his family were the last people to live in the rectory. The rectory burnt down on the 27th February 1939; apparently the ghosts were seen in the flames.

This means that from 1927–39 there were at least five different people in charge of the building and at least five different sets of experiences to compare.

The number of rectors, owners or renters was only, however, the very tip of the iceberg, as when Price leased the property in 1937 it was not for his use but for that of the 48 independent observers/paranormal investigators he had advertised for in *The* (London) *Times* – some of whom had very strange experiences there.

After the rectory burnt down strange experiences still took place, and have continued on and off in Borley Church and on the rectory site to this day.

Borley therefore has a vast pool of witnesses that have experienced apparently inexplicable things.

The full scope of Borley is far outside this book (though more will be said of it later in relation to fraud), however, I think it helps prove an important point. Once the legends and myths of long inactive or 'never-were' active ghosts have been tenderly but firmly pushed to one side, what you tend to be left with is a fascinating mix of ghost and poltergeist phenomena intertwined. This could possibly even make ghost sightings in some ways a subset of poltergeist phenomena.

Other than a thorough analysis by Gauld and Cornell, the nature of the 'Intermediate Case' has been very much neglected. In fact I had not even heard of or considered the term myself till a few years ago. Perhaps that was because in 2010 such a case was to literally fall into my lap, which I have kept an active watching brief on ever since.

On Tuesday 20th July 2010 I received an email via the Society of Psychical Research website of an unusual but rather compelling honest nature in what it was asking. A close approximation of its contents is summarised below:

Hi my name is Vanessa Mitchell, I am the owner of The Cage medieval prison... I lived there for three years and have rented it for the last year... but yet again my tenants are in the process of moving out... No one ever stays there long... there has also been a suicide [in the fairly recent past prior to Vanessa moving in]. I am thinking of letting in paranormal groups. [It subsequently emerged that she felt uneasy renting her house out to yet more 'unsuspecting' people when she didn't feel able to live in it any longer herself.] I have seen many ghosts in there in broad daylight, also a huge amount of [paranormal] activity – including me getting slapped hard on one occasion... any advice would be great.

Vanessa Mitchell, owner of The Cage, who could no longer stay in her home due to the apparitions and poltergeist type phenomena she experienced there. A good example of an 'intermediate' (haunting and poltergeist) case as defined by Gauld and Cornell. (Photo Credit Peter Ladanyi)

I replied on the 21st July along these lines:

Hello Vanessa,
Thank you for your interesting message. I am curious as to the type of advice you need. I wouldn't necessarily see letting your house out to voluntary paranormal groups as a long-term solution

to your genuine problem... Please, however, tell me more about the
phenomena that has happened.
My very best regards
John Fraser

I think I remember hoping at this point that she was not the only witness to these events, as however genuine the experience and the person – accepting the testimony of just one person takes a great leap of faith.

The next exchange of emails unleashed a large list of things that had thankfully happened to others as well as to her – and whilst it would be a few years until I fully researched this, the seeds of a project emerged.

The Cage, St Osyth – Old lock-up jail extended into a private home
and a subject of an in-depth report by the author because of the
phenomena reported there.

Two particular things are worth noting about this case. Firstly unlike the case mentioned in Chapter 1 regarding the single mother in the South London council flat, Ms Mitchell has never at any time requested anonymity about the events. In fact an interesting account of her own chronicle of happenings can be found in her book *Spirits of the Cage: True Accounts of Living in a Haunted Medieval Prison* (Llewellyn, 2017), co-written by the respected Anglo-American ghost hunter Richard Estep, and including his thoughts of his own investigation over several days.

My process of research and investigation was to prove a very different type from spending the night there surrounded by electronic equipment. It was to culminate in a project attempting through very thorough witness testimony to analyse the nature of the haunting. Below is an abridged and edited version which keeps the finding in the context of what was known about the place in 2015. It also fits in with many of the concepts we have discussed so far in this book. I add a few comments about this in [brackets] but many others are simply self-explanatory. Like any 'good' ghost story, however, it continues to evolve and fascinate. Perhaps I was wise to call it an interim report?

The Cage St Osyth: Interim Report
A Project of Witness Testimony Analysis of a Traditional Haunting Investigated in 'Modern' Ways.

ABSTRACT
This property caught the imagination of the popular press in 2012 when it was reported that the owner, Vanessa Mitchell a single mother of one, decided she could no longer live there or rent it out, due to the experiences both of her and other residents. Mitchell took the decision to try to hire the house out for paranormal investigation. Like most other reports of active paranormal activity there was a danger that anything valid could become second-hand hearsay in time, or for that matter hearsay could become reported as fact.

This project therefore set out to report on efforts to make a record of first-hand witness testimony beyond that of simply the owner, to see if any meaningful theories can be found when this testimony is brought together, and to explore the strengths and weaknesses (in an evidential sense) of short periods of observation and measurement by differing people – which is in effect the style of modern paranormal investigation most often seen today.

METHODOLOGY

Witness testimony with regards to the Paranormal in itself can be a controversial issue, particularly when involving individual paranormal investigation teams. Sceptical arguments would for example state that due to the lack of a common methodology and other factors such testimony counts for little.

Alan Murdie Chair of the Ghost Club and council member of the SPR who is also a qualified barrister tends to disagree. Pointing out that even:

The courts accept that collections of what may appear to be isolated facts or reports, emerging from the testimony of different witnesses... can constitute cogent proof to a standard beyond reasonable doubt.

And that:

Similar fact evidence... enables separated collections of isolated testimony to be taken together to act as cogent proof.

Murdie then goes on to argue that it is logical that evidence that can put someone in jail should also be evidential at least in establishing a case for evidence of the paranormal.

I believe Murdie's argument to be relevant in this project especially as the point of this exercise was not to try to prove anything beyond reasonable doubt – that would be too ambitious in this stage of our understanding of apparent paranormal phenomena, but simply to ask whether any evidence is of a strong and compelling nature or not – and if it is shown to be just that, what is it evidence for?

As far as I am aware relatively few attempts have been made recently to try as comprehensively as possible to trace back to original witnesses. Perhaps the first modern type of collation of witnesses was the tenancy of Harry Price at Borley Rectory. Here, however, the observers he chose were given instructions in advance sometimes of a leading nature via what became known as the 'Blue Book' of instructions. Such a scenario is of course very different to going back to a case and picking up information later. Perhaps the most witness-focused case recently was that of the Enfield Poltergeist (Playfair, 1980), where an on-hand presence of the two investigators Grosse and Playfair ensured any debriefing session happened quickly.

In many ways therefore such a process of gathering evidence of a fairly large number of past experiences is therefore experimental. For that reason I mainly kept to the report of anomalies that could be classed as being objective. Those for example involving any sixth sense or mediumistic ability I have dealt with briefly separately. This in no way comments on their validity or otherwise, it simply avoids any analysis being along well-trodden arguments about whether such experiences are subjective or objective and real.

For practical purposes as much as anything I also avoided data regarding EVP and other recorded phenomena as each would have needed to be analysed to decide its evidential worth.

Initially I optimistically thought a form could be devised for initial responses but quickly found out that quite frankly people's experiences don't fit nicely into tick boxes. Data was therefore gathered in several ways:

Key witnesses who lived locally to The Cage and who visited it or lived in it when it was used as a residential home were interviewed face to face with the invaluable assistance of Rosie O'Carroll of the Ghost Club. A summary of the interview was *then emailed to the witness to ensure the facts were interpreted correctly.*

Structured telephone interviews were used with other witnesses, especially those who had later investigated the cage. These were largely taped. Again a summary of the main points raised were emailed to the witness for confirmation or correction.

Some interviews were conducted purely by email; these, however, would consist of several exchanges to fully clarify points and understand the extent of what was experienced.

In a few cases where key witnesses have already stated publicly on film or online their report of what occurred and when what occurred was significant and clear, notes have been made of these experiences as well.

In all cases not already out in the public domain the option was given for witnesses to remain anonymous. That option was only taken in a few cases.

Care was also taken to identify the location within the premises of an unusual event. The property was ideal for this being in effect a fairly small cottage. It consists of two bedrooms, a bathroom, a staircase, the 'Cage' room (built around the original holding cell – thus getting its name) including an extended kitchen area, and a separate reception room off a small entrance hall.

Only what were interpreted as significant events were included, and in the case of the actual residents especially many significant events of a similar type were summarised. This excluded what were clearly events of an ambiguous nature such as noises that on the balance of probability may have come from outside or creaks in floorboards that may not have been anything sinister.

INTRODUCTION

The Cage as it is dramatically called is [debatably, as the true age of the cage is unclear] an 18ᵗʰ century property in St Osyth, Essex built over a [possibly] much older smaller shell which was used as the local holding jail up until 1908. Its most famous prisoner was perhaps the local 'witch' Ursula Kemp who it is thought was kept there amongst other similar accused before being tried and hung at Chelmsford in 1582.

It was purchased in 2005 by Vanessa Mitchell, despite a local reputation for being haunted, which is perhaps not so unusual in an old property of this type.

In 2010 Ms Mitchell initially contacted the SPR's Spontaneous Cases Committee reporting that phenomena had made the house uninhabitable and making the unusual request of asking for advice as to what to do with a property no one could any longer stay in, and whether in our opinion it was ever possible to let out a house as a haunted site for research purposes?

I visited Ms Mitchell in 2010, taking with me a colleague, Rosie O'Carroll of the Ghost Club. Whilst nothing unusual happened at The Cage during our time there, Ms Mitchell appeared to be a credible witness giving consistency of testimony and accepting that some facts may appear difficult to believe at first. The timeline above gave me the impression that she genuinely believed the place to be haunted, and that any appeal regarding letting the house out to paranormal researchers was a purely last resort option. Her thought process (in my opinion) being along the lines of 'I have a haunted house that I can't live in and don't feel morally able to let out again – what can I do with it?' I attempted to dissuade Ms Mitchell from this option [of letting out her house for research purposes] partially on the grounds I thought it unlikely to be a practical solution to her issue of what to do with the premises.

Shortly after our meeting Ms Mitchell did indeed offer her house open to paranormal research groups. This reached the national press and TV which reported it in their normal sensational way. However, on a short-term basis at least from a practical point of view my advice was incorrect. My understanding is that she received investigations over a period from many paranormal research groups of various types (and more likely or not of varying belief models as well). During this period it could possibly be claimed that The Cage became the most talked about active haunting in the country.

INITIAL EXPERIENCES OF THE OWNER

When Ms Mitchell moved into 'The Cage' in the late spring of 2005 she was almost immediately joined by a close friend Nicole Kirtley as her lodger. J.C. (pseudonym), a male friend of Nicole Kirtley, joined them in early 2006.

Ms Mitchell has stated that prior to buying the property she was aware that it had, like many old houses did, a reputation for being haunted. She had previously lived in the area, and knew of a middle-aged couple who claimed that books flew off their shelves whilst they were there. (Ms Mitchell admits that she didn't know them that well and as they are long gone it has not yet been possible to establish this first hand.) She was also fully aware that there had been a suicide there in the not too distant past which took place on the stairs landing next to the bathroom. [As this suicide is within living memory all details to it are omitted, other than to say we have tracked down sufficient proof to show it is not a local myth.] Mitchell states that on her first day there she turned and saw a figure of a tall dark male walk from the Cage room into the Lounge. In the following weeks and months amongst other things she recalls doors slamming or opening with no wind to push or pull them, footsteps upstairs. Ornaments would fly of the mantelpiece, the old chain from the original prison building would swing back and forward and the hall stairs door would crash open in a forceful almost violent way, taps turning on and off, door latches rattling through the day and night (as if someone was going to come in the room, but never did), a Coke can whizzing across the table, objects disappearing then turning up in unusual places or not turning up at all, objects turning up out of the blue that did not belong to her, something walking up and down the stairs in the night. Amongst other apparitions she viewed a transparent lady carrying what seemed to be a bowl of herbs from the Cage room to the living room, a sighting which may have had some association with one of the 'witches' that was held there? She also stated in initial correspondence that she ultimately entered a state of dark depression which only cleared up quickly after she finally moved out.

What made the final decision for her to move was when she saw a man standing at the top of the landing with modern day clothes on... "he wasn't a burglar he was a ghost of a man and standing very near my son's cot."

When Ms Mitchell moved out she first tried to let the property to a long-time friend. The new female lodger reported to Mitchell that she also experienced phenomena to the extent that she had requested the help of a psychic who had ultimately refused to enter the house on arrival. She also reported that she felt a similar dark depression while resident there.

This tenant moved out after four months and the next tenants a young couple with a baby lasted half that time; during that time it was rented out by an agent so it cannot be conclusively known the reason these tenants decided to leave quite so quickly.

At that point Ms Mitchell decided based on her own and others' experiences that the house should not be let out for residential purposes again and attempted to rent it out for investigation by paranormal groups and individuals with a reasonable amount of success. It was also at this time the press started to take an interest. The house is still sometimes used for this purpose and is currently now up for sale.

CORROBORATION AND ANALYSIS OF THE INITIAL TIMELINE

It was clear when investigating the credibility of these interesting initial reports that as things stood, most of the reports were coming from one witness, the owner. That is of course hardly surprising, but from an evidential view based on witness testimony it is of course not ideal. So part of this project included a further visit to the village again with my colleague Rosie O'Carroll. The point of the visit being to interview others who had unusual experiences at the time the house was occupied. In this case interviews were conducted face to face and on tape, [An interesting twist here was our choice of venues. With hotel bars being too public, and The Cage itself too foreboding and hardly a neutral venue we took the choice to hire out a nearby caravan on a small holiday site, which despite its unconventional nature actually suited its purpose well.] and involved Nicole Kirtley, resident for part of the time with Vanessa Mitchell, Kirstine Blackwell a frequent visitor and cousin of Ms Mitchell's, 'Nick' (pseudonym) a friend of Ms Mitchell's, Neil and Kirsty Williams who were also friends. J.C. the male resident at the time of Ms Mitchell's residence was unavailable for interview. He, however, has given several interviews previously including on video, and his comments are nevertheless useful for comparison purposes.

Whilst none of the witnesses had experienced quite the intensity of the phenomena as the owner, their testimony did in fact prove very interesting indeed.

Nicole Kirtley who moved into The Cage almost immediately after Ms Mitchell experienced the door latch being undone in her bedroom room (later used as Ms Mitchell's child's nursery/ bedroom) and the door swinging part the way open on numerous occasions. She also had numerous occasions of JOTTs objects (normally clothes) disappearing and reappearing in places where they were most unlikely to have ever been put. An interesting point to note here is that Kirstine Blackwell who sometimes kindly visited the property when no one else was at home reported experiencing exactly the same phenomena – thus negating the possibility of practical jokes (at least by a physical entity).

As well as the day to day mysterious events Nicole was also witness to some significant one-off incidents. This in particular included the strange appearance of an important document relating to a past resident on the kitchen surface. This was not the immediately previous residents and so could not have been put down to something simply having been left behind. She also sighted orb-like lights filling the living room along with Vanessa, and was witness to the Coke can sliding across the table in the living room that has previously been mentioned. She also reported that after she had stopped living in The Cage, on one of her return visits she had found it extremely difficult to enter the premises. This was beyond being just nervous – more like a feeling of having to "wade" through the door. By itself this is an interesting but somewhat subjective incident – the reason why it may be evidential will be more fully explained later.

Perhaps the strangest and for that matter the best witnessed incident of all was when Nicole, Kirstine and 'Nick' were helping Vanessa move out of the premises. There was a loud bang from upstairs heard by the three ladies who were all on the ground floor which happened at the very instant that Nick had pulled up outside in his van and seen the shadowy figure of a lady in one of the bedroom windows. It is this sort of coordination of testimony that can very much help to strengthen a case.

As previously mentioned Kirstine Blackwell tended to often visit the premises when the residents were out to help tidy up. As well as the incidents previously mentioned there were at least two other unique incidents that Kirstine reported as being totally inexplicable.

The first involved when she was tidying up in the kitchen alone and was hit by two soft objects on the back of the head.

On turning round she found that two sugar sachets (previously stored with others on the opposite work surface) were lying on the floor and had apparently been the objects that had struck. This was sufficiently unnerving for her to have the urge to ring up Ms Mitchell to report it. The other incident of special note was after stacking up books in the Cage room again when alone, found them shortly afterwards to be randomly-strewn all over the floor – in a way that could not have happened if the stack had simply collapsed.

Kirstine also reported the feeling as if she was about to be pushed from the top of the stairs.

'Nick' a friend of Vanessa's also tried to help around the house when he could, and during one of these times when repairing an electrical fault at the top landing he also felt a force physically trying to push him down the stairs.

On leaving the living room for a short while, he also found that a large vase had repositioned itself without explanation from the floor of the living room into a hole that he was helping dig beneath the floorboards in a search for interesting artefacts.

Perhaps most interesting, however, his witnessing of the door latch move in the nursery/bedroom and the door being opened at such an angle that it appeared to be being violently moved. This not only corroborates Nicole's testimony but gives a sense that this was not simply a badly-hung door – something we found no evidence for during a basic inspection during our recent visit.

As mentioned previously it was not unfortunately possible to talk to the other resident of the house during the time Ms Mitchell lived there. J.C., however, has appeared on camera to be interviewed about his experiences (North London Paranormal Investigations, 2012) confirming the high level of activity in the house and specifically talking about seeing a figure "as clear as day" behind him in the bathroom on one occasion.

Before finishing this section regarding the initial outbreak of phenomena it is worth pointing out the extended timeline *of these events. Since The Cage no longer has any permanent residents it has gained a good deal of publicity, a professional website and undoubtedly a fair number of bookings both from serious paranormal investigation groups and those who are simply curious. It would therefore be possible to think in passing that an 'old mysterious' house was purchased just for that purpose. This is why it is so important to point out that every effort was made to live in the house for several years, after which it was rented out while the owner Ms Mitchell has lived in rented accommodation at different addresses including at one stage in a caravan. This hardly seems to in anyway be an obviously planned lifestyle choice.*

When she contacted the SPR in 2010, it seemed clear in my opinion Vanessa Mitchell fully believed that her house had significant paranormal activity. The question which this report needs to continue to answer is whether that belief can be justified to an outside investigator, which as previously stated can only be really achieved with a wide variety of other witnesses.

FINDINGS AND OBSERVATIONS OF PARANORMAL TEAMS AND SUBSEQUENT VISITORS

Let us first go back to the debate about whether it is a useful tool of analysis to have a series of differing people spending time at a place of paranormal reputation. Hayley Stevens a sceptical blogger in a critical review of phenomena at 'The Cage' has this to say:

You can't conduct an investigation in one day as there are so many data variables that you have to try and account for before you even begin to investigate allegedly anomalous phenomena. How can you study the mean temperature of a location in just one day? How can you account for regular electromagnetic fluctuations in a building in just one day?

How can you map out the normal movements of the building in just one day?
(Stevens, 2015)

Stevens is actually strictly speaking correct if the aim of an investigation is to totally overcome accepted scientific theory in just one visit and prove a place as haunted – but [I believe] incorrect in the sense that most investigations should and do not even aim to achieve this. [If you expect to overturn all known science with one night in a possible haunted house yes quite frankly you are deluding yourself.] Most investigations simply should aim to observe and add to any relevant data, and to gauge the strength of a case through measurement and observation. As the pioneering scientist [and believer in some aspects of the occult] Nikola Tesla better puts it:

> The scientific man does not aim at an immediate result... His work is like that of the planter – for the future. His duty is to lay the foundation for those who are to come, and point the way.
> *(Tesla, 1934)*

Where a weakness may actually lie is that in apparently haunted places where this type of multiple investigations takes place there has been to date no central point in which any agreeing or conflicting data can be collated. This is actually why I thought this exercise in at least partially doing this was long overdue.

There is one advantage, however, in not really knowing what happened in previous investigations. This means there is far less potential with regards to suggestibility of specific phenomena. This was of course the mistake made by the 'Blue Book' of instructions at Borley.

Without a complex narrative of what has been or should be seen any correlation of events becomes far more significant in the evidential sense. The limited narrative that exists about 'The Cage' was as a former witches' holding cell in which strange events took place. However, very few observers saw or picked up much to do with what might be witches, which is actually much more in line with the known history. Ursula Kemp and her associates (if staying there at all) would have likely only spent a few weeks imprisoned there before going to Chelmsford for trial and ultimately the execution of Kemp and one of her colleagues Elizabeth Bennet.

Before looking at events that did indeed have a high degree of correlations I list a random series of anomalies which show that what the residents experienced seemed to continue after they had left.

K B (male) of S E Paranormal Investigations (SEPI) reported that he and part of his team heard bangs coming from the bathroom wall partially on request as if something was trying to make communication. Amongst other things they also experienced a pebble fly across the room whilst in the main bedroom.

Investigator M K (female) heard a growling sound in the kitchen and a woman's crying coming from the lounge.

Donna Harris while leading the investigation group 'Ghost Search UK' reported that her group heard a noise as if a heavy object was being dragged across the floor in the main bedroom (when in the nursery/bedroom next door). Nothing was found to be moved on investigation. Muffled thuds were also heard while in the living room.

S L (male) an experienced television producer heard distinct voices in the main bedroom and also experienced the swinging chain that was hanging in the Cage room which had been reported at times when the place was still inhabited.

D M (male) who organised investigations in 'The Cage' on various occasions reported amongst other things an iron moving along the floor of the downstairs cloakroom.

Added to this there is a selection of very unusual phenomena, on public record on the Internet. This includes an investigation and film made by Chris Halton of **Haunted Earth** *where while during their filming in the living room a loud noise was heard and a Ouija Board (one used in other investigations and not the type of equipment they wished to use) was found to have been thrown across the Cage room when previously standing in the corner (Halton, 2012).*

North London Paranormal Investigations reported and recorded footage immediately afterwards of a table moving in front of the inwardly opening nursery bedroom door when the bedroom was empty (North London Paranormal Investigations, 2012).

It is fair to say that not all groups had active nights. The Ghost Club for example found very little phenomena during the night of their investigation.

Overall there was a significant selection of events with on the face of it no obvious normal explanation (and only a small proportion of the unusual things that were reported during the interview and information gathering process). This in my opinion by itself shows that the phenomena in The Cage can certainly not be dismissed. Over and above these one-off events, however, there were certain trend events the sort of 'Similar Fact' evidence that has been supported by Alan Murdie's paper.

'SIMILAR FACT' OCCURRENCES

The Staircase

The staircase is only unusual in that it actually has a door at the bottom. Otherwise it appears normal for a house that is stated on an estate agent's specification to be largely early 1800s – possibly extended over the original older holding cell.

Footsteps on the staircase seem to be the most common type of phenomena. These have been experienced by the Ghost Search team, S E Paranormal Investigations, the **Haunted Earth** *filming team, and separately by investigators D P (male) and D M (male) amongst others. Such footsteps were also a common occurrence when the house was inhabited. In the case of D P (male) his experience of the footsteps was reported to occur when the door to the staircase slammed, a phenomena also reported by Nicole Kirtley when she lived there.*

Whilst such footsteps were part of the original phenomena, they were not a 'headline' event that was likely to have given a predisposition for any researchers to let their expectations run away with them. There is of course still a possibility that there may be something in the natural fabric of the building that causes footstep-type noises to occur (although that would not explain any incident of the door to the stairs slamming at the same time). Now that this phenomena has through multiple witnesses been identified as being so common, it should give any future investigators with an understanding of old buildings a specific project to concentrate on – which in itself shows the usefulness of such gathering together of data.

However, collective evidence on the staircase does not end with this auditory phenomena, with 'Nick' and Kirstine Blackwell identifying the sensation of something actually trying to push them down those stairs.

Could such feelings of being pushed, however, simply be subjective? This of course is a possible answer. When we look at the national press report regarding the investigator Chris Palmer – who was actually pushed to the extent that he fell and landed on a fellow investigator (**Daily Mail Online, 2012**) *the subjective theory regarding such experiences starts to fit far less comfortably with the overall data.*

Lifting of Latches – Opening of Bedroom Doors
This was a phenomenon that was predominant when The Cage was inhabited by Mitchell, with all three of the initial

inhabitants confirming this. The nursery/bedroom door (actually Ms Kirtley's and J.C.'s bedroom at the time) seems to have been the room where this was most frequently witnessed. Again any future investigative teams should look for normal explanations relating to uneven floors and faulty latches etc. However, 'Nick', long after the house had stopped being occupied, described the movement of this door as opening up at an angle as if being violently pushed which would not sit quite so comfortably with the 'quirks of an old building' theory. The **Haunted Earth** film team also captured a very decisive movement on video (Halton, 2012). This when combined with their experiences of hearing footsteps on the stairs (mentioned earlier) makes a 'quirks of an old building' theory less likely to be the full explanation.

Poltergeist Scratches

This refers to physical scratches on the skin (as opposed to scratching noises) and is a relatively rare type of phenomena. [Perhaps the best-known case was that of Eleonore Zugun, the Romanian peasant girl which we fully discussed earlier in Chapter 5.] It is perhaps quite surprising therefore that I have to date reported four separate incidents of such occurrences at The Cage. These cases are of course very different to that of Zugun, however, whose phenomena seemed centred around her rather than because of a person's presence in a particular building.

The first occurred to S L (male) who noticed a pain in his leg immediately after leaving the building and photographed the back of his right leg as soon as he could, which shows significant scratching and redness when it is viewed.

The second is stronger evidentially on the basis that the lady, a member of S E Paranormal Investigations, was more aware of the point of impact (on her arm) as being during part of the investigation that took place in the bathroom. A photo was taken shortly afterwards and shows that blood had been drawn.

The third, however, is the most impressive of all involving

a colleague of Donna Harris named 'Emma' who was assisting during an investigation. When Emma was sitting on the easy chair in the living room (wearing boots with jeans tucked inside thus protecting her legs from any likely normal source of abrasions) she suddenly felt a pain in her legs and later found that blistering and scratching had formed. The blistering was later examined by a doctor and diagnosed as being burn marks.

Potentially related to these is a fourth example – a severe stabbing pain in his leg that an investigator felt when in the lounge at The Cage which caused some bruising. This will, however, be discussed in the next section.

Extreme Emotional Reactions

This could potentially be the most controversial 'Similar Fact Occurrences' that took place, as by their nature emotional reactions are phenomena internal or subjective to the person. In much the same way, however, as if mediums had independently received a particular message not in the public domain, internal experiences that correlate between non-associated groups of people at the very least can be deemed to be of 'interest' in the gathering of evidence sense.

There is undoubtedly a psychological factor in being placed in a house that is reputed to be haunted. I have, however, conducted investigations in such places as the haunted underground prison cells – which can be definitely categorised as more psychologically 'atmospheric' than The Cage. If we call a degree of nervousness the normal 'baseline' effect in such places, The Cage seems to extend this normal effect exponentially.

A female investigator who had been to The Cage several times before was suddenly reduced to tears on the stairs, could not stay in the building and had to immediately arrange a lift to come from close to London to take her back home.

D M (male investigator) also stated he was reduced to tears after being prodded and bruised on his leg in the lounge...

TV producer S L (investigating in a private capacity) has described to me in detail as to how he hit one of the darkest moods he could imagine shortly after a visit.

Though perhaps not as intense as those stated above, members of the S E Paranormal investigations suffered from chest pains and headaches shortly after entering the premises.

The next two examples are so very similar as to be especially significant. Mr Kim Sondergaard, founder of Dansk Parapsychologist Aspect, one of a relatively few active research groups in Denmark, was visiting The Cage as a possible prelude to making a television documentary. When he entered the main bedroom – to put it in his own words:

I began to feel as if my legs would not carry me anymore... I bumped into the wall, into the door and could not stand still... at one point I suddenly felt a strong hatred towards 'Jette' (a member of his team).

Sondergaard's strange behaviour caused the others to evacuate the building with him. He then goes on to explain that:

Standing in the courtyard... Then I broke down... I started to cry uncontrollably.

Sondergaard, an experienced investigator, ultimately believed he had become possessed in some way.

Let us compare this further experience of the same female investigator who was once reduced to tears again who whilst also in the main bedroom had been filled with a rage for no reason and had wanted to punch a fellow investigator in the face. Both experiences also strangely included the unusual perception of facial 'shape shifting' as well i.e. the belief that the facial features of another had changed to something unworldly and bad. [This is interesting but inconclusive with regards to our *previous discussions about Tulpas, or thought forms in Chapter 6.]*

If we refer back to the dark mood experiences of Ms Mitchell and potentially other residents, there does seem a strange pattern emerging. When all this is pulled together the reactions of those in The Cage seem I believe to go far beyond the normal baseline of feeling 'on edge' in a house that may be paranormally active. I therefore feel that such reactions when taken together are potentially significant of something very strange.

What that 'very strange' thing is, is of course open to debate. It could be something paranormal or even an unusual but natural atmospheric effect in the building, but whatever they are, such a collection of extreme emotional reactions which cannot be dismissed out of hand as not being related.

N.B. A collection of all raw data is shown on the chart below.

Name	Organisation/ Purpose	Source	Incidents	Notes
K.B. (male)	S E Paranormal Investigations	Email interview	**Noises:** Footsteps+: Movement:+, (Pebble flew across room) Movement +(Clockwork Toy)/ **Noises:**+ (Communicating bangs) /	
Blackwell, Kirstine	Visitor to house when occupied. Cousin of Owner	Face to face	**Touching:** Scratching (of lady's arm blood drawn) /Intense: Chest pains/ Headaches +/ Movement:? Cushions rearranged on Couch, Movements: (Sugar sachets hit head). Stacked books found on floor Intense: Feeling as if about to be pushed, Movement: JOTTs Clothes disappearing found elsewhere. Noise-Loud Bang Upstairs	

Darnell, Sarah	Ghost Club	Face to face	**Intense:** Felt unable to be there alone in bathroom without someone close by outside	Otherwise uneventful night.
Halton, Chris	Haunted Earth	Internet Film	**Movement:+** (Of unused Ouija Board) / **Sounds:** Footsteps+ / **Visual:+:**Light Phenomena, / **Movement:+:-** Door Opening	
Harris, Donna	Ghost Search UK (Since disbanded)	Tel Interview	**Noises:? +** (Muffled Thuds). **Touching?-**Scratching-painfully of colleague's leg **Noises:** Footsteps+ **Noises+** (As if heavy objects moved whilst in bedroom 2), **Touching** (Colleague's shoulder). **Noise+** Hissing sound	
J.C. (Male)	Former resident	Internet	**Movement:+:** (Of Coke Can on table)*/**MovementS:** Bedroom door swinging open/ **Visual:** Apparition seen. Touching: Feeling like spray on back of neck/	*See Nicole Kirtley:
M.K. (female)	Independent investigator	Telephone Interview	**Noises:** -Woman's cry/ **Noises:-** Growling/ **Intense:** Burst into tears* / **Uncategorised:** Wet patch on floor. **Intense:** Intense Anger at fellow investigator/ **Noises:** knocks	*Visit was aborted
Kirtley, Nicole	Former Resident	Face to face	**Visual:+**(spherical lights),/ **Movement: +2**(Coke Can)* / **Uncategorised:+**(Document of former resident appeared from nowhere) / **Noise:** Stair door violently slamming / **Movement:** Door coming off latch and opening (various occasions) / **Noise:** Loud Bang Upstairs** / **Move**mentS JOTTs on numerous occasions clothes etc. disappearing / reappearing	*Coke can flew across table in front of all the residents eyes. **As reported also by Kirstine Blackwell

S.L. (Male)	Independent investigator/ television Producer	Telephone Interview	**Electrical:** High EMF Variations. Movement: Chain swinging* / **Noise:** Distinct Voices / **Intense:** In one of his darkest ever moods after one visit. Footsteps coming from upstairs	*Have been told anecdotally this phenomenon is fairly frequent
D.M.	Independent investigator	Email interview	**Movement:** Iron Moved across floor in toilet/**Intense:** Reduced to tears after sensation of being stabbed in the leg **Noise:** Footsteps	
North London Paranormal Investigations	North London paranormal Investigations	Internet footage	**Electrical**: High EMF variations partially on command / **Movement:** table moves in front of door when room is empty / **Intense:** GP a Medium is panicked and refuses to enter / **Intense:** G.P. a Medium has to abort investigation feeling girl in agony	
Nick (Male)	friend of Owner	Face to face	**Touching:** Feeling of being pushed on stairs / **Movement**+; Door Swung open off latch. **Visual:** Apparition *Saw shadowy female figure from outside at window / **Intense:** Stated strong dislike of atmosphere in the bathroom	*This occurred at the same time as residents heard loud bang.
Potter, David	N/A	Telephone Interview	**Movement:** JOTT? (Training shoes disappeared. Found in Cage Room) / **Touching:** Tap on Back/ **Noise**+:Banging Door Footsteps +Taut rope swinging / **Noise:**+ (of window frame Shaking). **Visual:** Shape Shifting colleagues face became wizened & old. **Visual:**+ Blue Laser Light: **Visual:**+ (Blue Sphere) **Electrical:** Equipment malfunction?	

Sonder-gaard Kim (Mr)	Dansk Para-psykologist Aspect (Danish paranormal investigations Group)	Email inter-view	**Visual:** Apparition seen **Intense:**+ (Strong feeling of hatred towards fellow investigator, loss of memory uncontrollable tears)* / **Visual:** Shape shifting(Momentary shape shifting of fellow investigators face into a 'skull like mean looking face') / **Touching:** General sense of being touched	Notes* Investigation was temporarily aborted at this point; breakdown actually took place in the courtyard.
South West London paranormal	South West London paranormal	Internet	**Electrical:** High EMF variation * equipment malfunctions. **Touching** : Being pushed / **Electrical:** High EMF variations. Touching: of legs *	*These two phenomena happened at about the same time: Many 'communications' through séances.
T.W. (Male)	Independent investigator	Telephone Interview	**Electrical:** High EMF meter variations partially on 'command'/**Noises:** Bangs from walls+ Childs groan? / **Electrical:** Torch flickering on off to command	
N. & K. W (Male / Female)	Owner's Friends	Face to face	**Uncategorised:** - Blood trail on Corridor floor with obvious explanation	

Key

Phenomena is categorised into:

Visual / Noises / Touching / Electrical / Movement / Intense (Unusual high impact emotional reaction) / Uncategorised (fits none of these categories)

+ Sign after phenomena category means reportedly witnessed by others who I could not interview.

Capital **S** after category is stated means that this phenomena happened more than once over a period.

? After category means witness less adamant that phenomenon was inexplicable but both witness and myself thought it to be significant.

Other Data

Information Psychically Retrieved

As I mentioned during the methodology at the start, information picked up from séances, mediums etc. was excluded from the main comparison points of this project. There was a large amount of such information but it did not tend to fit a particular pattern. Entities reported to have been communicated with included 'Marcus', 'Joshua' and Matthew Hopkins the infamous Witch-Finder General but with no obvious similarity of communication between groups. Perhaps surprising Ursula Kemp was also only reported the once. There was, however, an underlying feeling that a former more recent resident may have been trying to communicate, though nothing was specifically gained in communications that was not already known.

Perhaps the situation from a psychic's point of view was best summed up from the medium Donna Harris, who stated that she felt that any 'spirits' she picked up during a table tilting experiment were not centred on any particular place and could have been picked up similarly in other venues.

CONCLUSION

This was a fascinating experiment in witness testimony in many ways, particularly because it took the recorded phenomena in directions not really expected. The lack of a 'Witches' angle in the apparent phenomena and a relative shortage of apparitions was more than made up for by the strength and repetition of differing types of 'phenomena'.

A number of the initial witnesses including Ms Mitchell seem primarily convinced by an 'afterlife' paranormal theory [which as previously stated seems to be the one favoured by those closely involved with phenomena] and this is of course a clear possibility – but without an identifiable intelligent source it would be impossible at this stage to favour one 'paranormal' theory over another.

It has many of the facets of a poltergeist but seems to be centred round a building rather than any one person, which would make it closest to what Gauld and Cornell refer to as being an 'Intermediate Case' (Gauld and Cornell, 1979), one that contains elements of poltergeists and traditional hauntings.

It is also possible that while differing groups of people may be able to experience the same phenomena, any attempt at communications may only come (assuming an afterlife theory) when both parties become more familiar with each other. Referring back to the Enfield Poltergeist for example it was only after a spate of apparently meaningless random marble and bricks being thrown and chairs being moved that some kind of communication was established.

Perhaps one of the closest matches to the phenomena so far at 'The Cage' is one discussed by Gauld and Cornell also affecting a smallish house at Prestonville Road, Brighton between 1882 & 1889 and which again had a suicide in the not too distant past. Gauld and Cornell state that:

A woman had a few years before hanged herself in the upstairs bedroom... The story was discovered from reports of the inquest to be true.
(Gauld and Cornell, 1979, pp. 187–189)

Phenomena in this case extended primarily to what Gauld and Cornell described as "imitative noises" – differing sets of witnesses heard such things as footsteps, doors banging, sounds of furniture moving as well as seeing door handles turn. What they call "imitative noises" is surely no different to the 'Similar Facts' evidence we have been discussing. As with 'The Cage' no *clear connection was ever established between any one 'entity' and the phenomena in the Brighton case. The fact that such similar trends have been noted in the past again strengthens our current witness testimony.*

Whilst witness statements in themselves should not be expected to overturn the views of current science, the fact that 'similar fact' evidence has clearly been shown should show beyond doubt that a case such as this should in no way be dismissed even by those of a sceptical nature [based on the depth of evidence and the discussions in all of our predating chapters, this in my opinion would simply be unscientific].

To summarise my conclusions in this report, whilst I did not go quite as far as Harry Price, when he gave a certificate of paranormal authenticity to Rudi Schneider, or Guy Playfair by implications when he named his book on Enfield This House is Haunted, *my report made it clear that I found many of the events to be strange and definitely inexplicable at this time, and quite possibly of a paranormal nature as well!*

The author giving a presentation of his report of The Cage, St Osyth to a central London audience. (Photo Credit Peter Ladanyi)

If 'research' can send shivers down a paranormal researcher's spine – then the specific bit that did was the extremely close fit between the phenomena at The Cage, and the 19th century house in Prestonville Road, Brighton. Right up to the fact that the strange events happened reasonably shortly after a suicide. You do start to think, when such similar facts occur, there must be something behind it. There seems to be a trigger such as this to such outbursts of poltergeist phenomena in so many cases.

I have also made some interesting discoveries since my original report. Much of the narrative surrounding the phenomena is based on the fact that the 'witch' Ursula Kemp and her colleagues were kept in St Osyth prior to being taken to Chelmsford for trial. This witch trial is well documented and factually correct. It is also, however, recorded clearly on an old 'Local History' plaque on the house. So everyone who enters is very aware of the fact. This plaque reads as follows:

The Cage
Medieval Prison
St Osyth residence Ursula Kemp
was imprisoned here before being
hanged as a witch in 1582.
It was last used in 1908.

However, The Cage itself is a strange hybrid place. The old holding cell and the then much smaller cottage being joined together in a building project in the mid-1970s. (The prison cell itself never had special or listed status.) This leaves 'The Cage' as a unique combination of an as yet undated holding cell attached to a house which is old but likely at best only a couple of hundred years – with a more modern (likely) 1970s extension built on above! I suspect the old local history plaque was put on at the time the house and the holding cell were merged into one – though I haven't been able to find the source of the plaque for sure as yet. Other than the plaque, however, there is no other reference to this particular holding cell being used for the imprisonment of these particular witches.

What the plaque does is to act as a compelling narrative right in the face of anyone who enters the house, and we have seen from other cases how compelling narratives can also seem to literally provoke phenomena be it the perceived threat of vampires or black magic, or witches. (Though more likely in this case a wise herbalist caught up within local hysteria – or a traumatic event, such as a death or a suicide.) With 'The Cage' these trigger factors simply seem to be abundant. This has been compounded by the media narrative such as TV shows which have given it the title of 'Witches Prison', and which after some thought I decided to keep in the subtitle of this book as well. The 'Converted Lock-up Cell' at St Osyth has already long been renamed in people's eyes as the 'Witches Prison' and as I think a compelling narrative can potentially add to real life phenomena, in some ways it is important to keep that already existing narrative intact. We will see a case in Pontefract in the next chapter where a narrative may have been actually created by a local investigator – which is something different entirely.

So the King Kong vs. Godzilla analogy is in the end not strictly accurate. The phenomena of ghosts and the phenomena of poltergeists are not in competition. A much better analogy would be like powerful twins such as Romulus and Remus, the mythological babies who were brought up by a she-wolf prior to becoming the all-powerful siblings who founded the city of Rome, and ultimately created what became the Roman Empire.

Now there is also of course that old saying that 'Rome wasn't built in a day', but perhaps so far I have been starting to hint at just laying some of its basic foundations – in suggesting that the cause of poltergeist phenomena and possibly other phenomena as well is something internal though also potentially something 'super-normal'. That is not to say that any theory is as yet a perfect fit, and those who would follow an afterlife theory would be in at least as good if not better company than me. I claimed at the start of this book that there may have not been a major publication that explored the Poltergeist for about thirty years, and in the UK at least none since 1981 since an excellent book from the self-styled "Existential Philosopher" Colin Wilson, *Poltergeist! A Study in Destructive Haunting*.

Yet despite the fact that in so many other books Wilson hypothesised about the hidden powers of the mind, when it came down to the powers that a poltergeist had he ultimately opted for an afterlife theory.

The question is, was he in this case correct?

Chapter 8

From Without or From Within?

(Is the poltergeist a human agent or truly a noisy spirit as it was named?)

I still remember the particular day when shortly after having arrived at Keele University as a first year (freshman) student, I took the monumental decision, for a nineteen-year-old, not to go down to the students' union bar to have a few drinks, but rather to finish a 600-page plus book I had gradually but enthusiastically been ploughing through.

I always think that if you can remember where and when a book has been finished years later it does say something rather special about that book itself. (So please note where you are when you come to the last page of this publication.) The only other time I can distinctly remember where and when I finished a book was one with a curious but fascinating title called *Zen and the Art of Motorcycle Maintenance* by Robert Pirsig, which I finished while travelling on a very slow train between towns in Germany while following England in the 1988 European soccer championships.

Yes that was the same trip where I should have been reading my infamous accounting textbook ('JOTT') which disappeared from my bag (see Chapter 4) ... but I digress!

The book in question that I had a sudden urge to complete that particular night at Keele was none other than one called *Mysteries*, written by Colin Wilson.

I can still (more or less) remember the last few phrases of the final chapter where he stated that:

Yet if the ecstasies of the romantics meant anything they meant that man has a far greater control of his inner being than he ever realised. He is enmeshed in all curious misconceptions about himself... the chief of which is that he is a poor helpless creature.

Going on to say:

Consciousness is intentional: its destiny is to become more intentional. Through a gradual deepening of intentionality, it will re-establish contact with our 'lost' levels.

And finally:

Instead of wasting most of its energies... consciousness will recycle its energies into its own evolution. The feedback point will mark a new stage on the history of the planet earth. When that happens the first fully human being will be born.

Now Wilson was never one to doubt his own certainties – but these were certainties that certainly made an impact on a nineteen-year-old, looking for new possibilities in life. What they also made clear was Wilson's belief in the power of man's own consciousness to hit new peaks and find new or long-hidden powers. Nor was this particular book an aberration to what he normally wrote; it was in effect a follow-up to his first work on the paranormal *The Occult*, which very much had the same overlying theme.

How possibly then could a man who believed in the power of the human mind **NOT** finally consider it a strongly possible cause of poltergeist phenomena? It seems to be a case, at least when it came to the poltergeist, of Wilson suddenly losing belief in everything he had written previously.

Wilson nearly admits this in the latest edition of his book *Poltergeist!* (republished by Llewellyn in 2009). Here he states in a 'Prefatory Note' that whilst in 1978 when asked to write an article for *The Oxford Companion to the Mind* on *Paranormal Phenomena*, he cited the 'Philip Experiment' and concluded that:

Poltergeists are probably a creation of the unconscious mind.

But he admits to now being:

In the embarrassing position of having to admit that I no longer agree with what I wrote then.

And putting this sudden switch down to the findings of Guy Playfair to which he dedicated the book, and also the curious case of the 'Black Monk of Pontefract', which will be revisited later in the chapter.

Such though was Wilson's transformation from exploring the inner powers of the mind – to his belief in an outside force – that by 1985 he wrote a full book on the evidence for the *Afterlife* entitled simply that. This is a good solid review of existing cases but without any real 'breakthroughs' as such, in which he concludes by saying:

It is not my purpose to convince anyone of the reality of life after death: only to draw out the impressive inner consistency of the evidence, and to point out that in the light of the evidence, no one should feel ashamed of accepting the notion that human personality survives after bodily death.

Like any good 'New Existentialist Philosopher', Wilson did not go as far as stating he knew the truth for sure. But the direction of travel is so very different from what he had written previously as to show he had changed his views. Was that change based on the evidence or merely on the fact that witnesses to the evidence so often have the afterlife interpretation of events? We will look into this further just a little later!

The first 'spiritualist' afterlife theory of poltergeists developed in the second half of the 19th century was simple – that the phenomena was caused by dead people trying to communicate both with and through the living. Even in those earlier days of poltergeist investigation, many (normally male) investigators came up with an alternative theory – the biggest proponent of which was Frank Podmore of the SPR who came up with the rather sexist 'Naughty Little Girls' hypothesis. This consisted of the obvious (to Podmore) fact that basically girls of a certain adolescent age had a propensity to seek attention and play tricks by throwing objects.

Through the years this (thankfully) became refined to the possibility that female pubescent energy itself might provide a potent force for object movement.

Harry Price was one who took on the more refined theory and dismissed Podmore's version by pointing out in his *Poltergeist Over England* the unlikelihood that a young girl could:

Smash half the china in the house, break the furniture, set fire to the baby, and make twenty bells ring simultaneously – and without a single occupant in the house detecting her.

He instead speculated that:

Poltergeist phenomena are... not fundamentally dissimilar to ordinary physical processes involving energy changes... One might tentatively suggest... [one energy source being] the adolescent child. In numerous cases it has been noticed that phenomena are produced most vigorously when the child is lying or sleeping in bed. The conditions may then be rather favourable for the removal of energy from the child by the Poltergeist; the child under these conditions approaches more closely the state of a medium when in trance.

Whilst Price did not speculate as to how the energy was removed, the possibility of the removal by the child's own subconscious was definitely there. It was found though that far too many cases did not fit the strict causal effect of having a pubescent teenager on the premises when events took place. So this simplistic theory has more recently gone more out of favour again, with the pendulum swinging back towards the afterlife theory. We have already mentioned Gauld and Cornell's guarded preference for such a theory, and in the early 1980s the American researcher Stafford Betty seemed to find a case which he believed could go some way to proving this pendulum swing.

I have never met Mr Betty but do know of his reputation for being a very experienced researcher in the field. His own publishers even go further, describing him on a major book site as:

Professor of Religion at California State University in Bakersfield, CA, Stafford earned his PhD in theology from Fordham University
Which further concludes that Betty:
"Is a world expert on afterlife studies."

Perhaps a little over the top, but I guess if a major book site ever describes me as a "World Expert" I would not object

The case in question actually happened in his university's town of Bakersfield, which helps prove my point made in Chapter 2 about the relative commonness of poltergeist phenomena, and about it not being too difficult to find this type of event even close to your workplace or home. It became subsequently known as the Kern City Poltergeist due to the fact that it took place in an upper middle class retirement community of this name. A community most unlikely to be conveniently filled with adolescents fuelled with poltergeist powers.

Betty was contacted in January 1982 by an acquaintance of Frances Freeborn. Freeborn was a wealthy widow of 63, who had moved into a house in the community as recently as November 1981. Upon moving in, Freeborn had immediately been faced with an onslaught of strange phenomena. Even on her first evening there were thumping and chafing noises that came from the kitchen, and by the next day Freeborn found three previously closed doors wide open without explanation. A pink vanity bench that was left in the premises by the previous owner was found on multiple occasions to be pulled out from where Freeborn had left it previously, and over the coming weeks there were multiple doors swung open and drawers pulled open as if potentially another entity was living in the house. This was most unlikely to be put down to normal traffic vibrations as even an earthquake 90 miles away during that time, whilst shaking Bakersfield, had no effect on either doors or furniture, which in itself was an interesting event that very much backs up the induced vibrations experiments of Cornell at a condemned house in Cambridge (see Chapter 2).

Every time Freeborn tried to hang up a picture it seemed it would be removed or taken down, and by 25th January 1982, after a night of windows and closet doors swinging open and shut in a violent way, Freeborn was to confide in her acquaintance who in turn contacted Mr Betty – who very sensibly from an ethical point of view visited the premises accompanied by two female colleagues. Both these colleagues, however, were known to believe themselves to possess psychic powers.

One of the 'psychics' was to immediately pick up the presence of an elderly couple and a younger woman. Whilst the psychic was trying to communicate with them, Freeborn – in a separate room (and apparently sceptical about the project) – experienced a dining chair move in front of her eyes.

The two psychics then performed what Betty himself can only describe as an exorcism. It was one, however, of a more subtle nature than the fire and brimstone 'Evil get out of the house type'! This 'exorcism' consisted more of a gentle persuasion of whatever entities were there to, at the very least, leave their negative energies behind, and explaining to Freeborn that things could only happen if she 'allowed' her energies to be used. Now this may be true or not but as a psychological device it allows a victim of poltergeist activity to feel more in control of a situation – so as belief-led rituals go was likely of the less harmful variety, and may even have been helpful. This belief-led process seemed to be similar in some ways to the more practical advice any investigator should give that there is virtually no record of such phenomena causing actual harm.

Whatever our views on 'clearances' – and mine are very mixed – it appeared to bring two months of very intense phenomena to an end, with only the slightly odd occasional incident in the future.

The significance of this case is not so much about the intense but short burst of poltergeist activity, but more about the interpretation Mr Betty put on to it when reviewing it in depths for the *SPR Journal* (October 1984).

Prior to Freeborn moving into the premises, it had remained unoccupied for several years since the death of its long-term owner that Mr Betty gives the pseudonym of Meg to in his report. Betty strongly believed that only the discarnate theory truly fits the facts – and the likely discarnate was Meg herself on seeing her house disrupted.

The thrust of his argument being summarised in the points below:

1) That a random force might have rattled doors but not moved them or many other objects around with care.
2) That there was no adolescent present and as Betty also points out in his experience poltergeists often follow a death or divorce.
3) That an exorcism would have far more chance of actually working if there was a discarnate who could be persuaded

to leave.

4) That Freeborn wasn't under any particular stress – which could be seen to trigger a poltergeist style phenomenon.

5) That Meg's son – who had sold the house to Freeborn – subsequently stated that he remembered doors being opened that he had thought he had closed when he visited the house occasionally, before selling it on sometime after Meg's death. Her son also was fascinated by the fact that a picture that was not taken down by the poltergeist was of the same style and put in the same place as one chosen by Meg.

6) That Freeborn was sure that she in no way contributed to the phenomena.

I would like to look at each of these points in turn.

1) There is an assumption made by both Betty and others that only an external intelligence can behave in a rational and coherent way, and that someone's subconscious can only produce random and chaotic events. It is true of course that the subconscious is not fully understood. However, it is clear both to sleepwalkers, and to those who suddenly drive their cars on autopilot finding they are at home without remembering a familiar journey (admit it, those who drive, we have all done it), that this simply isn't the case that the subconscious is 'chaotic'.

Colin Wilson, in his book *Mysteries*, when still a believer in the ultimate power of consciousness makes it very clear this isn't the case as well. In a chapter called "How Many Me's Are There?" he conducted a fascinating study of multiple personalities. In particular he referred to the 1910 case of Doris Fischer whose multiple personalities started to emerge when she was as a young child thrown to the floor by her father in a drunken rage. Fischer started to intermittently be taken over by a very different personality known as Margaret. This personality influenced her through her formative life, to the extent that Doris' urge to go to college was thwarted by Margaret who wished to become a seamstress. This case is very multifaceted and was investigated in depth by the Pittsburgh psychiatrist Walter F. Price who came to the conclusion that:

"Margaret was aware of Doris but NOT the other way round, in some ways very much the dominant personality."

So who can possibly say that our own subconscious can't behave in an organised way, and without us knowing?

Wilson himself states that:

"These recognitions are not a discovery of modern 'depth psychology'. They are part of an esoteric tradition that is older than civilisation. Oddly enough its name is magic."

This only makes my point a little more clearly as there is surely enough undiscovered 'magic' in the human mind to at least have the hidden potential to use its inner energies to open a door or take down a picture frame.

2) Betty correctly notes that there was no presence of adolescents. He is also correct that the notion of adolescence being the cause of the poltergeist syndrome is a very outdated thing. However, this is not an either/ or argument, for either the cause being 'subconsciously naughty girls' or 'discarnate spirits'. We have already seen how so many other events can apparently trigger a poltergeist, and it is clear that any subconscious trigger theory has to include more than just one factor. Even Betty states that unpleasant divorce can also be a trigger event – here of course only a relationship has died, and the conscious ghost of a 'dead' relationship is surely a step too far.

3) Betty refers to a successful exorcism being an event that is

only likely with a spirit to exorcise. We have already seen how it is possible that the removal of a fear can put the phenomena to rest. Sugg makes that point when discussing so-called vampire cases. The fair-minded 'Betty' actually makes this point even better referring to a case when Tony Cornell carried out a fairly unique experiment – by promising to exorcise a spirit in a poltergeist-infested house through the process of:

"*Taking mysterious odds and ends into one of the bedrooms.*"
And then he:

"*Sat inside the bedroom smoking a cigarette. After fifteen minutes he emerged... and dramatically stated it [the poltergeist] would not come back.*"

It was reported later there was no further phenomena in the house.

Betty relies on calling this case a fluke. Having read the rest of this book so far I will leave you to your own judgement on that. The final crucial point, however, is that even the psychics in this exorcism did not identify 'Meg' as the spirit and referred to three spirits, an older couple and a younger lady.

4) Betty states that Freeborn wasn't under any particular stress. Freeborn had just completed a house move which is, short of bereavement and possibly divorce, one of the most stressful events in most lives. A survey in *Which?* magazine (2016) showed moving house more stressful than arranging care for an elderly relative or even having a child. Possibly of interest is the fact that the same survey showed that 73% of females found house buying very stressful compared with 67% of males. Add to that the fact that Freeborn was a widow and at 63 possibly fairly set in her ways, and the lack of stress factor doesn't really add up at all.

5) The fact that Meg's son subsequently reported what

may have been minor poltergeist incidents is certainly interesting, and doesn't fit with the theory that the phenomena may have been caused by Freeborn. Any honest investigator (Mr Betty included) should admit that no theory is currently a perfect fit on the reported facts, and I am more than happy to do the same with mine. However, if you cast your mind back to Chapter 1 and the psychological tricks the mind can play – especially after a longer period – witness evidence long after an event is seen as being fairly weak, especially if not thought important enough to report at the time. It is possible then (but by no means definite) that Meg's son may have been subject to 'confirmation bias', remembering the facts in a way that suited his (likely) favoured theory that his mother was still in some way present in the house.

Mr Betty also makes a great play on the fact that one of the few pictures taken down was of a type and in a spot of where Meg would approve according to her son. However, in doing so he overlooks the significance of one of his earlier observations, this being that:

"When Frances [Freeborn] was first shown the house by her agents, it was in the condition that Meg had left it five years earlier. Her family pictures were still mounted on the walls... even her underwear was folded in dresser drawers."

So it seems equally likely that Freeborn felt that at least on a subconscious level she was somehow intruding, and she certainly knew the favoured places where Meg would approve of pictures to be hung.

6) With regards to Freeborn's insistence that she was not the cause... This is a perfectly natural one. It is counter-intuitive and against everything the 'ego' stands for to think that thoughts, let alone powers, you are not aware of are going on in your own head. Yet it is clear from what we have said earlier that the subconscious can work on an

intelligent basis, and therefore no logical reason why it might not possess some hidden powers as well.

It is equally counter-intuitive for any non-physicist to believe that time can slow as we get to the speed of light – but that has been proven by Einstein and we should accept it even though most, including me, can't really get their heads round it in everyday life. I suspect that some centuries back it would have been counter-intuitive to think of the earth as anything other than flat? Our intuition seems to be a jump to an immediate conclusion based on our current understanding of things.

Wilson also understands this concept well, citing the example of the hunter James Corbett in Wilson's book *The Occult* who for no apparent reason:

"Had walked over a culvert whose parapet was eighteen inches high. As he approached this, he had crossed the road to the other side, walking through the red dust at the side of the road. He crossed the culvert on the right-hand side, then re-crossed the road to the left again as he continued on his way home. Corbett was baffled; he could not imagine why he had absentmindedly crossed the road like this. The next day he retraced his footsteps. In the sandy bed of the culvert, on the left-hand side, he discovered the pug marks of a tiger that had been lying there."

I would also claim that as a hunter his intuition was on the lookout for telltale signs of dangerous beasts, and that it is likely if one of us had taken that walk we would have walked straight into the tiger and been its spontaneous feast. Likewise when Freeborn's or anyone else's intuition tells them they have no connection with the poltergeist happenings, the happenings themselves are so 'alien' to her experiences to date, it is very much as if our instincts are in that unexplored jungle in which they have not yet been taught to function.

Whilst I therefore disagree with Betty's conclusions, let me also point out how detailed his research and report were to allow me to come to alternative conclusions. I also fully agree with a postscript, in which Betty discusses and rejects a third theory of source of poltergeist power. This theory being one put forward by Professor Ian Stevenson, who in his 1972 study "Are Poltergeists Living or Are They Dead?" came up with the basic conclusion that some are but others are not! This is surely a case of expanding a theory so wide that it fits all the available facts to date.

Betty objects to this approach based on the methodological law of parsimony possibly better known as Occam's razor, a methodology first clarified by the 13th century theologian William of Occam, which states basically that when deciding between theories the simplest solution tends to be the right one. I also object on a more readily understood assumption – that in most areas of research a researcher should not try to have his cake and eat it. Sooner or later it's time to stop sitting on the fence and see where the evidence really points.

In my opinion Betty's case of the Kern City Poltergeist is not the groundbreaking one to swing the pendulum back to the afterlife theory, but the case is well researched and the conclusions thought-provoking – and is the sort of case we need much more of in our field, if we are ever going to get a true understanding of what the poltergeist syndrome really is all about.

We should now return to Colin Wilson's sudden change of theory which did not come about through a few doors opening or a few windows swinging.

It came about quite possibly by a poltergeist dragging a girl up the stairs by her hair!

The Black Monk of Pontefract is a strange case indeed – happening largely unnoticed in the late 1960s on a road called East Drive in the small town of Pontefract in Yorkshire, UK. It did not take place in a creepy old mansion but in an average council house lived in by a family of four called the Pritchards. At the time it achieved only regional news through the regional paper the *Yorkshire Post* and through its even smaller counterpart the *Pontefract and Castleford Gazette* – yet it now makes claims to be possibly the most violent poltergeist incident in recent times in Europe. These are claims that may have some substance based on the recorded evidence.

It involved an entity who was nicknamed 'Fred', a rather un-clerical name, and ran its course as a major poltergeist in two stages. The first bout of phenomena started in August 1966 and fairly quickly subsided. The second more major burst of phenomena happened in 1968. Apart from one of two sightings of a man apparently dressed in a long gown, towards the end of the second episode of activity, no one identified 'Fred' as being a monk. In fact Fred despite being a very active entity for a time did little in the way of communicating intelligently at all. The naming of the poltergeist as a Black Monk only happened about ten years later, when a researcher called Tom Cuniff reviewed the case and, spurred on by the description of the long-robed man, explored the theory that the poltergeist may have been a long dead monk. This was no ordinary long dead monk but an evil monk who had been hung for raping and killing a child.

The house in East Drive, Pontefract, where the poltergeist activity

came to be identified with the spirit of a murderous Black Monk.

As it happens, Pontefract had no less than two priories, both now totally destroyed. These were the Cluniac Priory of St John and the Dominican Friary of St Richard. The former were a closed order, the latter an open order that went about the countryside in pairs, preaching. These were actually known as Black Friars from their black robes. If the poltergeist was indeed to be a monk, the Dominican Friary of St Richard would have been the most likely candidate as monks that are able to venture outside a priory would fit far better into Cuniff's grizzly and rather speculative interpretation.

However, whilst Cuniff did interview the poltergeist victims more than ten years after the events, his subsequent theory was based on in effect 'Chinese whispers'.

This consisted of 'hearsay' information that was given by Mrs (Jean) Pritchard, in which she had been told a neighbour had found from a book in Pontefract public library that mentioned that a Cluniac Monk had been hanged for the rape and murder of a girl at the time of Henry VIII.

Cuniff's research apparently showed that the Pontefract gallows had stood at that time at the top of the hill where East Drive was and the house had stood on a bridge known as Priest's Bridge.

Quite the relevance of that is rather unclear as a priest is not a monk and why in any case would a bridge be named incorrectly after a disgraced rapist monk? This is a case surely of finding evidence for a fanciful theory that Cuniff had already formed. The use, however, of Cuniff's further research was to bring this case back into the public eye, and he happened to contact the well-known author Colin Wilson about the case just at the very point when Wilson was contemplating his *Poltergeist!* book.

Wilson himself visited the Pritchards and obtained good

first-hand testimony of the poltergeist incidents. He also tried to research the Black Monk theory, and could find no evidence at all for the neighbour's claim to have found a reference to a monk who raped and was hanged. However, Wilson continued to refer to the case as the 'The Black Monk of Pontefract', and named a whole chapter after it in his book. Because of this, the case will forever likely be referred to as this. It is possible that given the choice many authors would have been tempted to do the same. The entity never claimed to be called 'Fred', and 'Fred the Phantom (Poltergeist)' simply doesn't have quite the same ring. Nor would such an ill-defined entity likely have led to a feature film which we will hear more about a little later.

I have spent some time dealing with the context to the story without going into the details yet, as the context I believe with regards to cases is everything in an evidential sense. The context of the monk may be wrong but evidentially the case appears to be fairly well documented. Though most of the 'documentation' comes from interviews conducted ten years after the events, there is a least an apparent presence in the local papers to act as corroboration from witnesses taken nearer the time.

The actual 1966 phenomena began in a strange way with most of the family on holiday. Mr and Mrs Pritchard had taken their younger daughter Diana (aged 12) on vacation, leaving the maternal grandmother (Sarah Scholes) as a visitor to look after their older son Phillip who was then aged fifteen.

The first phenomena consisted of a strange white powder forming in the lounge. Whilst this was not a typical poltergeist phenomenon, more traditional manifestations appeared the very same day. Pools of water were found, spontaneously appearing on the kitchen linoleum, but when the linoleum was lifted up the floor beneath was found to be dry. The tea dispenser was found to work by itself, the button being pressed by an apparently unseen hand, till it was totally emptied over the draining board. A potted plant found itself relocated halfway up the stairs, while a crockery cupboard was to repeatedly rattle for no apparent reason. By the time a wardrobe started tottering neither Phillip nor Sarah Scholes wished to stay at the house overnight, and ended up staying at a neighbour's. When two neighbours subsequently investigated, they found pictures had fallen from the walls and a wedding photo of Mr and Mrs Pritchard had been slashed from one end to the other.

Other than very minor manifestations when the rest of the family returned, that was basically it – at least for another two years, at which time the Pritchard family would start to realise that whatever they had in their home had just been 'warming up' previously.

If poltergeists don't like change it was possibly the redecoration of Diane Pritchard's bedroom that may have set off the second bout of activity in 1968, and certainly the fact that paintbrushes and paste buckets were suddenly thrown across the room seemed to indicate a dislike of the Pritchards' taste in wallpaper. This incident was witnessed by Jean Pritchard, Phillip and also Diane. Other events during that night included a levitating 'carpet sweeper'. From these incidents began nine months of intermittent but frequent phenomena, which included the local Vicar, a Reverent Daly, apparently witnessing a candlestick levitate from the mantelpiece into the air when the Pritchards invited him over to discuss the possibility of a 'clearance' or 'exorcism'. This exorcism was never followed through; likewise the intervention of a Catholic priest Father Hudson only resulted in family and friends being left with holy water to attempt to clear the entity themselves. Whilst this was unsuccessful, it did show the possible belief system of the family at that time that a 'traditional' fix might just lay their spirit to rest.

The entity was first nicknamed Mr Nobody by the family, and later got the new nickname of 'Fred', and there were times when they could live with the phenomena, a bit like a naughty house guest. However, 'Fred's' energies at other times were of a frightening strength, and included pinning Diane to the stairs with a heavy oak hall stand. In a separate incident, it knocked over and ruined a grandfather clock that fell down the stairs. However, Fred seemed able to control his energies to the point that, whilst the family were shaken up, no one was actually hurt.

It is interesting to note that whilst she had been on vacation at the time of the first poltergeist outbreak, Diane Pritchard now fourteen, or at least her bedroom, increasingly became the focus of the phenomena. Her bedclothes would be pulled from her, and in one case she was actually tossed out of bed. Gradually everyday life became more surreal, when following interest from the local press, people began to congregate in front of the Pritchards' home waiting to hear some kind of crash or bang.

As I mentioned earlier towards the end of the phenomena a dark figure in a long robe was seen on a few occasions. This was a prelude perhaps to one last effort to lay the spirit, and having tried clergymen of both faiths perhaps something a little basic and even more traditional was called for?

Yes... believe it or not a 1970s Pontefract family, like the superstitious Romanian peasants that we have talked about in previous chapters, went out to buy some garlic and placed it around the house – having read it could ward off a spirit and finally after nine months the spirit was gone.

The garlic apparently worked!

Wilson makes some interesting observations about these strange and fascinating events, pointing out in his book that:

Jean Pritchard kept no diary as to the sequence of events.

The implication of course being that after ten years things could get out of order and exaggerated.

He also speculated:

Whether the 'monk's' first appearance... was before or after their neighbour had borrowed the book from the library. [The book which may or may not have contained details about the Monk who raped and who was hung on the site of the house.]

The implication again being that giving the poltergeist a personality may have either paranormally or psychologically triggered off the sightings.

In addition he speculates as to possible family tensions between a sporting father and a more 'bookish' son, and stated that:

Presumably it was because of that tension that Phillip stayed at home [in the 1966 outbreak] when the rest of the family went [on holiday] to Devon.

The point being that this type of tension or stress within a family has in various cases been a potential phenomenon trigger.

And also that:

Fred's first appearance may have been a subconscious expression of Phillip's resentment towards his father.

This is 'traditional' Colin Wilson theorising, looking for the hidden powers of the mind.

However, based on just one incident not yet mentioned in detail, Wilson's whole theories were to change. The incident happened when the lights went out for no apparent reason, and, as Wilson describes in his book, although groping around for a torch, there was enough light for Jean Pritchard to see:

Diane was being dragged up the stairs... her cardigan was stretched out in front of her as if Fred was tugging at it, his other hand was apparently at her throat... [later]. In the light they saw that her throat was covered with red finger marks.

Wilson totally changed his views that a Poltergeist was an expression of RSPK, on the basis that no subconscious would possibly want to drag oneself up the stairs!

There is of course, even at a glance, a contradiction with the lighting conditions described. Wilson reported it was only dusk but that Jean Pritchard had to grope around for a torch, yet it was still light enough to see Diane being pulled up the stairs (so why grope for a torch) ... but not light enough to see marks forming on Diane's neck until later.

An even more fundamental objection to Wilson's transformation of theories can be given by actually using the exact same reasoning he gives.

Wilson claims that it's absurd that Diane's subconscious would act in such a way. Is it not equally or more absurd, in the same common-sense way, that (outside of horror films) a once living spirit would try to communicate in such a destructive way? What would be the point of it all, spending nine months throwing objects and making sounds, but saying absolutely nothing of use? Wilson is left speculating that what you might be dealing with is not a straightforward 'afterlife' spirit but some kind of mischievous 'elemental'. This is a collective name first coined by the 16th century alchemist Paracelsus as taking in the concepts of gnomes, sylphs and salamanders, and if Wilson means these he might as well add duendes and vampires as well as pixies and elves. Each term is as meaningless as the next in giving us insight into what a poltergeist actually is.

In this one instance it seems Wilson falls into the same trap that has plagued us for hundreds of years – that of conjuring up 'demons' to explain what is yet not fully understood.

In the UK *Guardian* newspaper 9th December 2013, Wilson's obituary stated that:

*For a few dazzling months, Colin Wilson... was taken at his own
valuation in his diary as "the major literary genius of our century",
a writer destined to be "Plato's ideal sage and king".*

I would not want to argue with Wilson's self-styled 'genius'
tag, but simply point out as I have done in earlier chapters that
genius isn't flawless. If the *Guardian* wishes to compare him
with the great philosophers of ancient Greece, we have already
mentioned their fallibility (Chapter 4) with Aristotle's belief that
the elements of the world were simply earth, air, fire and water.
It is further worth pointing out that one of Plato's predecessors
Alcmaeon firmly believed that goats had a talent of breathing
through their ears!

**You can, however, forgive the odd mistake when an author is
memorable enough to make you remember, over three decades
later, where you were when you finished reading his book!**

When Wilson wrote about the Black Monk of Pontefract he
was fully of the opinion that he was revisiting a historical case
where the activity was complete. However, there is at least one
further twist in this very strange tale.

Jean Pritchard's sister's sister-in-law was a Rene Holden, who
had a boy called Patrick.

As he also was brought up in the area, Pat Holden would
often hear his mum talk about her encounters with an infamous
poltergeist. When he grew up he entered the world of television
and ultimately movies, his first credit being writing and directing
in 1997 a short film, *The Golders Green Formation Leaning Team*
starring Sacha Baron Cohen, who is better known to us these
days as the impersonator of Ali G and Borat.

Holden also made the movies *Awaydays* (2005) and followed
up with *The Long Weekend* in 2009, to mixed reviews.

However, I suspect he had realised for some time that there
was some excellent subject matter right on his doorstep, and in
2012 he adapted the experiences of the Pritchards for the big
screen with an 'Inspired by true events' movie called, *When the*

Lights Went Out.

The movie itself was brought forward a few years to be based in the early 1970s, the time of a long miners' strikes and power cuts in the UK. This was obviously done for artistic reasons and to justify the ambiguity of the title. It excluded the son Phillip and had most of the phenomena based around a single female child. It also had two bouts of phenomena as in the real case, with the initial bout being the longest rather than the shortest, and the subsequent short bout the most intense to allow a 'Hollywood-style' finish. Tom Cuniff the researcher was written in as the local teacher – with a very good resemblance as well. Despite all of the above, however, if you are not interested in the exact order of incidents and not worried by a little poetic license, the movie portrays what happened, based on Cuniff's and Wilson's notes, fairly well.

This would not of course be the first time a 'true' paranormal tale was adapted for the big screen. It was, however, to be the first time that the movie actually had its debut in the haunted house itself. When Bill Bungay, the producer of the movie, was looking for ways to publicise it, he discovered, likely through Holden, that the house itself was on sale. It was fairly cheap so he simply decided to buy it, and then ran a competition to have two lucky winners get the red carpet treatment with a unique film debut in an anonymous Pontefract suburb. Subsequently a neighbour called Carol informed Bungay that all the activity around the house had triggered the phenomena again. Carol continued to report knocks coming from next door, seeing balls of blue light and even hearing a television on when the poltergeist house next door to her was deserted.

Bungay was to experience his own phenomena when making a documentary about the house, stating that he found:

The kettle switching on and 'superheating' of its own volition, the case of the constantly missing thermostat (the remote kind that you

*sit on the mantelpiece), the researcher being pinned down on to the
bed in the small room (might have been a night terror?).*[31]

He also described a possible 'walkabout' JOTT when a set of
keys could not be found until someone opened a non-working
vintage vacuum cleaner that was being used for filming purposes
and found the keys inside.

On another occasion, when visiting the house alone, Bungay
was to find a domino materialise and fall to the floor along with
showers of glass marbles. He realised that he might have a house
that was difficult to persuade people to buy, but far easier to
persuade interested people to spend a night there, to see what
they might experience. Very much along the same lines as 'The
Cage' in St Osyth, the house at East Drive, Pontefract started to
open up for hire by investigators with one strange proviso on
the website that:

Theoretical physicists can visit for free.

I had realised early in this book that it would not be quite
complete without a visit to the premises where such a significant
case took place. A case that rightly or wrongly had changed the
entire way Colin Wilson viewed the subject.

At the beginning of 2018 I therefore filled in the website
application of the East Drive web page explaining that potentially
a few members of the SPR wished to hire out the premises and
do some background research.

I then waited for a reply and resent the post again – still
nothing was heard back!

I then decided that it was possible that whoever was at the
other side of the web page may have not had an affinity for my
organisation, and asked my colleague and often co-investigator
Rosie O'Carroll from the Ghost Club to resend the application
purely in her name.

All I can say is that it was not 'Fred' running the website as this seems to have been the first time East Drive had nothing to say for itself – there was still no response.

We were on the point of giving up the project when out of the blue on my twitter account there came a message along the lines of

Want to join @Dale_Makin and @paranormalmonk at an investigation at 30 East Drive? We have FOUR places up for grabs. Simply comment below why you should join them.

Without even thinking about it I responded

John Fraser@GhostFraser
Replying to @paratruthuk@Dale_Makin@paranormalmonk
Because myself from the Council of the Society of Psychical Research [and] @RosieO_writer from the Ghost Club would be fascinated to see how a responsible independent paranormal group operates. Also recently researched similar phenomena at @thecagestosyth
5:10 AM – 3 Jun 2018

Dale replied promptly explaining that he had:

Noticed [my] comment on the competition we are running and would like to invite you in addition to the competition winners and allow you to arrive the day before. It would be great to have someone like you [and Rosie] involved let me know what you think?

Then I suddenly thought I had better check out just who I have been twittering with.

It turns out that Dale and his colleague who twitters as @ paranormalmonk run a small research project known as

'Paranormal Truth', primarily consisting of a series of YouTube films based on healthily sceptical attitudes. They had been to East Drive before and had got some mysterious knocking that I thought might be interesting to put under sound analysis as well. So after a few more exchanges of messages I spoke to Rosie and we thought, why not?

It also struck me that this case was long overdue a full review as it was fairly unique in only becoming famous a good decade after the strange events apparently occurred. I decided then to travel to Pontefract the day before we were due to spend the night in East Drive, to attempt to get some context to the case at source.

Pontefract is an interesting place, perhaps very slightly run-down in places, but still with an impressive and historic town centre, and in the past surrounded by liquorice fields that gave the very distinctive flavour to the local speciality of Pontefract cake. Its ancient and very ruined castle was deliberately blown up in the 17th century to stop it becoming again a strategic focus for any civil wars. The locals were so successful in this aim that barely the walls of a tower remain and even the nearby church of All Saints was partially destroyed by the blast.

After my arrival there I spent most of the afternoon taking photographs of potentially interesting sites such as the sites of the two priories previously mentioned. Whilst both sites are well signposted, St John's is just open fields whilst the site of St Richard's has been turned into a rather beautiful park. As I was to discover, these were not the only two places that monks could call their home in Pontefract – which also has a 'Hermitage'. This consisting of hand-dug underground caves used at times by monks who wanted to totally cut themselves off from the world. The most famous occupant of this hermitage, 'Peter of Pomfret', was executed by King John in 1213 for predicting his downfall. This event was mentioned by Shakespeare in his play written about King John. For a small town of just 28,000 people,

Pontefract had three major and ancient ecclesiastical centres within its vicinities. So if looking for a way to express and justify an inexplicable event, a 'Mad Monk' would be pretty high in the things that either the conscious or subconscious might choose.

As I had arrived during an August bank holiday none of the local records offices were open, so after I had done as much productive work as I could I was drawn to a local hostelry, the Red Lion in Market Place, to listen to a tribute band playing songs from musical ghosts of the past. Whilst very much an unplanned diversion, I was later to find out (but sadly not investigate) the fact that the musical ghosts were not the only variety and that phantom figures have been reported standing behind the bar, including a ghostly young boy. Loud footsteps have also been heard, while poltergeist-like activities include bangs, and glasses which fly off the tables.

The rest of the evening was spent talking to my hosts in the small Barley Mow Hotel – who informed me that some of their guests had also been staying at the East Drive poltergeist premises but that they had found the feedback mixed – with some experiencing little at all. Whilst of passing interest this is of course in no way conclusive; it is impossible to tell if a place is 'haunted' in just one night.

The next morning I visited the archives of the local but rather comprehensive library. The first thing I wished to establish was that there was actually an independent reference to the events taking place in the late 1960s, and this I finally found in the 12th September 1968 edition of the *Pontefract and Castleford Express*. On the front page a headline stated that:

Invisible Hand Rocks Family

It went on to explain the opening events of the second and more major poltergeist outbreak. This included the grandfather clock falling down the stairs and also included the local vicar hearing noises. Incidents such as Diane being pulled up the stairs were of course still to happen at that point. Whilst the article was on the front page, it was very much a secondary story, being eclipsed by an "Appeal against a Refusal to Allow Limestone Quarrying" and even by a lucky lady who had won £2,000 on bingo – which to be fair was a lot of money in 1968.

So the cases definitely existed but without quite setting the media of Pontefract alight at that stage – though the story also confirmed that even at this early stage people were knocking on the Pritchards' door to investigate further. So like many things the media might not have been in tune with the everyday interests of a community.

What was also clear from old library maps was that the area of Pontefract called Chequerfield where East Drive is situated consisted basically of just liquorice fields until the mid-20th century, when it became in effect a large housing estate. This was a place comfortably outside the centre of town and hardly a place that would be logically used for hangings. A Priest's Bridge did exist in the area and it may well have been that monks once owned some of the land nearby, but in a town that could potentially have once humorously been nicknamed as 'Monksville' (having three major centres of worship) this was hardly a compelling connection. What was interestingly very close to East Drive was an 'Old Leprosy and Fever Hospital', standing along in the area. This was used from Victorian times until the mid-20th century, and certainly a place where some died in unpleasant ways, and potentially a much more likely source of any paranormal activity than a monk.

Though I browsed through ancient texts including *The History of the Ancient Borough of Pontefract* by Benjamin Boothroyd (1807) and later *The Black Friars of Pontefract* by Richard Holmes (1891), I could find no reference to a rape or hanging of a monk.

After a short lunch I went to the local museum – very conveniently situated next to the library where a local historian confirmed my doubts stating that the traditional hanging spot was in a street called Woolmarket just outside what is now The Windmill Pub.

The museum very conveniently also had both a box of newspaper cuttings on the Chequerfield area, and pleasantly surprisingly a whole box of cuttings on the paranormal as well. Giving the impression that Pontefract had more than its fair share of inexplicable incidents.

From these I discovered that:

1) The Chequerfield area had a very bad history of housing subsidence since the houses were built over local mines. Headlines from the 1980s included:

   "Mining Damage Claims Pour In" (*Pontefract and Castleford Gazette*, 12th January 1984) where it also stated that:

   "*Total of outstanding claims were well of 1000 [houses]."*

   This would certainly be a potential explanation for creaks or noises in a housing structure. As we have seen though from both Tony Cornell's experiments on derelict houses in Cambridge, and Stafford Betty's investigations in Bakersfield which happened during an earthquake, environmental factors do not tend to produce actual poltergeist type phenomena, so if a poltergeist is in effect 'earthquake proof', some subsidence can't be the full explanation.

2) The Chequerfield area is one that is particularly liable to flooding due to the fact that numerous rivulets run underground in the area. This is potentially of some interest as it has been theorised by the likes of the dowser and writer TC Lethbridge that fields from water could be a factor to triggering paranormal activity, in his book *Ghost and Diving Rod* (Routledge & Kegan Paul, 1963). I was still wondering in the final edit of this book if this was too

much of a speculative link for inclusion, when a gentleman I had met a few months previously sent me a selection of old SPR journals he had no further use for. Strangely the very first article I opened was from 1955 and entitled "Poltergeists: a physical theory" by GW Lambert.[32]

In this long-forgotten piece of research Lambert had taken 54 poltergeist cases from sources where the exact location could be verified and had found that nearly half of those had taken place within three miles of tidal water. He also noted that in 33 of these cases where the month of the outbreak was stated, in 27 of the 33 the outbreak began in the wet and wintry half of the year. Lambert hypothesises a natural explanation that:

"The only force that answers to that specification [of causing at least some poltergeist symptoms] is that of flood water, and as the water has never actually been being seen 'at work' it must be moving under an unsuspected subterranean stream underneath the building that is affected."

This would account of course for bangs and some falling items but not necessarily for items that are thrown a great distance or for that matter JOTTs. By making the correlation, however, Lambert has given credibility not only to a natural explanation, but to hidden water sources such as rivulets also being in some way a 'paranormal' trigger. The fact that Pontefract has such sources can be therefore noted as potentially being of significance.

3) I perhaps in jest referred to Pontefract as 'Monksville' earlier, but I did subsequently discover that a ghostly monk has actually been seen in living memory, except that it was a black monk seen at Pontefract Castle. This was seen amongst others by castle tour guide Michael Holdsworth who stated in the *P and C Express* of 3rd October 1996 that: "I saw a man in black near the castle keep. He looked to be wearing old woollen clothing and reading a scroll."

4) A second hospital potentially for contagious diseases was in the area in much more ancient times and known as Foulsnape. It went out of use and was finally demolished as far back as 1507.

5) Of interest, though not strictly speaking evidential with regards to the identity or existence of the poltergeist, is the fact that there were numerous press cuttings indicating that the main researcher in the case, Tom Cuniff, had aspirations to become a full-time paranormal author. In fact one article from the *P & C Gazette* of 17th December 1981 talks of there being tension between himself and Wilson due to the fact that:

"The first edition published by New English Library does not [properly] acknowledge the work he put into it."

Other press reports talk about him moving into a 480-year-old cottage called Dovecote in Darrington graveyard to get greater inspiration.

Both his aim to become a full-time professional writer and (in my opinion) to live in a cemetery are admirable ones. According to the press reports Cuniff's ideas seemed to be wide ranging, from potential TV programmes to having his own design of tarot cards printed by a Swiss company.

Whilst there is nothing wrong at all with selling yourself and aiming high in your chosen profession, any approach to an established author such as Wilson would need to be one that immediately caught Wilson's eye. I am left wondering to what extent then Cuniff himself believed the 'Black Monk' angle or was just using it as a selling point?

The tentative conclusion I made from the five points above is that if a place in Pontefract was going to have a 'malevolent' presence or poltergeist, it was as liable to be identified as a monk, as one seen in Romania is liable to be identified as a vampire. If one is looking for an outside entity to be involved in the East Drive poltergeist case, it would be far more likely to look for a poor unfortunate leper who at least can be shown to have lived and died in the immediate vicinity.

Later in the afternoon I met with my colleague Rosie O'Carroll. Our intention, before meeting the Para-Truth team of Dale Makin and his mysterious twitter companion the aptly named @paranormalmonk, was to visit a pub right next to East Drive called the Chequerfield Hotel. This was to simply make subtle enquiries as to whether the Pritchards had used the pub's facilities and how seriously their story had been taken at the time. Whilst the publican knew of the story well he diverted us to the nearby Pontefract Sports and Social Club, which the Pritchards had been known to frequent when it was a private members bar. We found no drinkers there that were old enough to go back to the late 1960s, but were fascinated when the bar

Pontefract's historic town centre including the Red Lion Pub (left). A town that adds credibility to the theory that poltergeist activity might possibly happen in clusters.

lady was happy to explain that the club itself had a more recent history of poltergeist activity. The activity since she and her family had taken over the premises includes strange tappings on the dance floor and movement of empty beer glasses. These were potentially put down to a former homeless man who had previously frequented the place and who was to some extent looked after by the locals.

Perhaps this says something in favour of Lethbridge's and Lambert's theory that rivulets and other water sources can attract paranormal events for whatever reason. When you add this to other poltergeist incidents such as at the Red Lion Pub, and the thick file of cuttings within the museum archives, we were by the end of the day left wondering if this effect might actual cause geographical clusters of poltergeists?

After a thorough day's research and new thoughts buzzing in our head, it was perhaps fair to say that our visit to 30 East Drive whilst fascinating was something of a minor anti-climax.

Dale and Justin (yes @paranormal monk does in fact have a name) turned out to be excellent hosts and fascinating people. Perhaps just a little bit even more sceptical than we were, they had apparently been banned from the chat room of the *Most Haunted* TV series for scurrilously coming up with possible natural explanations for some of the phenomena. They used fairly high tech equipment but only in the way of cameras and motion detectors, believing that much of the rest, especially spirit boxes, were of little use.

The building itself has been furnished as of the late 1960s, including a new baby grandfather clock to represent the one that had been pushed down the stairs. This may be valid as an experiment to create the right environment to bring 'Fred' the poltergeist back, but what do not have any scientific validity are the creepy dolls and pictures around the house and a porcelain clown surely designed to give even the most hardened investigator strange and intensive nightmares. So the place does undoubtedly prime some people to psychologically experience visual phenomena.

The format for the evening was to set up the equipment and then hold a live podcast with discussion about the place, and the paranormal in general, until something actually happened. This was something we were happy to assist with. However, by about 3am nothing had happened at all and we retired to bed perhaps a little disappointed but hardly surprised. Paranormal investigating is much like a fishing trip, you go there for the experience, perhaps hoping but not expecting a 'catch' and you are happy that you went there either way.

We left Dale and Justin soundly asleep when we went to catch the morning train as they had a second night there which was to be attended by some of their podcast followers who has been the lucky 'competition' winners that I had spontaneously entered myself and Rosie into on a whim.

After the second night had passed I sent a twitter message to Dale thanking them for their hospitality, and got the reply along the lines of

> *Great to spend time with you and @RosieO_writer, we need*
> *to talk about what we experienced the night after you left.*
> *It's changed my opinions on the place forever,*
> *30 Aug 2018.*

I am just starting to clarify what happened to Dale and Justin on the second night, with the group of four 'competition winners' – the loud bangs that came from an empty room, and other events which appeared to truly change their views. Research like this can go on for many months, and short of extending this chapter to ridiculous length will go beyond the scope of this book. However, what this clarifies for sure is that just when you are starting to doubt a historic case, something new occurs to make you think and reflect. Whilst the balance of what I have seen and experienced indicates to me that any poltergeist phenomena comes from within, could it have been the new group of people visiting the house with Dale and Justin whose expectations might somehow have triggered off events? I can't help thinking that had I been there for the second night it would have felt to me that an outside entity or spirit was truly there.

Would I too have 'flipped' my theory just like Colin Wilson did?

Chapter 9

Fiction and Fakes – Ethics and Protocol

(Is there a better way that things can be done?)

9.1 Fiction and Fakes

I stated in the beginning of this book that if a poltergeist incident can be verified as happening, it boils down to a case of it being fact or fraud. This statement has been further strengthened throughout this book with natural phenomena – even as extreme as earthquakes – not being able to replicate the poltergeist. If an object can be shown to have moved from one place to another (a walk-about JOTT), it was either moved there by a human hand or a paranormal one. This is even more obvious when an object is shown to fly across the room or when communicative rapping is heard.

Whilst this gives poltergeist phenomena its provability and strength, it also means that we have to be particularly thorough when investigating a case. Misleading others for various reasons has been proven to occur in everyday life; if we are being honest it is in all our nature to do it. Poltergeist events whatever our belief have not yet been fully proved, so by way of investigation potential fraud should always be a theory that needs to be addressed, and which initially should often take precedence over a paranormal one. Certainly on the face of it, there is incentive both for fraud and exaggeration. The need for attention or fame or more recently the 'commercial' nature of having a ghost or poltergeist in your premises can give owners an incentive to exaggerate things. It can also do the same for authors – and to a certain extent you simply just have to take it on trust that a book such as this one is relying on the facts, and hopefully an interesting turn of phrase or two, to appeal to the reader.

I would suggest that such an incentive is similar in any discipline that attempts to discover something new. Psychologists and scientists are in far better paid professions. In these professions it is certainly not unheard of for some to overemphasize the results of their own particular piece of research.

Is red meat good or bad for you? Does fracking cause damage to the environment? Do man-made greenhouse gasses cause global warming? (At least certain high ranking American politicians are not yet convinced...) These are all questions that cause debate amongst qualified experts, sometimes commissioned by one side or the other and therefore potentially incentivised to stress particular points of experimentation and theory.

Perhaps the most blatant example both of fraud and gullible experts wanting to be part of a great discovery was that involving 'Piltdown Man'.

Between 1910–12 Charles Dawson, a part-time geologist and qualified lawyer, claimed to have 'found' in Piltdown in Sussex what appeared to be fossilized fragments of an ancient jawbone and skull. He took the fragments to no less than the British Museum. Here Arthur Smith Woodward, keeper of the museum's palaeontology department, stated that the find was a previously-unknown species of early man. In effect the 'missing link' between man and ape that many in that science had been seeking. This claim was endorsed by other prominent scientists and those directly involved became famous.

Strangely over the years no further remains of 'Piltdown Men' were discovered. It started to seem that this ancient 'missing link' lived an unfeasibly lonely existence in Piltdown, Sussex. This prompted a re-examination in 1953, which showed that the skull was a skilfully disguised human skull about 600 years old, combined with the stained jaw of an orang-utan and tooth of a chimpanzee. This mishmash of remains had kept 'experts' enthralled by a new great discovery for decades.

Perhaps to the credit of the paranormal community, I can't think of an example quite as blatant as that. The examples I give in this chapter are certainly less conclusive but give an insight into legitimate doubts that need raising, before apparent strange events can be thought of as a potential 'paranormal fact'.

In Chapter 2 I gave a few examples about poltergeist activity in my home town areas of Thornton Heath and Croydon, to try to show how common the phenomena were. As I have continued the book I have also received further information on these cases, all that is but one for which a consistent flow of 'non-information' seems to exist.

Let me explain a little further!

My intention was to fully research the well-known 1930s case of the Thornton Heath Poltergeist. This is a case for which I found local newspaper cuttings, and a full-length book written by Nandor Fodor – a case in short which very clearly happened. While doing further Internet searches on this I found a fairly common cross-reference to a 1970s case also known as the Thornton Heath Poltergeist. This was the story of an ordinary family being haunted by previous 18th century residents of the house, named as the Chattertons – which has subsequently become retold in a small budget movie called *The Thornton Heath Poltergeist* (2017).

This sounded fascinating enough to include in my list of local cases so I did. I also contacted the movie's 'producers' for more information into the background of the case. At the time they indicated they were particularly busy in organising the movie's launch, and so would respond back shortly. However, when they finally did make contact, they simply made references to the fact that the story had been fully sourced from the web.

I then looked to the various web sources which in most cases were very close to being a 'copy and paste' from whichever was the previous source. Following that I started adding to the comments sections of the websites that were publicising the tale.

This included 'Real Paranormal Experiences', where on asking for the source of the story, 'Chris' the administrator said he would get in contact with the author to find out the source, but following a delay admitted that the contributor called 'Glyn' was no longer contactable. I also noticed that a lady from the film project was posting comments. She was asking for people with first-hand experiences of this poltergeist, and also obtaining no response.

I saw virtually the same copy and paste story on 'MindSetCentral.com' where 'Kenton' also from Thornton Heath was asking where the house was located, stating he was very familiar with the area and that he could not imagine where it was. There was no feedback either to his or the comments I added.

This story continued to have an (after?) life of its own, being copied and pasted on site after site. When I looked at YouTube, I saw no less than four or five video renditions of the same material, most of them recent. These included a presentation by a USA video blogger known as 'Lady Invasion', who to her credit had got as far as obtaining an old map of Thornton Heath and was speculating as to where the poltergeist house could be. Just as interesting was the fact that my local (likely non-existent) poltergeist had acquired international fame with a YouTube presentation *El Poltergeist de Thornton Heath* made by video blogger Dark Kruck.

I have a colleague from my time in the Ghost Club called David Saunderson, who runs one of the best-known paranormal websites in the UK, www.SpookyIsles.com, which I frequently read. When the Thornton Heath poltergeist cut and paste appeared even on that site, I must admit to getting a little irritated and posted a comment to the author requesting he take the post down if there was no original source to the story. I was pleasantly surprised that when the author was good enough to reply, it was actually a correspondent from Chicago, USA, called

Rick. He accepted his source was the Internet and quoted the site www.realparanormalexperiences.com. This was my original source (apart from the movie as well). In effect I had come full circle and reached a dead end.

There is no indication as to where this story may have originally emerged, whilst there is still just the slimmest of chances that it might be based on some kind of fact. Taking into account that:

1) There is no discovered original source of the tale.
2) No address of the house.
3) The fact that Thornton Heath barely existed in the 18th century and few if any buildings from that time remain.
4) That the story has 'too good to be true' (fictional?) touches such as a ghost coming out of the TV as per Spielberg's *Poltergeist* film, and a shaking Christmas Tree (as per archetypical Christmas Ghost Stories).

It seems to me far more likely that someone is sitting back amazed that their little ghostly 'creation' now has a full-length movie and numerous worldwide presentations both on paranormal blogs and visually on YouTube. I said in a previous chapter how this type of (non-existent) ghost story was rather common when it came to historic apparitional ghost stories. These normally refer to tales that appear to come from far further back than the 1970s. As (relatively) recent poltergeist cases go, the fact that this case may be 'non-existent' may be a first. A first for my home area of Thornton Heath and the town of Croydon – not bad for a town that has been ridiculed by some as being such a bland place to live in!

So it seems when you hear of a potential poltergeist case it is actually good to establish whether the events even happened at all. This is the very first most basic level of faking of course. What I would call the second level of 'faking' is when the people and place existed but the events by and large did not occur. Thornton Heath doesn't have such a case, nor does Croydon. To find the most famous example that some at least would claim fits this criteria, one would need to cross the Atlantic to Suffolk County, New York State – to a small town known as Amityville. A seaside town of just under 10,000 inhabitants, known as the 'Friendly Bay Village' and according to the current Amityville website once the haunts of:

> Stage and theatre personalities, prominent members of society including businessmen, artists, writers and the so-called "rich and famous" Manhattanites.

It was also once the haunt of 'something' that became known as the Amityville Horror!

My thoughts on this case had been refreshed by a quote I had read when researching the case of the Black Monk of Pontefract for the previous chapter. I had spotted a quote from the researcher and writer Tom Cuniff in the *Pontefract and Castleford Gazette* stating that:

> The idea [of becoming a paranormal writer] came to him after seeing films and reading books, The Exorcist and The Amityville Horror, not because he was impressed by them, but because he found the latter so implausible that he felt he could write far more convincing material.

Any reality in the Amityville case has been clouded by so many movies which vaguely claim to be inspired by true events, which have surrounded the place in myth and legend even more.

What is undoubtedly true is the fact that in November 1974, the DeFeo family were murdered in their beds at 112 Ocean Avenue in Amityville – father, mother, two girls and two boys shot to death with a .35 calibre rifle. Ronald DeFeo, their remaining son, who likely had problems with drugs and drink, finally confessed to the murders. His attorney mounted an unsuccessful insanity plea claiming he had been hearing voices telling him to kill. He was sent to prison to serve six concurrent sentences of 25 years to life.

This event at the time was obviously very newsworthy and the house itself became a notorious place of death that was tricky to sell. That was until a year later, when George and Kathy Lutz spotted a bargain price of $80,000 and moved into the large family home with their three children in December 1975. Their residency there was to last all of 28 days – by which time they claimed to have fled in terror never to return.

What happened in those 28 days has been controversial over the last 40 years. Gauld and Cornell as I have mentioned before have invented the useful criteria of an 'Intermediate Poltergeist' case, where poltergeist and other phenomena are mixed up together. But it could be said that the phenomena in Amityville was simply 'mixed up', and followed no common pattern at all. These included a very significant walkabout 'JOTT' in the shape of a **4-foot-high Chinese lion** which appeared in the living room after George Lutz had taken it upstairs. George Lutz also claimed that when he tripped over the lion he found 'bite' marks on his leg – though we have no photographs of these possible poltergeist marks and a four-foot Chinese lion could likely leave a significant bruise! George would also wake up to the sound of the front door slamming, and claimed that locks, doors and windows in the house were damaged by an unseen force. Overall he may have got off lightly compared with the experiences of Kathy Lutz, who levitated off her bed and found an unseen hand giving her welts on her chest.

So far we have some elements that have something in common to such cases as 'The Cage' (bruising and marking by an unseen entity) and the Enfield Poltergeist (possible levitation of at least one of the girls). From here though the phenomena takes on a life of its own and included a demonic pig that became an imaginary friend of the Lutzes' five-year-old girl, and cloven hoofs possibly from the pig appearing in the snow.

Though in an interesting Internet article by the track expert Jonah Evans, he points out that:

Tracks can become distorted and expand dramatically as snow melts. In deep, melted snow I've actually seen people mistake squirrel tracks for those of a bear![33]

There were also swarms of flies and smells of excrement though it seems quite plausible that one could be the cause of the other. In addition to this, green 'Goo' ran down the walls and crosses turned upside down. From 'The Cage' and 'Enfield' there is suddenly a touch of *The Exorcist* added – the 1973 ground-breaking movie which shocked the public far more than even the real-life murders at Amityville did.

Kathy Lutz also had nightmares about the murders and George kept waking up at what he perceived to be the time of death of the previous household. Both events are quite possible to conceive without any paranormal cause. It is quite believable that the family may have been freaked out by the house and took a paranormal slant on growing unfortunate events. Certainly when a demon is seen by the Lutzes to be 'burned' into the back of the soot in the fireplace – one would expect them to find the image of Jesus on a slice of burnt toast next. Both are of course 'Pareidolia', when the mind gives meaning to a simple pattern when nothing actually is there. Did the Lutzes, however, freak themselves out to the extent that their fear may have even triggered some poltergeist episode – or is this a generous assumption for me to make?

Because of the notoriety of the house, when the Lutzes vacated the premises after 28 days they very much walked out into media frenzy. Ronald DeFeo's lawyer William Weber even looked to the possibility that some natural electric force might be 'screwing up' people's heads in the house as possible grounds for a retrial.

Weber was also to discuss the possibility of a joint book with the Lutzes, though no book deal was ever done with Weber, and the bestselling *The Amityville Horror* was ultimately written by Jay Anson in 1977. The numerous movies were to follow.

Weber was later to claim that over several bottles of wine he and the Lutzes discussed embellishing the facts – well who wouldn't in that inebriated state? This has led to a claim that the whole thing was a hoax from beginning to end. A claim that might well have some substance based on the following reasoning...

We have been discussing how useful witness testimony is throughout this book, but unlike the cases such as The Cage and Enfield and even the Pontefract Black Monk – where in all cases the pool of witnesses goes fairly deep, in the case of Amityville the witness pool barely gets past the Lutzes themselves. The one key witness other than the Lutzes in Jay Anson's book is a Father Mancuso who amongst other things was told to 'Get Out' by a strange voice when he tried to bless the house. The real priest in this instance was actually Father Ralph Pecoraro who has signed an affidavit stating he only spoke to the Lutzes over the phone but subsequently mentioned he may have visited them but saw nothing strange. Finally, however, in his only TV interview he admitted that the incident actually occurred. Such contradictions of course, whilst not falsifying the Lutzes' story, make this witness testimony weak.

The witness pool is shallow enough to take seriously the possibility that few of the strange events took place at Ocean Avenue (and it does therefore fit well into a section about possible 'made-up' cases); it does seem strange though that many of the events when stripped of their 'horror story' setting seem so totally trivial. Much was made of George Lutz waking up at

3.15am nearly every night – but if a move of house is stressful, a move to the house of a former mass murderer is potentially more stressful still. Add to that the fact that (according to Jay Anson's book) even the Lutzes admitted they were looking for property in the $30–50,000 range before seeing 112 Ocean Avenue at the bargain price of $80,000. This common mistake of overextending a budget to buy a dream house would have added to the stress factor as well. There are so many psychological reasons that would have made George Lutz wake up in early morning panic that a paranormal one comes very low down on the list of explanations.

George Lutz himself pointed this out in a story for ABC News, which reported that:

> *He denies making anything up, saying that if they had, they would have come up with a better story.*[34]

Footprints in the snow are not proof of the devil, and invasion of flies and smell of excrement are more likely to be indicative of the need for a good plumber than anything else. Perhaps it's not such a coincidence that 'Plumbers' and 'Paranormal Investigators' seem to sometimes be one and the same these days![35] If a story was to have been purely invented why would the Lutzes have come out with such atypical paranormal events? Far more likely they felt real fear and panic for whatever reason, looked at all the odd things that had happened to them and put them on the 'paranormal' list.

Another common line of attack on the Amityville Horror book has been the fact that Jay Anson decided to write the book basically using the formula of one chapter for each day in the house. Some have dissected each day and discovered apparently that there was no snow on the day that footprints were found in the snow or no storms on a particular day when the book said there were. I have not checked the accuracy of this research but would point out that there were no claims by the Lutzes to keep a diary of the events. What event happened exactly when, after a significant lapse of time, would certainly have been an approximation at best. The reader should try writing a detailed diary of what happened to yourself over each day for the month before, and you will quickly find I think that whilst the events in your life might be remembered, the exact day they happened perhaps only approximated. To therefore try to dissect Jay Anson's book like some scientific notes and call out fraud if the facts don't quite fit the right day would in my opinion be unfair.

Until his death in 2006 George Lutz stayed adamant that, with the exception of one or two literary embellishments in the book, and a few more in the film (No surprises there for a Hollywood 'Inspired by True Facts' horror movie!), the events basically took place as stated. Both George and Kathy Lutz took a lie detector test which they both passed. This again lessens the possibility of this being a case of out and out fraud – which is commonly argued by many. Danny Lutz the eldest son of Kathy and stepson of George appeared in a documentary in 2013 in which he backed up the stories of his parents. As was reported in the UK newspaper the *Daily Mail*:

> On the 'paranormal activity' in the house, he [Danny Lutz] says furniture would move around, voices would whisper to him and he experienced 'bodily possession'.[36]

So if not a case of fraud as commonly thought – is it simply a case of misinterpretation of normal events as paranormal? Or is there just a possibility that the poltergeist type events may have been caused by the stress of the situation the family found themselves in – as stress and even fear throughout the cases we have studied in the book seem to be such good 'bedfellows' for the poltergeist?

We have noted two types of (possible) fraud that are often

underestimated or ignored, cases where the whole facts are totally made up and which are fiction masquerading as fact, and cases in which even though the basic facts are true the paranormal bits are added in or at least incorrectly interpreted. The third main type of fraud that occurs is perhaps the most common of all, when the poltergeist events did occur as stated, but were made by human intervention as a deliberate attempt to deceive. I have given several examples of this in the fifth chapter referring to fraudulent mediums who tried, and in some cases succeeded, hoodwinking paranormal investigators. There are, however, also cases where the facts of the matter can become even more tangled, because it is the paranormal researcher himself that may possibly have been fraudulent.

So much has been said about England's most famous haunted house – Borley Rectory in Essex, UK, that originally I had wished to keep it out of this book – but have failed abysmally as it is a fascinating case. There were two books written by Harry Price: *The Most Haunted House in England* (1940) and *The End of Borley Rectory* (1946). Price had no psychic ability though when he named his second book *The End of Borley Rectory*, because the saga of Borley Rectory, despite the building itself being demolished, had not ended in any way, shape or form. Many other books followed over the next sixty years.

I am sure this list is not exhaustive but it makes the point:

Henning, Rev AC (1949). *Haunted Borley*. An intriguing collector's item written by the Vicar of Liston and Borley – which I am lucky enough to have a copy of in my collection.

Turner, James (1950). *My Life with Borley Rectory*

Dingwall, EJ; Goldney, KM; Hall, TH (1956). *The Haunting of Borley Rectory*

Tabori, Paul; Underwood, Peter (1973). *The Ghosts of Borley: Annals of the Haunted Rectory*. A collaboration between the Chair of the Ghost Club (Underwood) and Price's literary executor (Tabori).

Wood, Robert (1992). *The Widow of Borley.* A book which unfavourably analyses the character of Marianne Foyster, the wife of Lionel Foyster, who lived in the rectory during part of the 1930s, when the phenomena was at its most active.

Downes, Wesley (1993). *The Ghosts of Borley*

Banks, Ivan (1996). *The Enigma of Borley Rectory*

Mayerling, L. (2000). *We Faked the Ghosts of Borley Rectory*

O'Neil, V. (2001). *Borley Rectory: The Ghosts That Will Not Die.* An e-book published by the son of Marianne Foyster.

Babbs, E. (2003). *Borley Rectory: The Final Analysis.* The most far-fetched name of all – Did Babb's really think he was going to have the last word on the subject?

Adams, P.; Brazil, E. and Underwood, P. (2009). *The Borley Rectory Companion.* A voluminous effort to sum up all the data using the notes and knowledge of a by now aging Peter Underwood and the thorough enthusiasm of Adams and Brazil.

For a full recollection of this century plus old 'intermediate' ghost and poltergeist case please refer to the list of books above. My particular interest in the subject is that much of the phenomenon relies on the reporting and investigation skills of Harry Price, and that those skills after his death were critically reanalysed by some.

The re-analysis became outright accusations of fraud in Dingwall, Goldney, and Hall's book *The Haunting of Borley Rectory* in 1956 – published after Price's death and so with no risk of being sued in English law. This was in part a character assassination for which Price was always going to be vulnerable to as he really was quite a 'character' – and which started with accusations that Price might have exaggerated about his upbringing and his social class.

Paul Tabori, Price's literary executor, states explicitly that Price was born on 17th January 1881 in Shrewsbury, while both Hall and others have shown that his first home was actually 37 Red Lion Square, Holborn, a poor area at the time.

It does seem likely that Harry Price's father, Edward Ditcher Price, when aged over 40, had to shut his grocery business in Shrewsbury and moved down to London after being obliged to marry a 14-year-old girl Emma Randall-Meech, who was at the time pregnant with Harry Price's older sister – above the age of consent in those days but hardly respectable behaviour.

However, Paul Adams and Eddie Brazil (keepers of the Borley archives which they inherited from Peter Underwood) actually point out that Price made no explicit comment to where he was born, simply referring to himself as a 'Shropshire lad', when both his father and grandfather came from there. (Please note that I often refer to myself as Scottish – the home of all my Fraser Clan's ancestors – whilst I was also born in London as well.)

As Paul Adams has further explained:

There seems to be an amount of hazing by Price in his memoirs, as with hindsight we would suggest he was embarrassed about his London roots… In a class-divided Britain of the 1930s perhaps that was not surprising.[37]

At no point according to Adams does he ever say he was born there.

For any American reader it is worth emphasizing that the British class structure in Price's time was still very obvious, so the glazing may have been seen as a necessity to overcome these false and unfair barriers. Remember what I said at the start of the chapter – that we all find justification for little white lies. The question is when does that justification cease; when does a slight embellishment cross that acceptable red line?

Far more important in Hall's (et al.) accusations are the

potential examples of actual fraud in Price's paranormal research at Borley. These include two particular incidents – an accusation of throwing stones to deliberately mimic a poltergeist and an accusation of deliberately misleading when a flying brick had an obvious natural cause.

The first incident dates back to 1929 when Borley had first captured the media's attention, but again only came to light in 1948, after Harry Price's death. Charles Sutton, a reporter of the *Daily Mail*, had been accompanying Price and his secretary to Borley, along with Lord Charles Hope, Price's sometime sponsor. Sutton reported, in 1948, that during the 1929 visit he had seen Price throw a stone as if to try to replicate poltergeist phenomena and had then found Price's pockets to be full of stones and bricks. Lord Charles Hope subsequently confirmed that Sutton had made the accusation at the time, though could in no way verify its truth. It becomes the word of a (possibly) 'story-hungry' newspaper reporter after a story against the word of a ghost hunter, well known for his love of publicity as well, but whose reputation at that time was based far more on scepticism than actively promoting the existence of phenomena.

As to who can be believed in such a one against one statement of conflicting facts is by definition a very delicate balancing act. Price, however, had a possibly surprising supporter who came to his defence. This was none other than one of his main research rivals Nandor Fodor (whose investigation of the real Thornton Heath Poltergeist is detailed in Chapter 2).

In a review of Hall's (et al.) book, and particularly about this incident, Fodor stated that:

> *Anxious as the exposures [authors] were to examine minutely every story for the slightest contradiction or slip up when it could be turned against Price, they have no comment to make on Sutton's palpably absurd statement that he found Price's pockets,* **"Full of Bricks and Pebbles."**

The implication being that a suit pocket full of bricks and pebbles is an absurdly obvious attempt at fraud and one very unlikely to be used by an amateur conjurer such as Price was. Fodor also later stated that:

> *Anything can happen in a haunted house. Journalists may frame an investigator just as an investigator could frame a journalist.*

Here we have the paranormal researcher's conundrum, when dealing with paranormal incidents the evidence of fraud is rarely clear cut!

Similar comments may also be applied to misreporting of events in our second example of a flying brick both seen and photographed when the rectory was a ruin after it burnt down in 1939. In this instance Price visited in 1944 again accompanied by a journalist and photographer, in this case Cynthia Ledsham and David Scherman who were representing *Life* magazine.

During the visit Scherman photographed a picture of a brick in flight at the rectory which he claimed was just taken as a photographic effect of the sort of thing a poltergeist would do, as in his view it was clearly thrown by workmen slowly demolishing the building. Ledsham also backed up his account of the incident, and although the photograph did appear in the magazine it was made clear that this incident had been staged to recreate a typical poltergeist event.

However, the photograph was also to appear in Price's second book on Borley, *The End of Borley Rectory*, and he has been accused of passing it off as a real poltergeist incident. Again the truth or otherwise of the accusation is far more subtle in nature, as what Harry Price actually said (*The End of Borley Rectory*) was this:

> *The three of us saw it [the brick] and, as I said, we were at least a hundred feet away from it. We all laughed and called it 'the last*

phenomenon', and said the poltergeists were 'demonstrating' in honour of our visit. We walked over to the passage, where there were many bricks lying about. I picked up several, and all appeared normal. No string or wire was attached to any of them, and we saw no workmen at all on that side of the Rectory.

This is a likely factually correct rendition of what happened, three people saw something in a haunted house that had an obvious natural explanation and had a laugh about it; but by spinning the tale to be about checking for strings and wires, he is blurring the factual events and making it seem like a potential real poltergeist incident – **without actually saying it is**!

Did Price cross that red line between colourful narrative and pure dishonesty simply by the way he implied an incident without actually stating there was one?

I personally believe in this instance he did, although whether implying something without actually saying it amounts to outright fraud is something open to debate. Perhaps I am still being a little too generous to Price because I have a memory of doing this to a much lesser extent many years back, when I had visited and researched the remote and desolate Sandwood Bay and ruined Sandwood Cottage thought to be the 'haunt' of a ghostly bearded sailor.

On my return from Sandwood I sent a detailed report of the case to Peter Underwood, the then President of the Ghost Club, who I simply then knew by reputation and by the interest he had taken in Sandwood Cottage in his previous books. This was very much in the same sort of way the less experienced Tom Cuniff had approached the established writer Colin Wilson regarding the East Drive, Pontefract case. I guess we all want to impress the people whose books we read?

Except as well as a detailed report I also included a nice piece of 'Pareidolia' that I had photographed at Sandwood Cottage, the face of a bearded man on a crumbling plaster wall taken in the dark by flashlight. Clearly not a ghost (where was his body?) but I had seen far worse published in paranormal books of the time. Underwood didn't publish the photo but spent a whole chapter discussing my experiences and the case in his book *Nights in Haunted Houses* (1994) in which he gave my fine piece of Pareidolia a good few lines stating that:

> *There is a clear outline of a head of a bearded man which resembles the head of a statue. However, as John explains… as it is surrounded by flash reflection it seems likely to assume that it is just a clever trick of the flashlight. This, however, has not been confirmed and until it is the photograph remains interesting.*

All totally factually correct but between Underwood and myself (he was mainly using quotes from my own report) there was enough ambiguity added to keep the photograph an 'interesting' event with just a hint that it could be paranormal.

The report (not the photograph) subsequently got me an invitation to join the then 'members by invitation only' Ghost Club – so not a bad result overall, and whilst I personally think that both myself and Underwood stayed more or less on the right side of that fine line in the sand between 'literary embellishment' and 'literarily misleading', it remains a fine line all the same.

I think the way this 'fine line' can be best summed up is by revisiting Fodor's book review on the Borley book by Hall (et al.) which he completed by saying that:

> *No doubt Harry Price had his weaknesses, inconsistencies, confusions and mistakes… Nor is the tendency to embellish easy to resist in books written for the general public. It is not the details that matter in the story of Borley Rectory. Even if Price had thrown the stone of which he is accused, the grim story of the most haunted house in England would still stand.*

In other words, read between the lines, and look at the depth of witnesses and overall evidence, and by doing that rather than going round in circles about one (irresolvable) incident you become far more likely to separate an overall fraud from a potentially valid case!

When I previously was addressing this issue in my book *Ghost Hunting: A Survivor's Guide*, I stated that a good approach was to:

Believe nothing [and to] Check and question everything.

Also pointing out that:

Not to believe someone is not the same as disbelieving them. A good researcher is one that can get his mind in a state of suspended disbelief and let the facts do the talking unhindered from any preconceived ideas.

In effect we would make a lot more progress if we could all become good level-headed, open-minded 'psychic detectives'. However, there is one big proviso which in particular applies to poltergeist cases. By its nature being a detective can be quite an intrusive process. This is even more obvious when witnesses in poltergeist cases tend to be victims of, or even catalysts for, the phenomena – disconcerted and scared by events.

How far then can you intrude on a person and their home in your search for truth before the well-being of the people you are there to help is put in some jeopardy?

In short, is the way we investigate ethically sound – or how can we ensure it is?

9.2 Ethics and Protocol

In 1977 the SPR sent an inexperienced, upper middle-aged, male investigator alone to investigate a poltergeist that had been scaring the occupants of a private family home. The investigator had been given no training and had no prior experience in investigating – and with recent bereavement himself had the potential not to be in an objective frame of mind.

As luck would have it this investigator came in the shape of the highly professional and level-headed Maurice Grosse, who ultimately with the help of a more experienced Guy Playfair investigated this case of the Enfield Poltergeist which turned into quite possibly the best documented case of all time. However, despite the outcome it should also be asked if simply 'looking like a sensible well-educated gentleman' (Grosse had recently retired as a successful inventor) is sufficient criteria these days to refer someone initially unaided to a high profile and complex case?

Of course any lapse in ethics or protocol in the Enfield case was rather minor when compared to what has happened in the past. We have already heard of a poltergeist victim being strip-searched in the 1930s 'real' Thornton Heath case, and of intimate internal inspections taking place on mediums by investigators of the opposite sex. Such protocol should most definitely be out of bounds in the modern world, but until recently any real protocol with regards to the needs of witnesses/victims of phenomena has not been written down. Groups have debated at length the sensible use (or non-use) of equipment but often forgotten the fact that at least in 'Cry for Help' cases (when the witnesses are in a state of confusion or distress) it should be the needs of those witnesses that come first. This applies even if there may be a suspicion of fraud as that in itself could be a plea for attention for numerous reasons.

One thing that has totally changed since the times of the 'Gentlemen' Investigators is the fact that, since the popularisation of the paranormal on television, so many people and organisations have involved themselves in the discipline. It has been estimated in the UK that this might consist of up to 1,200 groups, and far more I expect in the USA.

This explosion of groups of course gives no sense of 'quality control' for paranormal research. Many groups I suspect are as respectful as possible but others are led by their own beliefs, and possibly even their own urges for paranormal thrills.

'ASSAP', a nationwide umbrella group based in the UK, made a unique attempt a few years ago to rectify this situation.

I was attending and speaking at the ASSAP 'Thirty Year Anniversary' special conference in 2011, when the organisers kept hinting that a surprise announcement would be made. This announcement was the fact that they had sought and gained government accreditation as a professional association. Which technically at least would put them in the same category as well-known organisations such as Association of British Travel Agents (ABTA), less well-known organisations such as British & International Golf Greenkeepers Association (BIGGA), and less well-liked organisations such as the British Parking Association (BPA) – the non-governmental organisation whose members hand out parking fines.

The reception and the impact of this announcement were mixed, as membership of a professional body does not necessarily mean that a person possesses qualifications in the subject area, and non-membership of such an association does not mean the opposite either. Nevertheless, this was a genuine attempt to try to assist the paranormal community to both look and act more respectably, and was combined with a criminal background check for those who wished to be accredited ASSAP investigators, as well as a need to first attend training sessions.

To follow up on this initiative ASSAP compiled a code of ethics to be followed specifically by members, but much of it is good guidance to non-members and to non-UK researchers as well. In this they categorised for different types of case:

1) Cases dealing with statutory vulnerable people such as when the:

> *"Client is under 18, is frail due to old age, has mental health issues or learning disabilities."*

In such cases of course a guardian or carer should be present.

2) Cases dealing with non-statutory vulnerable people which are defined as:

> *"Cases where investigation is of an individual's private home or where the client is emotionally invested in the case."*

Categories 1 and 2 are very close to my 'cry for help' case definition which I have used in this and my previous ghost hunting book.

3) Non-vulnerable cases. These are likely to be public venues, or places that have been well investigated in the past.
4) Cases with no client, such as an outdoor location or ruin. This would have applied to my visits to Sandwood Bay.

Whilst basic protocol is of course important for all cases, it is categories one and two where it is ethically most important. It is also categories one and two that are far more common when it comes to investigating poltergeist phenomena, so whilst these guidelines are for all cases they are often far more relevant to the type of case discussed in this book.

Most of the concepts ASSAP discusses in their ethical guidelines are extremely useful ones which we should all do well to remember. These include:

1. Not working in cases where someone has been bereaved of a close relative for less than six months.
2. A client's right to anonymity unless made clear by the client that no anonymity is required.
3. That 'people' should come before 'research'. To emphasize this ASSAP states:

> *"When working with vulnerable clients the investigator's primary concern should be reassuring that client. Research aims should be secondary to this aim."*

4. That ideally investigators should not work alone and that in many cases investigators of both sexes are best. This is particularly true when ensuring the investigation teams have someone as the same sex(es) as the client.

There are one or two points, however, where I feel that ASSAP's approach could tie an investigation up in knots when dealing with responsible adults of a sound mind, when a little more common sense is called for rather than pre-set rules. This applies in particular to ASSAP's recommendation that:

> *You do not research the history of a property as part of working with a vulnerable client. There is no proven association between historical events and anomalous activity.*

There is after all no proven association between **ANY** events yet as a cause of the paranormal so to use that argument would be an argument to do nothing at all. Most people want to try to rationalise what is going on around them and the more potentially relevant facts we have the better this process can be. If people think their home may have the presence of an evil 'Black Monk' such as was thought at one point in the Pontefract case, and if research can show the unlikelihood of such an event, is that not the essence of what a paranormal researcher actually is?

The SPR had not until very recently changed their investigation protocol notes since 1996. In 2018 we commissioned Steve Parsons of Para.Science in liaison with our Spontaneous Cases Committee to rewrite them. Our choice was not a code of conduct but a comprehensive guide extending to more than 50 pages. I should first say that it covers most of ASSAP's main points with regards to investigation ethics; the emphasis, however, is much more in encouraging techniques that get to the essence of the client's experiences. It therefore recommends that prior to an in-depth interview:

> *It is helpful in most instances to ask the witness to write down... a description of their experiences. The witness should be encouraged to include the dates and times and as much detail... as can be recalled.*

Therefore any subsequent interview can be carried out in a structured way based on the facts already known, and increase the chance of the investigator(s) getting a better understanding of what has occurred.

It also recommends that for any future events the witness keeps an investigation diary. Something I made the assumption was lacking (due to the fact I could find no mention of it) in the incidents reported by the Lutzes from Amityville.

Key questions to a witness being interviewed once they have been put at ease include:

1) The location of the witness during each event.
2) Information about what the witness was doing previously and their state of mind at the time.
3) What the witness did during the event and afterwards.
4) Who else was at the location – where were they situated and did they experience anything too?
5) The physical circumstances at the time of the experience such as the lighting and temperature.

Once facts like that are established the 'psychic detective' in us starts to have enough information to understand what **MIGHT** have been happening and offer some general reassuring advice. If there are further witnesses it is important to go through the same procedure with each.

The style of the interview is also important and the guide points out the importance of not asking leading questions such as when was the ghost first seen, as opposed to asking when the first unusual event took place.

With the client's permission it is also better to audio record the interview. Without this there is the danger of inaccuracies and excessive note-taking. Video recording should normally be avoided as it would put some witnesses into an excessive self-conscious state.

With regards to the historic perspective of an investigation, the SPR guide states that:

Researching the history of a location, the building and the people that have been associated with it, may in some instances reveal information that is relevant to the investigation process.

And that:

The history or appearance of a location may alter the perception of a witness... a figure in a religious setting [or town??] might easily be open to interpretation as being a monk!!

I couldn't have written the last quote better myself and guarantee you I had not read it before writing my findings on Pontefract – nor had Steve Parsons read my findings before he wrote this guide.

Overall, whilst the ASSAP initiative is perhaps the most workable for what is in effect an umbrella organisation, my personal preference is for the new SPR guidelines which avoids, as Parsons puts it, the process becoming:

A tick box exercise when questions are asked just because they are written on the paperwork.

Paranormal investigation may well be a science but dealing with people under difficult circumstances is very much in itself an art – any approach in my opinion should take strong account of that fact.

A guidebook available to all as opposed to a code only applicable to members also increases the chance of wider education outside of that group and with up to 1,200 groups this is surely what we have to be trying to achieve.

The above gives some sense of how some in the UK are starting to get to grips with ethical issues, which if not tackled would in particular hinder sensitive poltergeist cases. One of my claims in this book has been that the poltergeist is a worldwide phenomenon, and I have given some worldwide examples. I couldn't help but get curious as to whether other countries that take phenomena seriously were having similar protocol and ethical conversations, and therefore thought I would make a few enquiries.

I contacted The Institut Métapsychique International (IMI), famous for having Charles Richet as a member, and got a reply from a charming lady called Pascale Catala, who explained that since the days of Richet active paranormal research had become almost unknown in France until the new millennium, but that especially in the last five years it had gained a new lease of life. Protocols actually written by Catala herself were therefore more in the way of bullet points but appear to be sound and covering all main areas. With regards to the witnesses these protocols put emphasis on discovering their belief system and religion, the state of consciousness at the time of the strange event, whether they had prior knowledge of any strange events that had happened before and perhaps most importantly their emotional reaction to the phenomena. A witness should be treated in a different way of course if simply curious about what is happening as opposed to being scared.

She has also, with the help of her colleague Jann Alexander, produced easily measurable 'Scales' with regards to reported phenomena measuring such things as:

1) The intensity of the phenomena
2) The level of authentication by witness
3) How connected the phenomena are with a person or place
4) The psychological effect of the phenomena on witnesses
5) The psychological health of the main witnesses.

Each category having a rating from 0–4 depending on the strength of the effect.

With regards to these scales I found that the descriptions of what fitted into each level make them a useful categorisation tool that could help compare cases rather well – especially for poltergeist cases, and with the kind permission of Ms Catala include them in full below.

'HANTÉES' SCALES
Based on an idea by Jann Alexander

A - Scale of intensity of the disorders
B - Authentication scale
C - Scale of personalization / localization
D - Scale of psychological feeling
E - Pathology scale

A - Scale of intensity of the disorders
0 - No anomalies
1 - Sensations of presence, drafts, cold
2 - Slight noises, unassuming noises, undefined glimmers, self-starting devices, odours, appearance with a single witness
3 - Major noises, movements and breakage of objects, jets or puddles, improbable trajectories, appearance with several witnesses

4 - Clash, major destruction, fires, stone rains, displacement of heavy objects, people affected (displacements, bites, burns, scratches, receiving projectiles)

B - Authentication scale
0 - No investigation, no written or oral narrative
1 - Testimony of a person
2 - Collection of concordant testimonies of at least two persons
3 - Field investigation with verified concordant testimonies
4 - Field investigation with verified testimonials and observations of anomalies by a knowledgeable person (parapsychologist, police officer...), photos or films

C - Scale of personalization / localization
0 - Internal feeling of a person without objectivations
1 - Obvious focus on one person (ex: teenager)
2 - The phenomena reproduce elsewhere when the agent or the group moves / or the phenomena stop if the agent leaves
3 - The phenomena cease for the agent or the group that moves / or the phenomena persist in the place if a new group moves in
4 - Busy place: legends, history, tragic events. Several independent observations over several years, even generations

D - Scale of psychological feeling
0 - Ordinary everyday life
1 - Feelings of presence, slight anxiety, discomfort
2 - Surprise, perplexity, questioning, torment, concern
3 - Fear, desire to move, fatigue, need help
4 - Panic, flight

E - Pathology scale
0 - Ordinary everyday life
1 - Mild discomfort, expression of problems, proper management of the disorder

245

2 - Destabilization, need of listening and external help, takes into account advice, lucidity, questioning, phenomena related to a personal psychological problem
3 - Delusional interpretations that cannot be modified by reasoning, lack of lucidity, extreme mental agitation
4 - Need for psychiatric care of at least one subject, risks of violence.

The Cage for example would comfortably fit as a level three case with regards to the intensity of phenomena which is described as including:

Major noises, movements and breakage of objects, jets or puddles, appearance of phenomena with several witnesses.

(Possibly it is a borderline level four when you think of the poltergeist scratching incidents.)

But **definitely** a level four with regards to psychological effect i.e. severe panic and 'flight' (as Vanessa Mitchell and others have had to literally flee the premises).

Whilst the Black Monk of Pontefract case would be a level four case with regards to intensity of the phenomena including many of the factors in the category:

Major destruction, fires, stone rains, displacement of heavy objects, people affected by being moved, bitten or burnt or scratched, or having projectiles thrown at them.

A grandfather clock falling down the stairs is definitely a heavy object displacement while Diane Pritchard was not only 'moved' but dragged up the stairs and left with marks on her neck.

However, Pontefract with regards to Authentication would only rate as a level two case. Consisting of:

Collection of testimonies of at least two persons.

Further verification by trained investigators or outsiders was not of course available as the details were only put on record about a decade later.

The psychological health scale is a little more problematic, as it would really need a psychological expert to gauge such things, and even if one was available a level four judgement ('Need for psychiatric care') would likely have to be kept hidden from the witness of course.

However, with a touch of refining I believe that these sorts of categorisations could be very useful in making sense of our subject.

Pascale Catala has also written books on the subject, including *Apparitions & Maison Hantées* (2004), which could also give a useful insight into the French perspective. If only my language skills were better!

In Germany, where the word poltergeist actually comes from, there seems to have been no loss of interest since the times of Albert von Schrenck-Notzing. This was in particular due to the efforts that the German parapsychologist Hans Bender made in the second half of the 20th century.

Bender is in particular known for his investigation of the Rosenheim Poltergeist, a controversial case in Rosenheim in Southern Bavaria, Germany in the late 1960s involving a law office where the light fittings exploded and swung, and heavy office furniture moved without explanation.

Bender identified the likely focus of the phenomena as being a young secretary, 19-year-old Anne Marie Schaberl, who was unhappy in her job and had suffered a broken marriage engagement. He claimed that after she left her employment the phenomena ceased.

Whilst this particular case hit the headlines and caused controversy amongst some sceptics as well, even by 1974 Bender was claiming to have investigated 38 cases to date.[38]

With his background in psychology Bender was to favour a 'poltergeist' that comes from within us at times of stress rather than an 'earthbound spirit' or 'elemental' theory. Perhaps though his best achievement was in 1950 to set up the IGPP (Institute for Frontier Areas of Psychology and Mental Health), which is the only private foundation in Europe supporting research in parapsychology. This apparently well-funded institute appears to thrive, giving details of no less than 24 staff on its website.

On contacting the IGPP I was efficiently and courteously replied to. It was explained to me that the phenomena reported by clients was dealt with through a special documentation system developed by the Institute. I was referred to the Institute's latest report of activity for further information.

There I was immediately struck by a paragraph I read that:

*Depending on their cultural tradition or ideological background, "exceptional experiences" (ExE) are described as supernatural, super sensory, **magical,** paranormal, spiritual, transcendent, transpersonal etc. For ages, such experiences belong to the varieties of human experiences that are well-known interculturally.*

Not because of its immediate relevance to the topic of protocol and ethics, but because of the way it reiterated the theme running through this book that the same phenomena can be described in different cultural ways.

From 2014 to 2015 the institute took on 250 enquiries (cases) relating to potential paranormal happenings of which about 28% (57–58) involved phenomena which could potentially be related to poltergeist activity. These cases seem to have been dealt with fairly extensively, with each of them averaging just above five separate contacts with the institute's staff. Most of these contacts were made remotely, with 43% of all contacts being realised by email and 43% by phone, 12% were made by letter and only 2%

face to face at either the institute itself or at the home of the person.

Whilst this mammoth operation is likely to be extremely effective at picking up meaningful overall data and also providing reassurance to as many as possible, the remote aspects make it a bit less likely to investigate (in the old-fashioned sense) a potential 'breakthrough' case, in the way that for example the Enfield Poltergeist makes claims to be.

Moving across the Atlantic, perhaps the closest that Canada has to an organisation that tries to coordinate all the ad hoc active interest in the paranormal is the 'Ghost and Hauntings Research Society'. Started relatively recently in 1997 by Matthew James Didier as an online reporting facility for true ghost stories, it gradually expanded its subject focus into active investigation and research. The GHRS also expanded geographically into parts of the USA and UK as well, but operates primarily within its own nation now as part of 'Paranormal Studies and Inquiries Canada' (PSICAN).

PSICAN's protocol for investigations covers most of the basic points previously mentioned by others. Didier, however, makes great stress on the lack of a real theory to back up the use of equipment such as Electromagnetic Frequency (EMF) meters, pointing out that there is no accepted theory with regards to how they measure the paranormal; and that the theory could actually be based on a fictional 1973 movie called *The Legend of Hell House*:

> *Where a scientist theorises that if he bursts an EM [Electromagnetic] pulse through a haunted house it would dispel the ghost.*

This is interesting for as we will see later 'high tech equipment' seems to be on the whole taken more seriously on the North American continent as opposed to Europe.

PSICAN have also done some excellent research to allay people's fears about phenomena, pointing out that:

> Over the last 200 years... there are only 2 documented cases of ghosts being accused of harming people... One is the death of John Bell in relation to the Bell Witch Case [Tennessee, 1817]... The other is an attack on a woman known as The Entity Case [California – 1970s].

PSICAN also try to categorise levels of phenomena in much the same kind of way, but using a different scale, as The Institut Métapsychique International, IMI. This seems to indicate that an international classification is something that would be very useful in the future.

Our worldwide tour of protocol would not be complete without also looking at the USA. On contacting a trusted contact in the USA, however, he stated that there was too much dissention and egoism amongst members of the paranormal community stateside so that there was little in the way of agreed ethics or protocol. He did, however, say that the one exception to this might be 'TAPS'.

The Atlantic Paranormal Society (TAPS) was set up originally in 1990 by Jason Hawes and Grant Wilson as the Rhode Island Paranormal Society – so it was well established before the sudden influx of interest. The organisation became known as TAPS in 1994, a clever pun of the co-founders' previous jobs as plumbers, and initially helped pioneer the use of much higher tech equipment that was to take over investigation practices in the early millennium. This was in a large part helped by the fact that in 2003 they got their own long-running ghost hunting series on television called quite simply *Ghost Hunters*, which I must admit was my main awareness of them as an organisation. However, what their website (which states 40 million hits a year) makes clear is that the TAPS which takes on high profile cases on TV is kept separate from the TAPS that does private investigations where:

> *We will not share or publish any of the media or any details of the case outside of the close-knit TAPS group. More sensitive cases will be dealt with by the founders and be held under the strictest confidence.*

And will:

> *Bring a level-headed and comfortable atmosphere into your home, in essence, taking care of the most important thing, your discomfort.*

I would disagree with some generalisations their website makes about a poltergeist only being active when one specific person is present. (This was a once well-regarded theory but, based on this book, things are far more complex than that.) I would love to hear about the case experience that backs up the theory they mention that poltergeist activity happens:

> *commonly around a high limestone deposit location.*

This particular geological slant is as yet something not highly considered in the UK.

I would also agree with their advice regarding poltergeist phenomena that:

> *counselling the client while waiting it out appears the only real option.*

However, what my contact I think really meant when he mentioned the TAPS organisation is actually what is known as the 'TAPS Family', a network of TAPS-affiliated groups, much in the same way as ASSAP but in TAPS' case much larger and spreading across both America and other parts of the world.

In doing this they seem to have a reasonable extensive vetting process. This consists of a request for five years' verifiable investigation of the paranormal, two references from previous cases, declarations that no investigators within a group have criminal records and a further declaration that no fees will be asked from clients.

TAPS' focus on equipment such as EMF meters can be less relevant in poltergeist cases and hardened sceptics have been critical of what they regard as pseudo-science. Benjamin Radford for one criticized their research in his article on "Ghost-Hunting Mistakes: Science and Pseudoscience in Ghost Investigations". However, according to his own article his observations are based on:

watching episodes of Ghost Huntersand other similar programs.

It strikes me though as somewhat pseudoscientific in itself for Radford to come to such firm conclusions if these are based on a likely highly edited (and for entertainment) TV programme!

TAPS, to be fair, recommend the protocol of equipment coupling. This is trying to get unusual variations from two unrelated pieces of equipment at the same time, which would increase the possibility of a real 'anomaly' taking place. TAPS give the example of EMF variations at the time when a photo of anomalous mist is taken. Now if these two factors combined on a regular basis it would be evidence of something very interesting indeed. It's just that I can think of few if any occasions where such coupling has constantly occurred in this way. Nevertheless as far as equipment-led investigations go this is a protocol which I would also approve of and recommend.

The approach of TAPS emphasizes a slow but growing division in investigation protocol between the USA and the UK. With the USA still very much equipment-led.

As mentioned in Chapter 1 the American investigator Joshua P. Warren in his book *How to Hunt Ghosts* has perhaps taken the quest for the 'ultimate' equipment-led investigation even further. Suggesting the use of advanced devices such as:

Electrostatic Generators – These would enhance ghostly activity **IF** it is dependent on electrostatic charge.

Strobe Lights – Which **MAY** enhance one's ability to see a ghost.

Tone Generators – Where the 'standing waves' produced **MAY** encourage a manifestation.

He also says that:

Once we really find a complete understanding of spirits we can hope to combine many technologies into one 'Ghost Meter'.

We started this book discussing the pre-digital "Ghost Meter" called S.P.I.D.E.R. which never caught anything apart from cobwebs, now it is locked up in the SPR store cupboard. I think with this near random use of so much near 'random' equipment, Warren is getting equally carried down the wrong path.

Let's contrast this with what the then Chair of UK-based ASSAP Dave Wood said in 2012:

*Over thousands of investigations, no one has proven a link between gadgets and ghost experiences. In most cases, 'anecdotes' of EMF [electricmagnetic field] meters 'going off' when someone feels something unusual are presented. But no one has proven these to be anything more than coincidence... When it comes to investigating ghost cases, we are best off pre-warning our clients that we will be leaving the equipment at home **and just focusing on their experiences.**[39]*

There was also total agreement of a panel in 2013 at the ASSAP Conference – to the fact that most paranormal detection equipment was more of a hindrance than a help. I would of course claim bias as being a member of that panel but would point out that another member was Steve Parsons of Para.Science who is thought to be one of the best 'Paranormal Detection Equipment' experts this side of the Atlantic.

As for focusing on the experiences of the witness, Alan Murdie's concept of trying to find similar fact evidence in ghost and poltergeist cases does just that. So we find whilst there is agreement about basic ethics in paranormal investigations, other elements in protocol seem to be heading in different directions.

What way is wrong – what way is right? Who can possibly tell if we don't interact? To paraphrase my trusted American source we have to get rid of the "dissention and egoism among members of the paranormal community" and that applies to both sides of the Atlantic. Once that is done, start talking to one another – and once that is done, a whole better future for paranormal investigation in general and (for the purposes of this book) poltergeist investigation in particular.

Who knows – if we get to that stage we might even get two American plumbers swapping ideas with us at a future English SPR conference?

Chapter 10

Glimpses into the Future!

(Can we ever find the missing link to truly 'tame' and understand the illusive poltergeist?)

During the 2012 SPR conference in Northampton I was chairing a session of speakers. One of these was a fairly young researcher by the name of Dr Christopher Laursen, who had travelled all the way from the USA to attend.

His talk was entitled "Delusions and Distress: Therapeutic Approaches In Post-War Psychical Research". During it he mentioned aspects of some research one of our last full-time investigation officers Donald West had written about in the 1940s.

As Chair of the session I was responsible for taking questions at the end of the talk, and when looking around the room one hand was stuck up more eagerly than most, an elderly smartly dressed gentleman... by the name of Donald West. I can still remember Laursen's shock and then intrigue in realising that one of these historical characters he was discussing was still very much around – one of those times when you remember the people far more than you remember the details of the question itself!

I must admit that until then I had more or less forgotten the fact that the SPR used to have full-time professional researchers, and became curious as to how Donald West's function had worked. After the conference I emailed him, and he perhaps a touch modestly explained that as:

a young man just out of medical school he had become the paid Research Officer and divided his time between Rhine style cards based ESP experiments, following up on people's reported experiences and investigating psychometry readings by mediums.

West unfortunately had few positive results with regards to proving paranormal phenomena. Though his predecessor CVC Herbert, later Lord Powis, had also failed to make any breakthrough.

West also pointed out that:

In its early[ier] years the SPR was run by a rich elite who possessed the leisure and resources to organize research.

I suspect this extended outside the SPR where both Harry Price and Baron Schrenck-Notzing had wives of some financial resources, as well as in Price's case occasional benefactors such as Lord Charles Hope.

It left me wondering for a little while as to whether a 'golden age' of paranormal (and poltergeist) research really did exist. I do think on reflection though that likely it actually did! Despite the fact that it relied somewhat on a now outmoded 'old boys' network, there was actually some very interesting and ground-breaking research. From Price and Nandor Fodor in the UK, from Hereward Carrington to JB Rhine in the USA – and later in the 20th century a further generation consisting of the likes of Hans Bender in Germany and of course Guy Playfair for his ground-breaking research in Brazil and the Enfield case. The list should not of course exclude Colin Wilson – though he himself would admit to being more of a man of ideas than one who dug "at the coal-face" of research.

However, even this further generation of 'pioneers' in paranormal research has left us. A few years ago in 2014 I had also contacted my old colleague Peter Underwood, the long-time chair of the Ghost Club, with regards to a face to face interview for the *Fortean Times* magazine. He had replied politely stating that:

Sadly I must say no. I am afraid that the years are beginning to catch up with me – I am 91 and a half and some days I feel very under the weather and not fit for anything; other days I am OK but always apprehensive about making commitments for future activities...

Within a week I was shocked to hear reports of his death. This was just a year after Colin Wilson left us after a rather long illness as well, and Guy Playfair was to follow even more recently in the spring of 2018. All of them, to their credit, achieved significant obituaries in the more serious UK national press.

So the last few years have been something of a reflective time as to where paranormal research can go from here. In 2018 I attended a ceremony to mark the 70th anniversary of Harry Price's passing, held by his beloved Ghost Club at his grave in Pulborough Churchyard in typical English March driving rain. This was sadly followed by Guy Playfair's funeral, held at Mortlake Crematorium on Friday 4th May. He had been ill for a short period, and from the eulogies of those who had spoken to him shortly before his death, he had still been convinced that

The Ghost Club (London) at the grave of famous paranormal researcher Harry Price on a wet windy day and paying tribute to the 70th anniversary of his death (2018) – acknowledgement of that 'Golden Age' of international paranormal research? (Photo Credits Sarah Darnell)

poltergeist phenomena were real – but even then not quite able to make total sense and be sure of what caused it. If even Playfair with his dozens of cases couldn't be sure of a cause in the end, where it does leave those who now try to re-scratch the surface of this strange and recently neglected syndrome again?

Perhaps this passing of a whole generation was in part the impetus that I needed to help me finish this book – which started as a chapter plan in 2012 to be included in a series of books on the paranormal to be launched through the ASSAP organisation, which for various reasons sadly did not go ahead. It was a subject I was assigned as part of this project rather than chose, but this accident of fate gradually made me realise how much the subject had been neglected. After six more years of research and experience I thought this was something that I could in some way try to put right.

I have on balance over the last few chapters come down in favour of a 'power within us' theory as the best possible fit at this time. I fully admit that so far this still looks like a theory with a key ingredient missing. That 'missing link' which explains that once poltergeist phenomena have been triggered by one person it can then seem to be triggered by others when the original person is not there. A fair percentage of cases such as Borley, Pontefract, and St Osyth need that ingredient to start to make sense.

Logically speaking, assuming poltergeist phenomena is something within us, such a 'missing ingredient' can only be one of two things (or possibly both):

1) Some psychological state which can somehow make common poltergeist experiences more likely.
2) Something within the environment of the house or location which triggers such reactions within us, and therefore makes it more likely to be triggered with different people at different times.

There is as far as I can see no other logical factors that would make phenomena take place in particular vicinities, but not just take place when one particular person is present.

Looking first at a person's psychological state, it has already been made clear through this book that circumstances of stress or similar negative emotions such as distress or fear can be an individual trigger. In only the last few days I received notification of a further interesting case, where a group leader in a paranormal investigation sensed a malevolent presence and felt poltergeist type bite marks forming on her upper arm at exactly the same time. Short of accepting a flesh-eating demon (and the ever-present possibility of fraud) the most likely explanation is that this is a strange and unexplained way that some people's bodies react to stress or fear – very similar in some ways to the phenomena of stigmata (the manifestations of bodily wounds, scars and pain in locations corresponding to the crucifixion wounds of Jesus Christ).

But once such a poltergeist effect has been triggered in one person, how does it suddenly jump to another. Surely here the explanation is fear of the poltergeist itself – in the same way as we found out how Richard Sugg explained (in Chapter 3) how fear of the vampire triggered phenomena amongst peasants of Eastern Europe. Have we really changed that much in the last few hundred years?

Once phenomenon has been initiated through the stress of a house move (Amityville?), a broken engagement (Rosenheim) or even possibly a family argument (Pontefract), the fear of further phenomena in others not at first directly affected could potentially provide the trigger for that phenomena to continue. In effect it could be said that the 'Poltergeist Syndrome' is actually highly contagious.

For those not convinced that the human mind can work in this way, there is a powerful under-researched psychological effect which is commonly termed 'mass hysteria' or collective obsessional behaviour. This phenomenon can be defined as a condition affecting a group of persons, characterized by excitement or anxiety, irrational behaviour or beliefs, or inexplicable symptoms. One of the best-known cases of such mass hysteria, within the paranormal community as least, is the mass possession of nuns in 1634 in a convent in Loudun, France. Partly because this factual case was also written up as a historical novel *The Devils of Loudun* by Aldous Huxley in 1952, and which also managed to become an opera as well.

This initial trigger for this mass hysteria was possibly the immoral philandering of the well-connected and good-looking parish Priest Urbain Grandier. The phenomena though went far beyond those who may or may not have succumbed to his charms. Nuns at the convent were one by one to succumb to signs of being possessed by evil spirits, by fainting, or having fits and convulsions, holding their breath, barking, screaming, and perhaps worst of all blaspheming. This led to ineffectual mass exorcisms and ultimately to the indictment, trial and execution of Grandier. Even following this it took a full three years before all signs of possession were seen to fade in the nuns.

Of equal fame in the paranormal community, again because of its association with witchcraft, is the generally accepted mass hysteria that triggered the extended witch trials which happened in 1692 in Salem, Essex County, Massachusetts, which was then an English colony.

Here the superstitious colonists initially convicted two ladies, Sarah Good and Sarah Osborne, of witchcraft, after two young girls both from the same family started experiencing seizures and fits. It was claimed that the two girls had been put under a spell by the ladies.

This act was to prove a trigger to unleash the superstitious nature of the whole community, and people were to identify friends and neighbours as witches throughout the year, to the extent that by the end of the 'hysteria' over 200 people had been accused of witchcraft and twenty had been executed.

By 1693 things calmed down and the judiciary of Salem stated that the accounts in the trial had been false. Too late for the twenty who died, but this remains a powerful example of what happens when the 'collective mind' of a community gets into a panic.

Mass hysteria does not just occur with regards to outbreaks of witchcraft; some events can seem strangely mundane and include:

The laughter epidemic of Tanganyika (now Tanzania) of 1962:
Here a girls' school had to be closed because of an outbreak of laughter which affected half the pupils and which went on for up to 16 days. Children and young adults in nearby villages were also to be affected as well.

The fainting epidemic of Blackburn, England (1965):
Up to 85 pupils in one school were to spontaneously faint over a period of weeks. It is possible that a three-hour school parade had caused some of the initial fainting, but that the others were caused as a 'hysterical' reaction to the initial outbreak. This outbreak was made into a 2014 movie called *The Falling*.

Strawberries with Sugar, 2006, Portugal:
This intriguing case was named after a TV soap opera popular with Portuguese teenagers called *Strawberries with Sugar*, which had an episode where a life-threatening virus affected a school. Following this around 300 real life students at 14 different schools reported symptoms of this non-existent virus. These included shortness of breath, dizziness and in some cases rashes.

Whilst 'official' outbreaks of mass hysteria are relatively rare, it is likely that there are minor outbreaks of hysterical reactions, triggered by an incident, which do not officially get diagnosed and recorded. In most cases there is an (imagined or real) expectation of something to fear, which seems to in some way trigger the subsequent events. If this powerful collective force can to lead to convulsions and fainting, it is surely at least possible that it could provide the 'feeding frenzy' where the poltergeist syndrome starts in one person and then moves on to several, or simply starts to appear in the 'haunted' house where people would most expect it to be.

To emphasize this point it is also worth noting that:

1) Mass hysteria can include visual symptoms such as rashes (e.g. Strawberries with Sugar, 2006). This seems tantalisingly like a minor 'stigmatic' effect or even like the poltergeist scratching/biting/bruising that also seem to appear when the psychological fear factor is high.

2) There seems to be a higher propensity towards mass hysteria in pubescent young ladies. The exact same propensity found in poltergeist cases that made some paranormal investigators (incorrectly) claim that poltergeist phenomena was the **exclusive** domain of girls of that certain age.

We therefore have a working hypothesis with regards to how, through psychological effects, poltergeist phenomena can be 'contagious' even if there is no external agent setting the phenomena off. Looking next to potential environmental effects the situation is perhaps even more interesting and tantalisingly already explored to some extent by science and academics.

It has over the last few decades been argued that certain environmental factors associated with particular locations may cause susceptible people to experience strange sensations. Those experiences of phenomena may be induced by exposure to unusual geomagnetic and electromagnetic (EMF) fields. Pioneers in such research have included psychologists such as William

Roll (formerly of the University of West Georgia) and Michael Persinger of Laurentian University, Ontario, Canada. Persinger was one of that second generation of pioneering researchers who also died as recently as 2018. Research by Roll, Persinger and others have indicated that conditions which may cause significant variations in these fields include the movements of tectonic plates, geological factors such as quartz-based rock, and magnetic mineral properties, as well as of course man-made electrical devices. This is primarily put forward as a psychological explanation for ghost type apparitional experiences, which, as we saw in Chapter 1, shows just how susceptible to natural explanations these experiences really are. In layman's terms it is possible that certain doses of EMF or geomagnetic fields may slightly 'fry' the brain, increase the fear factor and feeling of being watched or even seeing something from the corner of the eye. Interestingly there is also some evidence for showing such fields may also have some kind of trigger effect with regards to poltergeist activity. In a study of 40 cases made by Persinger and Livingston Gearhart in 1986, they found a significant correlation between the poltergeist outbreak and the increase in the earth's geomagnetic activity immediately before the event. This was a simple statistical exercise as records have been kept on the earth's geomagnetic fields since 1868. However, these increases in geomagnetic activity seemed to simply be a catalyst to trigger the activity, which could then continue of its own volition. Within the context of this theory it is also interesting to remind ourselves that poltergeist cases are sometimes associated with interference with electrical power, which is something that can also occur naturally with changes in magnetic fields. I have in earlier chapters emphasized how frequently poltergeist and other phenomena go together, the case of 'The Cage', St Osyth in Chapter 7 being but one example. There is therefore at least a persuasive appeal with regards to a force of energy that can potentially trigger both.

In earlier chapters I have also light-heartedly stated that the poltergeist is in effect 'earthquake proof', as the disruption caused **directly** by an earthquake is so very dissimilar to the phenomena caused by a poltergeist. However, if the movement of tectonic plates can increase geo and electromagnetic activity, which in turn might trigger the powers within us to summon up poltergeist energies, we strangely may have an indirect correlation instead.

This would surely be difficult to test out in the UK, which fortunately suffers so rarely from significant earthquakes. Strange perhaps that on the one spot in which a significant earthquake struck a very interesting case was to emerge in its wake.

In his later years Peter Underwood perhaps left himself open to criticism that some of his books started to involve a repetition of cases he had previously written about. I imagine most factual writers would be doing the same if they approached the 40th book, and I guess there comes a point when you are into your seventh decade that you don't want to spend sleepless nights in abandoned cottages or castles or un-abandoned council houses. As Underwood reached his tenth decade before his death there are many who remember him as a kind of semi-retired spokesman on the paranormal, who mixed with celebrities, and in several cases signed them up to the Ghost Club as well. Such celebrities included occult novelist Dennis Wheatley, actors Peter Cushing (*Star Wars*) and Peter Sellers (*Pink Panther* films). Many newer paranormal researchers might have forgotten that in his time Underwood was an investigator of note. Perhaps the best way to truly assess the activity of his earlier days is to study his book *Nights in Haunted Houses* whose contents are very much encapsulated by the title, and show conclusively what an active investigator he was.

One of Underwood's earlier cases was a thorough investigation of events that occurred in and around the once desolately situated Langenhoe Church, in the little village of Langenhoe, Essex, UK. This was an ongoing investigation which began in 1947 until the sad demolition of the church in 1962.

Underwood was first informed of the case by his friend the author James Turner, who then lived at the nearby village of Borley. What made this case particularly intriguing were two interesting angles:

1) The Rector of Langenhoe since 1937, the Rev Ernest Merryweather, had kept a detailed account of all the strange events since his arrival.
2) That Langenhoe Church had been near the epicentre of what is regarded as Britain's most destructive earthquake, which happened in 1884, partially destroying the church and causing vibrations in the Houses of Parliament about 60 miles away.

Merryweather had never experienced anything paranormal, but his curiosity was aroused when in 1937 the big west door of the church slammed shut with such force that the whole body of the church seemed to shake.

He was shortly after to experience various occasions of the vestry door locking and then unlocking itself without any explanation. As in the place-centred 'Black Monk of Pontefract' case and the more person-centred experiences of Matthew Manning, the initial events were to cease and not return again for a period of time – in this case a rather long period of eight years. As with both these other cases, when the 'poltergeist' returned, it returned with much more energy.

On Easter Sunday in 1945 Merryweather and two helpers were trying to brighten up the church by putting some flowers in vases. When their backs were turned for an instant one set of flowers appeared to transport itself from a vase and was found to be lying neatly on one of the pews. This was one of several incidents of spontaneous 'flower arranging' that was subsequently to occur, and symptomatic of a very typical poltergeist 'walkabout JOTT'.

Merryweather was to discover that it was not just the church in which strange experiences took place. When visiting some of his parishioners in the nearby Tudor manor house, he was told by the householders that there was a particular bedroom in which they refused to stay for any length of time because there was something 'queer' about the atmosphere there. This is potentially relevant to our short discussion earlier regarding Roll's and Persinger's theory of the possible propensity for geomagnetic factors to trigger unease in particular areas. The theory of course also extends to the possibility of disorientating the brain sufficiently to experience what seem to be apparitions. This could possibly explain Merryweather's 'unique' encounter. When being left alone in this bedroom he turned around and experienced for a few seconds:

the unmistakeable embrace of a naked young woman.[40]

The phenomena at Langenhoe was to gradually increase, and Merryweather was to experience frequent overwhelming feelings he was not alone in the church, again consistent with Roll's and Persinger's theories, and was to experience an incident when his hat was to slowly revolve upon an iron rod he had placed it on. An apparition of a young lady (this time fully clothed) was to be seen walking across the chancel of the church, while thuds were to be heard by both Merryweather and his parishioners on no less than ten occasions.

These occasions were all at the exact time they were celebrating Holy Communion!

Of great interest to us in our search for 'similar fact' evidence is the fact that Underwood was to trace the phenomena back beyond Merryweather's time as rector to a former parish clerk.

He discovered there was a long-standing tradition of the bell of Langenhoe Church ringing without human agency and he [the then parish clerk] was among those who had heard disembodied heavy footsteps and other inexplicable sounds in the church.

Underwood's one attempt at a full investigation of the premises was made with his colleague John Denning and he took with him quite an impressive set of measuring devices (much in the tradition of his Ghost Club predecessor Price). These included measuring temperature, humidity, magnetic field and electric fields, and also sensitive recording devices. These would have been extremely useful in providing evidence for the then unexplored theories of Roll and Persinger. The actual night's investigation, however, took place in a raging thunderstorm whose noise and atmospheric changes may have made much of this equipment's use redundant, and nothing significant was recorded.

Despite renovations after the fearsome 1884 earthquake, the church was to become unstable again. It was to close its doors to parishioners in 1959, and be demolished only three years later. All that remains is a strange desolate field full of gravestones which in itself might be enough to trigger a panic in the most hardened investigator of the paranormal when visited at dusk. There may or may not remain another type of strange 'field', that of the geomagnetic type triggered by the earthquake, which could possibly have contributed to the triggering of the events. As no measurements were taken at the time this is of course just informed speculation, though the events do fit the theory rather well. For a real missing link to be shown to possibly exist, electromagnetic or geomagnetic variations would have to certainly have been taken at the time.

It would surely be expecting too much that during the thirty years of public silence about poltergeist phenomena such a case would actually exist. Except that when it comes to the poltergeist it is fair to say you should always expect the unexpected!

Whilst this final chapter pays tribute to the passing of the last generation of 'old school' investigators that is not to say that there are no new ideas or that no newer talent has emerged in the meantime. Whether Steve Parsons with his vast amount of investigation hours would automatically trigger the idea of 'emerging new talent' is perhaps a question for some debate – however, the in-depth and novel approach over the last two decades by himself and his colleague Ann Winsper through their 'Para.Science' organisation has potentially seen a major new under-publicised potential breakthrough in the field.

We briefly heard in Chapter 6 about Para.Science conducting 700 hours of research into phenomena at the Cammell Laird shipyard near Liverpool, UK. It is to another case, however, that we need to look at to bring our subject to some conclusions. That of an old farmhouse in Cheshire whose location is kept secret for all the right ethical reasons of client anonymity explored in Chapter 9, and perhaps for that reason it has not received the publicity it truly deserves.

In 2003 Parsons and Winsper were invited by the owners to lead an investigation into some unexplained incidents at O.H. [pseudonym] Farm in Cheshire, UK. This was an apparently fairly standard 'Intermediate Case' consisting of several apparitions, disembodied voices, and objects being moved. Even more 'standard' was the fact that the house was at the time inhabited by father, mother, and teenage son and daughter – an older child having moved away. All three children and the mother had reported phenomena with the possibility of some phenomena being experienced in the adjoining house next door. The house itself was of no great age built in 1954, and therefore initially very reminiscent of the Enfield, Andover and Pontefract cases.

Para.Science, however, happened to be familiar with the work and hypothesis of Persinger (et al.) when they took on this case and when doing some basic checks found that:

The building lies directly on top of a known geological fault line in the underlying rock.

And that:

The fault line is estimated to run directly beneath the house and penetrates from the surface to below 1800 metres.

This could be of significance to Persinger's theories or simply coincidence – however, during Para.Science investigations the idea of coincidence was to be stretched a little too far.

Members of the Para.Science team were to at separate occasions spend time at the house and found that the bulk of the phenomena they experienced were situated in the bedroom of the son of the family. As the excellent report from Para.Science explains:

The most frequently reported unusual event was seeing bright and vivid coloured lights when the eyes were closed and the subject lying quietly upon the bed beneath the window... Four investigators had this experience of the vivid lights although at the time of their experiences none were previously aware of the reports of their colleagues... On four separate occasions members of the investigation team reported the onset of a strong headache shortly after entering the bedroom, the headache persisting until several minutes after they left the room.

During one of their visits the Para.Science team found an unexpected hum emerge in one of their sound recordings:

The source was traced to a bundle of cables attached to the gutter board at the front of the house. An area of high reading [of EMF] – off the scale of the meter – was found right outside the son's bedroom window.

This exceeded what was normal to such an extent that the advice of an electrician was recommended.

These findings so far mirrored Persinger's theory nearly exactly!

Except that I might have also missed the most important point until the end! As well as experiencing coloured lights and headaches the sort of possible natural effect that Persinger would have predicted with high electromagnetic or geomagnetic activity, the team also experienced more objective poltergeist type activity happening in the same room. This included a cupboard door handle turning and cupboard door opening, which was caught on a night shot camcorder, and a small toy bear 'jumping' from the top of the TV and being found on the floor!

Whilst in the nearby daughter's room, also the scene to a lesser extent of nausea and headaches being reported, an investigator felt his hand being slapped twice, whilst his companion heard the inexplicable sound of slapping, in light that was dimmed but bright enough to read by. No cause for the slapping sound was to be seen.

Every aspect of Persinger's theory was nearly covered to perfection. Over and above Persinger's theories, however, was perhaps the most important breakthrough of all. This was the fact that unusual environmental conditions would not only give the perception of unease or fear or possible hallucinations, but that they would actually appear to trigger potentially real paranormal events in the form of noises or object movement.

It could also possibly be that the unease and fear and coloured lights are in some way paranormal in essence? Even if they are, though, proving it, even to yourself, let alone others, is by its nature nearly impossible. When theories equally fit the facts and the psychological one fits into existing science whilst the paranormal one does not, the common-sense approach is to opt for the accepted one until it can be cast aside. No such problem exists for the phenomena in the poltergeist syndrome. We have come full circle back to Chapter 1 where it becomes even clearer from what we have learnt – that it is only within the 'Poltergeist Syndrome' where proof of potential paranormal events might be found. If an object moves in a spontaneous way, if fraud can be discounted, something unique and very special has happened. If the sound of a hand being slapped is heard without other human contact this is something unequally inexplicable in straightforward natural terms. Even better with regards to finding this proof is if the poltergeist syndrome turns out as I speculate to be a power from within us. It will allow some of the 'braver' parapsychologists and other academics to become involved, an option that just isn't there with the (scientifically) unfathomable concept of afterlife spirits or demons and elementals. In September (2018) whilst completing this book, and completing a year of research in the subject, I gave a talk to the annual SPR conference entitled:

Proving the Paranormal by Prioritising the Poltergeist

The audience in such conferences consists of a cross-section of academics, parapsychologists and old-fashioned paranormal researchers, and I was fully expecting to split the audience down those lines. Despite part of me sometimes liking to be controversial, it was more pleasing I think to find that both sides of the audience were largely in agreement – to the extent that I had helpful thoughts and constructive advice passed to me from the attending academics. Those who already investigate PK in a lab can gradually, like Roll, be persuaded to investigate spontaneous examples of it (RSPK) in everyday life.

The future of paranormal research seems therefore to be clearly with the poltergeist, and with all those who care to participate in its responsible and ethical investigation. In some ways then it could be inexplicably interlinked with the future understanding of ourselves. If the cause does turn out to be internal to us, it will show that the human race is even more special than we already knew it to be. It would certainly make for a spine-tingling 'Faculty X' – fitting for any ending of a Colin Wilson book.

I occasionally 'joust' online with that friendly but very 'plain speaking' sceptic called Hayley Stevens, who runs a popular blog called 'Hayley is a Ghost' and occasional podcasts as well. When reviewing my previous book on ghost hunting techniques Ms Stevens stated that:

> As I read Ghost Hunting: A Survivor's Guide I gained the impression that Fraser knows his stuff when it comes to the history of paranormal research, but that he is doomed to repeat it and all of its mistakes by offering up defence after defence of unscientific methods of paranormal research.

I rather liked the "Fraser knows his stuff" bit, though would disagree with her interpretation of the history of paranormal research repeating its own mistakes again and again. I would hope that this book has shown that progress can and has been made over the last three decades.

More interestingly though Ms Stevens also concluded by stating that:

> It [the book] offers an interesting insight into contemporary paranormal research, but I wouldn't take the author's word as fact.

The reader might be surprised to know that I actually agree 100% with this second quote, and would recommend anyone who reads this current book does so in the same critical way!

The whole point about the paranormal of course, and about

poltergeist research in particular, is that we are still in the realms of making intelligent and informed speculations. It would be impossible for a book on the subject to do anything more than that. What I hope this book has done is to provoke you to as yet unproven possibilities and 'glimpses' as to where the truth might be. In addition though I hope it provides a useful framework to the important questions that need to be answered. From Colvin's theories to Barrington's classifications to Parsons' and Winsper's state of the art investigations.

The working hypothesis I have come to as to what poltergeists are might well have some validity. It does not fully explain every case so far, however. The Enfield case is a particular exception to the 'powers within us' theory in that the communications of Bill Wilkins who died in the house gave information that would not be obviously known by the current residents. Against that there are the cases in such places as Andover, Borley, Dalby (Isle of Man), Pontefract, even Amityville (assuming the genuineness of the case), where the phenomena were of a random mischievous and sometimes destructive nature and hardly evidential of any 'afterlife' presence. Even the Kern City case put forward by Stafford Betty as being strong afterlife evidence has been shown to be open to simpler interpretation. There is still though of course a possibility that my interpretation of a poltergeist as being within us might turn into an accidental version of a 'Poltergeist Piltdown Man' (see Chapter 9) and simply lead us to a dead end in this maze of unexplained phenomena. If this by chance turns out to be the case, even by falsifying my hypothesis we would have brought the subject forward.

From a working hypothesis there sometimes comes a theory, from a theory there sometimes eventually comes a fact – though even those things we call facts are often themselves incomplete interpretations of what is really occurring. Often a case of two steps forward, one step backwards – but progress nonetheless.

Will the future continue be more progressive or just a repetition of some of the controversies and unsettled debates of previous generations? That is an unanswered question which depends on the resources available and the open-minded enthusiasm of people – the sort of people that might just be reading this book.

If you believe like me that in time there is a need for a 'Chapter 11' and beyond – perhaps it is up to you to write it or at least to advise as to your thoughts on what the next steps should be?

In either case let us not leave it another 30 years!

Jfraserpoltergeist@yahoo.com

Endnotes

Preface

1. *Poltergeist! A Study in Destructive Haunting*, Colin Wilson (New English Library, 1981, p. 171)

Chapter 1

2. <https://psi-encyclopedia.spr.ac.uk/articles/enfield-poltergeist>
3. *This House is Haunted*, Guy Playfair (Sphere Books, 1981)
4. "The Report of the Enfield Poltergeist Committee" (SPR archives)
5. Roll, William G., Nichols, Andrew. "Psychological and Electromagnetic Aspects of Haunts", *Journal of Parapsychology*, September 2000
6. *Journal of the SPR*, Vol. 79.4, No. 921 (October 15), correspondence
7. The famous French paranormal researcher Charles Richet was a Nobel prize winner but this was for his immunology research and not for his investigations into mediums at the turn of the 20th century.

Chapter 2

8. *Poltergeist Over England*, Harry Price (Country Life, 1939, Chapter 1, p. 1)
9. *Guidebook for Tennessee*, Federal Government's Works Project Administration (1933) <https://www.thoughtco.com/the-bell-witch-2596741>
10. *Bealings Bells*, Major Edward Moor (Woodbridge, 1841)
11. *The Poltergeist*, William G. Roll (Nelson Doubleday, 1972, p. 34)
12. PSI Encyclopaedia <https://psi-encyclopedia.spr.ac.uk/articles/poltergeists-overview>

Chapter 3

13. *Gef! The Strange Tale of an Extra-Special Talking Mongoose*, C. Josiffe (Strange Attractor Press, 2017)

14. *The Haunting of Cashen's Gap: A Modern 'Miracle' Investigated*, Harry Price (London: Methuen & Co., 1936)

15. Pitt was famous for a series of Vampire movies in the 1970s made by cult UK producers Hammer House of Horror.

16. *In My Solitary Life*, 6 volumes, Augustus Hare (London: George Allen, 1896–1900)

17. *In Search of Dracula* (London: Robson Books Ltd., 1995)

18. <http://www.historytoday.com/blog/2013/10/vampires-and-poltergeists>

Chapter 4

19. *Treatise Concerning the Principles of Human Knowledge*, George Berkeley (Dublin: Aaron Rhames, 1710)

20. <https://psi-encyclopedia.spr.ac.uk/articles/jott-phenomena-spatial-discontinuities>

21. *On the Track of the Poltergeist*, D. Scott Rogo (New Jersey: Prentice Hall, 1986)

22. *Mitos de Antioquia*, Arturo Escobar Uribe (Minerva Editions, Bogotatales, 1950)

Chapter 5

23. *The Strange Case of Rudi Schneider*, Anita Gregory (Lanham, MD: Scarecrow Press, 1985, p. 12)

24. Woolley, VJ (1930). "Review of Harry Price's Rudi Schneider – A Scientific Examination of His Mediumship", *SPR Journal*, Vol. 26, p. 125

25. Schmidt, Helmut. "Observation of a psychokinetic effect under highly controlled conditions", *Journal of Parapsychology*, Vol. 57, December 1993

26. *The Link*, Matthew Manning (Henry Holt & Company Inc., May 1975)

Chapter 6

27. *Journal of the SPR*, Volume 72.i, No. 890 (January 2008, p. 9)
28. *Journal of the SPR*, Volume 72.i, No. 890 (January 2008, p. 18)
29. "The Acoustic Properties of Unexplained Rapping sounds", Barry Colvin <http://www.sgha.net/library/Unexplained_Rapping_Sounds.pdf>
30. *Paracoustics*, edited by Steve Parsons and Callum Cooper (White Crow Books, 2015, p. 199)

Chapter 8

31. Web page for East Drive <http://www.30eastdrive.com/today/>
32. "Poltergeists: a physical theory", GW Lambert, CB. *Journal of the Society for Psychical Research*, June 1955, Vol. 38, No. 684

Chapter 9

33. <http://www.naturetracking.com/the-5-most-common-animal-tracks-in-snow>
34. Previously accessed from: <https://abcnews.go.com/Prime time/story?id=132035&page=1>
35. Reference to The Atlantic Paranormal Society (TAPS). Perhaps the most famous investigation group in the USA, whose name TAPS is a play on the fact that its founders are also plumbers.
36. <http://www.dailymail.co.uk/news/article-2290279/Haunted-Amityville-Eldest-son-Lutz-family-reveals-living-possessed-Long-Island-home-ruined-life.html>
37. Adams, Paul; Brazil, Eddie. Harry Price Website: <http://www.harrypricewebsite.co.uk/index.html>
38. "Pursuing the Elusive Poltergeist". Allen Spraggett (*The Pittsburgh Press*, January 2, 1974)
39. ASSAP National Investigations Committee (2012). Professional Code of Ethics, "Anomaly" no. 46

Chapter 10

40. *Nights in Haunted Houses*, Peter Underwood (Headline Books, 1994, p. 206)

References

Adams, P., Brazil, E. and Underwood, P. (2009) *The Borley Rectory Companion*. Stroud: History Press

Anson, J. (1977) *The Amityville Horror*. New York: Pocket Star Books

Estep, R., Mitchell, V. (2017) *Spirits of the Cage*. Woodbury, MN: Llewellyn Publications

Fodor, N. (1958) *On the Trail of the Poltergeist*. New York: Citadel Press

Fraser, J. (2010) *Ghost Hunting: A Survivor's Guide*. Stroud: The History Press

Gauld, A., Cornell, AD (1979) *Poltergeists*. Abingdon, UK: Routledge & Kegan Paul

Gregory, A. (1985) *The Strange Case of Rudi Schneider*. Lanham, MD: Scarecrow Press

Holder, G. (2012) *What is a Poltergeist?* Exeter, UK: David & Charles

Josiffe, C. (2017) *Gef! The Strange Tale of an Extra-Special Talking Mongoose*. London: Strange Attractor Press

Manning, M. (1975) *The Link*. New York: Henry Holt & Company Inc.

Moor, Major E. (1841) *Bealings Bells*. Woodbridge, UK

Parsons, S.; Cooper, C. (2015) *Paracoustics: Sounds and the Paranormal*. Guildford: White Crow Books

Playfair, G. (1976) *The Indefinite Boundary*. London: Souvenir Press

Playfair, G. (1981) *This House is Haunted*. London: Sphere Books

Price, H. (1936) *The Haunting of Cashen's Gap*. London: Methuen & Co.

Price, H. (1939) *Poltergeist Over England*. London: Country Life

PSI Encyclopedia <https://psi-encyclopedia.spr.ac.uk>

Rogo, D. Scott (1986) *On the Track of the Poltergeist*. New Jersey:

Prentice Hall

Roll, WG (1972) *The Poltergeist*. New York: Nelson Doubleday

Underwood, P. (1973) *A Gazetteer of British Ghosts*. London: Pan Books

Underwood, P. (1994) *Nights in Haunted Houses*. London: Headline Books

Wilson, C. (1971) *The Occult*. New York: Random House

Wilson, C. (1979) *Mysteries*. London: Grafton Books

Wilson, C. (1981) *Poltergeist! A Study in Destructive Haunting*. London: New English Library

Wilson, C. (1987) *Afterlife*. New York: Doubleday

Acknowledgements

James Tacchi for full use of his report on "Poltergeist Rappings".

Lindsay Siviter, Sarah Darnell and Peter Ladanyi for use of photos.

Dominique Fraser for patiently rereading and making sense of my ideas.

Index of Main Case Reviews and Research Breakthroughs

6TH
BOOKS

ALL THINGS PARANORMAL

Investigations, explanations and deliberations on the paranormal,
supernatural, explainable or unexplainable. 6th Books seeks to
give answers while nourishing the soul: whether making use of the
scientific model or anecdotal and fun, but always
beautifully written.
Titles cover everything within parapsychology: how to, lifestyles,
alternative medicine, beliefs, myths and theories.
If you have enjoyed this book, why not tell other readers by
posting a review on your preferred book site? Recent bestsellers
from 6th Books are:

The Afterlife Unveiled

What the Dead Are Telling us About Their World!

Stafford Betty

What happens after we die? Spirits speaking through mediums know, and
they want us to know. This book unveils their world…

Paperback: 978-1-84694-496-3 ebook: 978-1-84694-926-5

Spirit Release

Sue Allen

A guide to psychic attack, curses, witchcraft, spirit attachment, possession,
soul retrieval, haunting, deliverance, exorcism and more, as taught at the
College of Psychic Studies.

Paperback: 978-1-84694-033-0 ebook: 978-1-84694-651-6

Divine Guidance
The Answers You Need to Make Miracles
Stephanie J. King
Ask any question and the answer will be presented, like a direct line to higher realms… *Divine Guidance* helps you to regain control over your own journey through life.
Paperback: 978-1-78099-794-0 ebook: 978-1-78099-793-3

The End of Death
How Near-Death Experiences Prove the Afterlife
Admir Serrano
A compelling examination of the phenomena of Near-Death Experiences.
Paperback: 978-1-78279-233-8 ebook: 978-1-78279-232-1

The Psychic & Spiritual Awareness Manual
A Guide to DIY Enlightenment
Kevin West
Discover practical ways of empowering yourself by unlocking your psychic awareness, through the Spiritualist and New Age approach.
Paperback: 978-1-78279-397-7 ebook: 978-1-78279-396-0

An Angels' Guide to Working with the Power of Light
Laura Newbury
Discovering her ability to communicate with angels, Laura Newbury records her inspirational messages of guidance and answers to universal questions.
Paperback: 978-1-84694-908-1 ebook: 978-1-84694-909-8

The Audible Life Stream
Ancient Secret of Dying While Living
Alistair Conwell
The secret to unlocking your purpose in life is to solve the mystery of death, while still living.
Paperback: 978-1-84694-329-4 ebook: 978-1-78535-297-3

Beyond Photography

Encounters with Orbs, Angels and Mysterious Light Forms!

John Pickering, Katie Hall

Orbs have been appearing all over the world in recent years. This is the personal account of one couple's experience of this new phenomenon.

Paperback: 978-1-90504-790-1

Blissfully Dead

Life Lessons from the Other Side

Melita Harvey

The spirit of Janelle, a former actress, takes the reader on a fascinating and insightful journey from the mind to the heart.

Paperback: 978-1-78535-078-8 ebook: 978-1-78535-079-5

Does It Rain in Other Dimensions?

A True Story of Alien Encounters

Mike Oram

We have neighbors in the universe. This book describes one man's experience of communicating with other-dimensional and extra-terrestrial beings over a 50-year period.

Paperback: 978-1-84694-054-5

Readers of ebooks can buy or view any of these bestsellers by clicking on the live link in the title. Most titles are published in paperback and as an ebook. Paperbacks are available in traditional bookshops. Both print and ebook formats are available online.

Find more titles and sign up to our readers' newsletter at http://www. johnhuntpublishing.com/mind-body-spirit. Follow us on Facebook at https://www.facebook.com/OBooks and Twitter at https://twitter.com/ obooks.